Each of these papers incorporates the interface between criminal justice and political philosophy and reflects the strong current interest in the development of the retributivist, or "just deserts", theory of punishment. They include a review of important issues in punishment and corrections, a rationale for the retributive theory of punishment, development of new theoretical aspects of retributivism, practical applications of the theory, and critical assessments of punishment focusing on the retributive theory.

Justice
and
Punishment

Justice
and
Punishment

Edited by
J.B. Cederblom
and
William L. Blizek
University of Nebraska
at Omaha

Ballinger Publishing Company ● Cambridge, Massachusetts
A Subsidiary of J.B. Lippincott Company

Copyright © 1977 by Ballinger Publishing Company. All rights reserved. No part of this publication may be reproduced, stored in a retrieval system, or transmitted in any form or by any means, electronic mechanical photocopy, recording or otherwise, without the prior written consent of the publisher.

International Standard Book Number: 0-88410-752-3

Library of Congress Catalog Card Number: 77-3378

Printed in the United States of America

Library of Congress Cataloging in Publication Data

Main entry under title:

Justice and punishment.

Papers originally presented at a symposium at the University of Nebraska at Omaha in May 1976.
Bibliography: p.
Includes index.
1. Punishment—Congresses. 2. Criminal justice, Administration of—Congresses. I. Cederblom, Jerry. II. Blizek, William. III. University of Nebraska at Omaha.
HV8683.J87   364.6   77-3378
ISBN 0-88410-752-3

Contents

Acknowledgments

In 1975 the Department of Philosophy of the University of Nebraska at Omaha was awarded a grant from the National Endowment for the Humanities (EP-21120-75-247) that facilitated the development of two humanities courses for professional education programs. One of those courses was designed for students in law enforcement and criminal justice. In conjunction with this course the Departments of Philosophy and Criminal Justice sponsored a symposium on criminal justice and punishment in the spring of 1976. The papers which comprise this volume were presented originally at that symposium.

We wish to express our appreciation to Chancellor Ronald W. Roskens, Provost Herbert Garfinkel, and Deans John M. Newton and Hubert G. Locke for their support, and to Laurie Hinz, Beverly Butterfield, and Pamela Glenke for their assistance. Special thanks is due Drs. Vincent Webb and Samuel Walker for their contribution to the arrangements for the symposium and the Department of Criminal Justice for its financial support. We also wish to thank Lynn Blizek for her encouragement. The University of Nebraska at Omaha Faculty Senate Research Committee provided financial support to Professor Cederblom for the writing of the introduction to this volume.

Justice
and
Punishment

Chapter One

Introduction

J.B. Cederblom

The chapters in this book were individually presented at a symposium on "Criminal Justice and Punishment," held at the University of Nebraska at Omaha in May of 1976. In light of the apparent inadequacies of the criminal justice system in America, and in response to the current debate over the direction in which this system should change, the contributors to the symposium were asked to present papers related to the question of whether any system of punishment can be made workable and defensible.

The amount of attention the various chapters give to retributivism, or the "just deserts" theory, illustrates the degree to which this theory has suddenly come to dominate thought concerning punishment. In contrast, the idea of "treating" or rehabilitating offenders, rather than punishing them, receives hardly a kind word in any of the chapters. The most that any of the contributors is willing to say, is that offenders should be allowed to participate in voluntary rehabilitation programs while they are being punished.

The revival of retributivism is somewhat strange, considering that until recently the direction of seemingly enlightened and humane thought has been toward the abandonment of punishment altogether, or *at most* employing it solely to avoid a greater evil, such as leaving dangerous offenders at large. For a theory to reassert itself which not only encourages punishment, but encourages it for its own sake, as simply fitting and just apart from its effects on crime, might seem to be a step backward into our less civilized past. As Hugo Bedau has remarked, "It is as though there were a vast conspiracy, Kant smiling from his grave of two hundred years; a conspiracy among philosophers, penologists, politicians . . . "

The resurgence of the idea of just deserts among the general public might be interpreted simply as a reaction to the increase in crime. To a public which feels threatened by and angry toward lawbreakers, the idea of "giving them what they deserve" is undoubtedly satisfying. But among scholars, the renewed interest in retributivism is surely not the result of anger over crime. One suspects rather that it results from a confluence of factors such as the growing documentation of the failure and abuse of rehabilitation programs, the general decline in respectability of utilitarianism (the chief rival of retributivism among philosophic theories of punishment), and the rise of contractarian and natural rights theories which might serve as an underpinning for a retributivist approach to punishment.

Not all of the chapters in this book support retributivism—three are critical of it and all are cautious about it. But retributivism is the most prominent concern which the chapters have in common. This continuing thread was taken advantage of in organizing the book.

Chapter Two, by John Hospers, is critical of retributivism, along with other theories of punishment. But Hospers believes that retributivism "has the most to be said for it." In Chapter Three, Hugo Bedau presses the critical attack on retributivism, but he makes certain concessions to it and, like Hospers, indicates a major area in which the theory is in need of development. Chapter Four, Edmund Pincoffs' study of desert claims, takes up the challenge of developing retributivist theory; and in Chapter Five, Martin Golding gives credit to retributivism for having something helpful to say about the problems of sentencing. The following three chapters—by James Q. Wilson, David Fogel, and Norval Morris—look at the practical problems of instituting a theory of punishment. In the cases of Wilson and Fogel, it is precisely a retributivist system of punishment which is under discussion. Norval Morris is less devoted to retributivism in a pure form, but the thrust of his recommendations is still largely in the direction of retributivism. The final chapter, by Richard Wasserstrom, returns to a critical assessment of punishment. He deals with a number of approaches to punishment, but a major share of his study is devoted to criticizing a recent and particularly defensible form of retributivism.

The following summary will attempt to highlight the main threads of common concern among the eight studies in this book.

Hospers: . . . *there is NO totally satisfactory theory, either of what constitutes penal justice or of who should be empowered to administer it.*

John Hospers considers three views which attempt to justify punishment and finds serious difficulties with each of them. But he also rejects the view that we should not punish at all. He believes that we are left with the dilemma of being forced to inflict punishment without being able to adequately justify doing so.

The pro-punishment theories Hospers considers are retributivism, utilitarianism, and the restitutive theory; the antipunishment view is a libertarian one. His objections to retributivism will be mentioned last, since they will be brought up again in the discussion of the succeeding chapters.

According to the utilitarian, or "results" theory, punishment is justified by its promotion of good or prevention of evil in the future. Hospers' most serious objection to this view is that the punishment which will have the best results is not necessarily the punishment which is just. For example, imprisoning an incurable nuisance maker for life might minimize social harm, but would not be just.

Some theorists have attempted to combine elements of retributivism and utilitarianism in order to avoid objections to utilitarianism alone, such as the objection that utilitarianism might justify the punishment of the innocent. John Rawls, for example, has suggested that while the judge should act as a retributivist by sentencing a person only on the grounds that he is guilty of an offense; still, the legislator should act as a utilitarian in determining how much punishment a law should assign to an offense on the basis of socially good results such as deterrence.[1] But, Hospers points out, his objection to the utilitarian theory remains also for this mixed theory: Why should the *legislator* follow the utilitarian theory, when the punishment which will have the best results is not necessarily the one which is just?

The restitutive theory concerns itself with helping the victim of an offense, stating that the offender's punishment should be to compensate the victim for his loss. The first difficulty with this theory is that in many cases, such as murder, the victim's loss cannot be restored. And the theory has the more profound difficulty that it cannot give consideration to intent. One person's minor negligence, combined with bad luck, might cause an entire city to burn down; while another might have threatened murder but not acted on it (yet). The restitutive theory would punish the former severely but the latter not at all.

Few philosophers have given serious consideration to the possibility that no retaliation for crimes is justified. One who has, Robert Lefevre, maintains that it is a waste of time and money to attempt to retaliate after harm has already been done. It would be preferable to make retaliation unnecessary by concentrating on *protection*. Hospers is somewhat sympathetic with this view, but sees telling difficulties for it. It is humanly impossible to prevent all crimes, and the criminal who does succeed will be encouraged by the fact that no one retaliated against him. Furthermore, it is not clear that protection (which *is* to be allowed) is completely different from retaliation. To set lethal traps to protect against trespassers would not really be different from retaliation (and besides, such measures would be undeserved by the inadvertent trespasser).

The theory with which we are most concerned, retributivism, asserts that a person who is guilty of an offense deserves to be punished in proportion to the seriousness of his offense. Hospers raises two objections which are fairly simple, but, he claims, extremely serious. First, there may be disagreement as to which offenses are most serious. And second, even if there *were* agreement as to the relative seriousness of offenses, there may yet be disagreement concerning what specific punishment is deserved for a particular offense. How are such disagreements to be resolved?

In addition to these criticisms, Hospers raises a general challenge to all theories of punishment which is rarely considered: Who has the right to administer a system of punishment? The state? The victim? Private agencies? Most people simply *assume* that the state has the right, and it is an indication of Hospers' libertarian sympathies that he challenges this assumption. The state doesn't do anything well, he says; if it can't run a post office or a school system, how could it run a judicial system? (And it *doesn't* run it very well, he reminds us.) Furthermore, it is not at all clear by what *right* the state imprisons those it suspects of breaking its laws. But the victim is also a poor candidate for administering justice—he typically overestimates the seriousness of the offense, and he follows no *rules* of retaliation. Private agencies might be more efficient than the state in administering punishment, but their first concern would undoubtedly be their paying customers; they would not be motivated to be impartial.

Hospers' arguments have been presented at some length because they pose a general skeptical challenge which will need to be faced by any theory of punishment. As was mentioned above, Hospers thinks retributivism has "the most to be said for it." His objections to it were not that it leads to unacceptable conclusions (as he argues the other theories do). Rather, he sees problems which the retributivist would have difficulty solving: How do we determine which offenses are the more serious? How do we tell what particular punishment is deserved for an offense? (And there is his more general challenge: "Who has the right to administer a system of punishment?") The challenge to retributivism is carried on in greater detail by Hugo Bedau, and although the tenor of his study is critical, he does make some concessions to retributivism.

> Bedau: *Although justice does require us to concede to the retributivist that the punishment must fit the crime, there is not much content and rigor in this abstract concession.*

Hugo Bedau characterizes retributivism much as Hospers does, as the view that features of punishment should be shaped by reference to features of offenses. Retributivism looks back to the offense in its justification of punishment (as it is often put), rather than looking forward to good effects of punishment. In order to see how much must be conceded to this approach to punishment, Bedau examines certain features of an ideally just society to determine what would be the rationale for punishment in such a society; who would be punished, and for what conduct; and what their punishment would be. Bedau argues that the rationale for imposing a system of punishment in a just society would be to secure compliance with rules that are just, and that this is *not* a retributivist rationale. Furthermore, if it is asked why a society should proceed to punish a person who has been found guilty of an offense, Bedau rejects the retributivist answer: "Because the guilty deserve to be punished." He claims that once society has laid down rules and threatened punishment in order to secure compliance, its reason for punishing a violator is not that he deserves it because of his guilt, but rather that society meant what it said when it threatened punishment in the first place. And "because it meant what it said" is not a retributivist reason for punishment.

Several of the concessions Bedau does make to retributivism are minor, and would be a part of other theories of punishment also. Among these are the concession that only harmful offenses should be punished; and that the sort of thing that would be appropriate to impose as a punishment would be the same kind of thing the offender inflicts—i.e., suffering or deprivation, and in this sense he is "paid back." Bedau does concede a weak version of the dictum that the guilty deserve to be punished; that is, he concedes that *only* the guilty should be punished. But he believes that even if a person is guilty, other considerations might outweigh the retributivist demand that he be punished. Bedau discusses the Kantian doctrine that a person "chooses to be punished;" and in the course of the discussion concedes that in order for an offender to be respected as a person, he must be punished rather than rehabilitated. He also acknowledges that retributivism can explain why punishment should never be imposed on a person who acts without *mens rea*.

Now we come to the most prominent feature of retributivism, and the one which Hospers calls into question: making the punishment fit the offense. Bedau does concede that "the punishment must fit the crime," and he explains this phrase by saying that "a punishment fits the crime when it matches in its severity what the crime involved in offender fault and victim harm." But he claims that we have no adequate measures of fault and harm, so we cannot give any content to this concession to retributivism. He examines in some detail the attempts by Andrew von Hirsch and Claudia Card to give substance to the principle of fitting the punishment to the offense, but rejects both attempts.

Bedau, even more explicitly than Hospers, is leaving us in the uncomfortable position of feeling that we should punish in a certain manner, i.e., in a way that is appropriate to the offense in question, but without knowing exactly what this amounts to. This puts us in a particularly uncomfortable position because the issue of how to deal with offenders is not one on which we can postpone action until the debate is settled or until all of the problems are solved. If it is true that we *should* punish offenders to a degree that "matches" the guilt of the offender and the harm to the victim, but that we really cannot measure the latter, where does this leave us? Not punishing at all because we do not know how much to punish? If we cannot "measure," can we estimate? guess? It is difficult to see how it could be *clear* that justice dictates fitting the punishment to the crime, unless we have some idea of what "fitting the punishment to the crime" means. And yet Bedau's claim that we cannot measure guilt and harm is compelling. In this context, we can see the importance of the analysis of desert provided by Edmund Pincoffs.

Pincoffs: *Desert claims . . . are intelligible and <u>in principle</u> defensible by rationally acceptable considerations.*

Pincoffs believes that it *makes sense* to say that a person deserves something (for example, that a person deserves a particular punishment for having committed a certain offense), and that such claims can be rationally defended.

If a person deserves something, according to Pincoffs, it is *because of* some fact or feature about the person. More specifically, a person deserves something by virtue of having done or suffered something which reveals his nature, as opposed to having done something by accident, mistake, or coercion. This feature of revealing the agent distinguishes desertmaking considerations from considerations which might *entitle* a person to something he may or may not deserve (such as being entitled to a prize because one's ticket is drawn); or considerations which show that the *outcome* of a person's receiving something would be desirable.

Pincoffs makes a helpful comparison of a judgment of desert to an appraisal of a house. An appraisal is not simply a description; it is a judgment which is based on a description. A statement of the square-footage of a house, qualified so that it would not mislead a judgment of value (e.g., part of the square-footage might be in an unfinished area), would form a part of the *groundwork* of an appraisal. Since an appraisal is a *comparative* judgment, a basis for comparison must be established. In the case of houses, the basis of comparison is the recent sale of comparable houses. In appraising the punishment a person deserves for an offense, the establishment of a basis of comparison is a fundamental problem.

The legislative problem involving the appraisal of punishment deserved for an offense, is that of relating two scales. The first is a scale of crimes from the least to the most serious. The second is a scale of punishments from lenient to severe. The problem of relating these scales has two parts: the anchoring problem and the interval problem. The anchoring problem is that of establishing a relation between the scales at some point. The interval problem is that of determining the intervals between crimes on the crime scale. Whereas the punishment scale, at least for punishments like imprisonment, is seen by Pincoffs to be a *cardinal* scale, with regular intervals between punishments; the crime scale is simply ordinal—three crimes adjacent on the scale will be of increasing seriousness, but the second may be only slightly worse than the first, while the third is much worse than the second. The interval problem is that of spacing out these crimes in relation to points on the punishment scale.

Again, Pincoffs' main object is to claim that judgments of desert are intelligible and can be rationally defended. The analysis of what is involved in a judgment of desert which was just summarized speaks to the question of intelligibility. What about defensibility? Breaking down the question of deserving a particular punishment as he does, into the anchoring problem and the interval problem, he must provide answers to the questions: "Why anchor the crime scale to the punishment scale at some particular point rather than another?," and, "How should crimes be spaced out on the crime scale?" As evidence that the anchoring problem is not intractable, Pincoffs points out that we do not have some idea where each scale should begin and why. We would not, for example, begin the crime scale with using a toothpick in public, and we would not begin the punishment scale with a fine of 3 cents. Our rationale for not doing this turns on the nature of the practice of punishment. It is necessary that the threat for unwanted consequences be taken seriously, and used for serious purposes. Regarding the interval problem we know that if the gap between two crimes is great, the gap in punishment should be great, too. But the problem of "how much" does not admit of an exact solution.

The crime and punishment scales may be coordinated so that room is left for judicial discretion. This may be done either by setting a maximum and a minimum, or by allowing the judge to depart from a presumptive sentence.

Pincoffs asserts that the question of whether there should be a system of punishment at all is separate from the question of what a person deserves for a particular crime, and has nothing to do with desert. It doesn't follow, however, that the justification of the system should turn on utilitarian considerations. It could rest as well on contract theory or intuitive principles.

This last point—that the question of whether there should be a system of punishment at all has nothing to do with desert—is similar to the point made by Bedau, that the rationale for imposing a system of punishment in a just society would not be retributive (Bedau thought that the rationale would be to secure compliance with rules). The main issue in punishment to which retributivism, or "just deserts" is seen as applicable both by Bedau and Pincoffs, is that of fitting the punishment to the crime.

Pincoffs is candid in admitting that the "interval problem" does not admit of exact solution. And he is modest in his claims about the solubility of the anchoring problem—saying only that we have some idea of where each scale should begin and why. The extent to which the critic of retributivism should be appeased by the state in which these problems are left, is open to debate.

Whereas the Pincoffs study deals to a large extent with the way in which retributivism might justify coordinating a particular punishment with a particular kind of offense; Martin Golding, in discussing retributivism, deals primarily with the way in which this theory could justify variations in punishments for similar offenses.

Golding: *Retributivism might have something significant to contribute on the problems of individualization and disparity in sentencing.*

In "Criminal Sentencing; Some Philosophical Considerations," Martin Golding asks whether the traditional theories of punishment have anything helpful to say about the difficult question: "How, and how much, may someone be punished?" He points to the tremendous dissatisfaction with current sentencing practices—the widespread belief that many offenders are punished for too short a time, the general loss of faith in rehabilitation, concern over disparities in sentencing—and, working on the assumption that the rehabilitation ideal must be given up, looks to the deterrence theory and retributivism for guidance. But he seems to find the deterrence theory beset with difficulties, while he sees retributivism as having something useful to offer.

The deterrence theory has traditionally been looked to as an answer to the problem of crime reduction. Some have challenged the claim that punishment can deter crime, but Golding sees the major problem for the deterrence theory *not* to be whether punishment can deter, but rather in answering the question: "How much punishment is it justifiable to employ in order to deter crime?" Golding poses the problem in this way: It seems fairly clear that using punishment to reduce crime is subject to some limitation; it would not, for example, be justifiable to use brutal punishment to reduce the incidence of minor offenses. How can the deterrence theorist account for this without resorting to the retributive principle of desert? If he merely claims that we should not produce more harm in punishment than we are avoiding in crime reduction, he is left in the position of counting harm to offenders equally with harm to victims.

There are further difficulties for the deterrence theorist involving individualization of sentences. How could the deterrence theorist justify giving a particular individual a lesser sentence or no sentence on the basis of mitigating or excusing circumstances, when such a practice might lessen the deterrent value of the threat of punishment? But on the other hand, since disparity of sentences is a major source of discontent, how can this problem be met without compromising individualization based on mitigation and excuse? Some have proposed maxima and minima for certain offenses, but even this policy would allow a range of discretion within which the problem of individualization must be addressed.

Golding thinks retributivism does have something helpful to say about the problems of individualization and disparity in sentencing. He makes an interesting comparison of retributivism to rehabilitation on the point of making a punishment appropriate to a particular offender. Golding sees retributivism as using punishment to condemn the offender as well as his offense. Since offenders are not all the same, individualization is justified on the grounds that each sentence should be imposed in a way in which the particular offender is caused to see that his conduct was wrong and that his punishment is just. If this rationale is carried out, it is not necessary that disparity of sentences appear unjust.

Golding acknowledges that a practical problem arises, once flexibility in sentencing is allowed for the sake of individualization, in preventing flexibility from degenerating into arbitrariness. He sees a possible solution in Marvin Frankel's suggestion that judges be required to state the basis for each aspect of the sentence, and how it adds up to the length of time or amount of fine which is imposed.

The double focus of retributivism on the offender as well as the offense is seen by Golding to be helpful in justifying sentencing alternatives which allow both culpability of offender and gravity of offense to be taken into account. But he allows that working out the details of this sort of retributive approach would be very complicated.

Although Golding seems optimistic about what retributivism might offer to certain aspects of the problem of sentencing, he concludes on a somewhat skeptical note concerning the possibility of providing an overall rationale for a system of sentencing. That is, he does not want to rule out the appropriateness of considerations of deterrence, or even (if it could be put on a more solid basis) rehabilitation; as well as retribution. But he is unsure whether it is possible to fashion out of these various approaches a system which "will reflect anything more than a crazy-quilt of inconsistent considerations."

The four studies that have so far been discussed have all been philosophical ones, dealing primarily with the justification of punishment. The following three, by James Q. Wilson, David Fogel, and Norval Morris, focus on more practical questions. Wilson investigates the political feasibility of instituting the just deserts approach to punishment; Fogel discusses the kinds of short range and middle range changes which would need to be made in prison facilities and sentencing policies to bring them in line with the model of just punishment; and Morris looks ahead to the problems of imprisonment which will confront us in the future. But each of the studies reflects a position concerning the kind of system of punishment which is justifiable.

Wilson: *The convergence which has developed of late between liberals and conservatives around the concept of 'just deserts' has profound implications . . . primarily for . . . sentencing policy.*

James Q. Wilson sees a "just deserts" approach to punishment as dictating a policy of more determinate sentencing. He believes that liberals and conservatives have a common interest in changing sentencing policy so that the minimum is raised and the maximum lowered. This would involve lessening the discretion of judges, making penalties for crimes certainly known, curtailing the power of parole boards, and abandoning the ideal of rehabilitation.

Wilson argues that if sentences were made more determinate, conservatives would be happy in seeing that convicted offenders would be certain to get *some* punishment; and liberals, in seeing that sentences were not too severe. Since sentencing would not be based on the likelihood of future criminality, liberals need not fear that judges would give long term sentences to those who would not recidivate, but conservatives need not fear that the offender who *would* recidivate would go free. The rehabilitative ideal, which liberals have come to see as too manipulative, and conservatives as ineffective, would be given up. Since sentences would be more certain, liberals would be less concerned about sentences being unjustly discriminatory. Conservatives might, however, have hoped for greater deterrence and incapacitation of offenders.

Besides satisfying many common interests of liberals and conservatives, raising the minimum sentence and lowering the maximum would have desirable social effects, according to Wilson. Since it seems to be the certainty rather than the severity of punishment which is more effective in deterring offenders, having a known minimum sentence is desirable, and lowering the maximum would result in only a small loss of deterrence. Furthermore, the incapacitative effect of imprisonment is only as long as the criminal career; and this, on the average, is short.

Wilson sees areas of intellectual disagreement which will tend to hinder this suggested alliance of liberals and conservatives, but he thinks it would be a mistake to let these issues prevent the alliance. One potential disagreement involves seeing crime as the result of free will, or as socially caused. Many liberals see it as unjust to punish a person whose criminal behavior was caused by social conditions. But, Wilson argues, to excuse the offender because his act was socially caused is to condemn the victim, whose position is also typically socially caused. To excuse the offender would be both unjust to the victim, and would give an incentive to would-be offenders to yield to temptation rather than resist.

The political obstacles which lie in the path of implementing the just deserts approach to punishment are seen by Wilson as more serious. First, the judges who presently have the power of discretion in sentencing would have to give it up, and it is doubtful that they would be eager to do so. Second, public funds would be needed for new, smaller, and better prisons. But although each citizen has some interest in combating crime, the benefit to each which would result from improving prisons is not enough to constitute an incentive to organize and lobby for such an allocation of funds. Paradoxically, in a nation beset by crime, little has happened that might affect crime rates.

The changes in our system of punishment which Wilson sees to be desirable are nearly identical to those proposed by David Fogel. But whereas Wilson's focus is on the political feasibility of effecting these changes, Fogel takes the prison administrator's viewpoint in detailing the actual structures and policies which would need to be brought about in prisons in order for the goals of the just deserts model to be attained.

> Fogel: *The prison sentence should merely represent a depriva-tion of liberty. All rights accorded free citizens but consistent with mass living and the execution of a sentence should follow a prisoner into prison.*

The measures which David Fogel proposes would bring prisons and sentencing closer to what he calls "the justice model." What lies centrally behind his proposals is a view of the offender as a responsible agent. He considers it a great irony that we take such pains during trial to establish that the accused acted voluntarily, but then treat the convicted prisoner as though he were incapable of responsible action. Fogel's most prominent proposals are a return to "flat time" sentencing, the elimination of parole, and the abandon-ment of the rehabilitative model, leaving rehabilitation programs voluntary.

Fogel lists several measures which could be implemented immedi-ately by prison administrators without legislation, which would make prisons more just. These include engaging convicts and guards in the governance of prisons; making legal aid available to prisoners (for civil as well as criminal problems); requiring that the bases of administrative decisions be made known to prisoners; and assigning the task of overseeing fairness in the prison to an ombudsman.

Perhaps the most important of Fogel's middle-range proposals is his plan for sentencing. He would *not* require that every felony offender be sent to prison. He would prefer that community-based punishments be used where the offender would not be dangerous to society. But once a sentence is set, it can be shortened *only* by "good time" credit. Fogel proposes that sentences be reduced one day for every day of lawful behavior. Infractions of prison rules *may* lead to a loss of good time, if this is so ruled by a hearing held with due process. But crimes in prison would be considered a matter of further criminal prosecution, and would not affect the original sentence.

Although sentences would be rather rigidly determined by the offense; certain factors, such as strong provocation or lack of serious harm, would be considered grounds for withholding a sentence of imprisonment, and for making a sentence shorter; while certain other factors, such as causing serious harm or being a repeated offender would be considered grounds in favor of mandating a prison sentence, and of making a sentence longer. For example, the presumptive sentence for a certain class of felony would be two years, but the allowable range of variation due to mitigating or aggravating factors would be plus or minus one year. This narrowing of range would help reduce plea bargaining.

Fogel points out that a flat time system such as the one he proposes has the political advantage of enabling us to predict prison populations and resultant costs. Some have objected that his proposed sentences for different categories of offenses are too short, but Fogel claims that the cost of supporting the prison population which would result from longer sentences would be intolerable.

As a part of his view of prisoners as individually responsible, Fogel favors paying prisoners a reasonable wage, and, if they are so paid, charging them for lodging, taxes, and victim restitution.

Fogel concludes that his perspective assumes that crime and criminals are not aberrations; that incarceration for some will be necessary. Rather than attempting to change people through rehabilitation, he claims we should attempt to make the conditions of incarceration just.

Fogel's approach to the problem of dealing with offenders has much in common with that of Norval Morris. Both see crime and criminals as something which must realistically be expected to remain with us, and both see the object of a system of punishment as being the just handling of offenders, rather than the manipulation of them. Morris sees this as a point of pressing importance as we look to the prison population of the future.

Morris: *The prison population will continue . . . to increase into*

*the mid-1980s and nothing we could do about it, even if we had
political power, would make much difference.*

Norval Morris sees Americans as having done well in encouraging
crime during the last two centuries. We are certainly the "home of
the brave," he says, and he predicts that matters will get considerably
worse. But in the face of this prediction he cautions us that the way
we run our prisons will really have little effect on crime rates; that
our reasons for running prisons one way rather than another should
be consideration of human rights; that individual freedoms should
not be sacrificed because citizens are becoming impatient about
crime.

Today, there are approximately a quarter million adults in prisons
in the United States. Morris predicts that this number will steadily
increase into the mid-1980s, and that there is nothing we can do
which would have much effect on this. Prisons will become more
crowded and more violent.

The reason why we cannot do much to reduce the prison
population is demographic. There is coming toward us a population
wave of the poor, minority youths between the ages of 18 and 30
who disproportionately fill our prisons. This wave will peak about
1985. In addition, there will probably be improvements in the
effectiveness of police and courts, and mandatory minimum sentences may be introduced, and these factors would also increase the
prison population.

Morris is, of course, unhappy over what he predicts to occur; he
finds caging hateful and requiring justification in terms of social
need. But he does not believe that any of the proposals by prison
abolitionists and reductionists would really affect the prison population. Decriminalization of certain offenses has been proposed, but
Morris points out that the offenders who would be affected do not
add much to the prison population. Diversion of less serious
offenders from jails and prisons is advocated, but according to Morris
these programs typically take under control people who were not
previously under control at all. Locking up only the dangerous is also
proposed, but the problem Morris sees here is that we are not able to
predict who will be dangerous.

Some have called for harsh punishment on the grounds that it will
deter crime, but Morris agrees with Wilson that it is not so much the
severity or duration of imprisonment that deters, but rather the fact
of imprisonment. As for rehabilitation, Morris urges that attempts at
rehabilitation *not* be given up; what should be given up is the *link*
between coercive efforts at rehabilitation and the duration of

detention. Rehabilitation should be *voluntary*. We should not send people to prison in order to cure them of being criminal; we are unable to cure them within the limits of proper regard for human rights, freedom, and dignity.

Morris believes that it is crucial for us to *recognize* that what we do with prisons will have little effect on crime rates. Neither humane nor brutal punishments would affect crime as much, he thinks, as would changes in such areas as education and employment.

Morris himself designed a new prison at Butner, North Carolina, which he thinks is important because it will take the most serious offenders, and will try not to brutalize them or make them worse men than they were. He hopes that the recidivism rate for this group will be lower than for the control group; but the task of real importance for Butner and for prisons generally, Morris thinks, in view of the minimal effects that can be had on crime rates, is to uphold minimum living conditions for prisoners. He describes procedures for intake and release, and for staff selection and training, as well as an institutional program; all designed to achieve conditions that will not make prisoners worse men.

Morris outlines a theory of punishment according to which we should punish only those whose punishment is *both* deserved by their conduct and necessary for the common good; the amount of punishment being only as much as is necessary to achieve social purposes. Within this theory of punishment, he suggests further restrictions on the use of *imprisonment* as the particular form of punishment. He concludes that, paradoxically, we will deal with the offender more decently if we recognize that we are punishing him, and do not pretend to be helping him.

So far, the studies discussed have become less and less critical of the institution of punishment, and generally more and more concerned with practical action. It seems fitting for the concluding study to return to a critical philosophical posture, and the contribution of Richard Wasserstrom is well suited for this purpose. Wasserstrom sees punishment as an unsolved problem: the pain it intentionally imposes requires justification in order for us to regard it as morally acceptable. But although there are justifications that work for some cases, no one theory, including retributivism, serves adequately for all cases of punishment.

Wasserstrom: *We do not, I think, yet have in retributivism a set of moral arguments sufficiently sound, convincing, and worked out upon which to rest the justifiability of punishment.*

Since some people think we should employ treatment rather than punishment, Wasserstrom argues, we should get clear on what punishment is and how this practice would differ from treatment. He criticizes a number of attempts to characterize punishment, on the grounds that they uncritically take *legal* punishment to be the standard case of punishment, while giving no justification for preferring this over, e.g., parental punishment as the standard case; and on the grounds that these characterizations typically rely on a notion of an *offense*. The problem with characterizing "punishment" in terms of "offense" is that there is no apparent way to explain what an offense is without saying that it is an act for which one is punished. Wasserstrom proposes that punishment be characterized by distinguishing it from other cases of unpleasant coerced treatment, and he cites as distinguishing features, that (1) assessment of responsibility is irrelevant in the case of treatment; (2) punishment must have an aspect of publicity; treatment need not; and (3) it does not make sense to treat a person for what no longer afflicts him.

Wasserstrom argues against both treatment and the use of punishment for the purpose of deterrence, on the grounds that in each case it is social control that is the object; the rehabilitationist seeks to control the criminal, the deterrentist seeks to control the noncriminal. Treatment, or punishment, is seen as instrumental here, and forward-looking. Both views fail, therefore, to capture the moral point of a system of punishment: that it is backward looking. This leads Wasserstrom to consider the theory which does acknowledge this point—retributivism.

The most important defense of retributivism which Wasserstrom considers is one made by Herbert Morris.[2] Morris has argued that a lawbreaker should be punished because he has taken an unfair advantage in benefiting from the fact that others have restrained themselves by obeying the law, while he himself has not shared this burden of restraint. Punishment is seen, then, as restoring the equilibrium of burdens and benefits.

Wasserstrom objects first that it is not always plausible to think of criminal and law-abiding behavior in terms of burdens and benefits. Tax evasion fits the scheme, but rape, for example, does not. Someone who is not inclined to rape, is not unfairly burdened if someone else decides to rape; and the same can be said for torture and murder. The retributivist could reply that everyone has an inclination to do *some* of the things the law prohibits, and that in this sense each person is burdened by restraint while each benefits from the restraints of others. But Wasserstrom has a further objection which would still need to be answered.

For Morris' scheme of restoring an equilibrium of burdens and benefits to work, punishment should take away the offender's undeserved benefit. We can take back *money*, but, Wasserstrom points out, this is restitution, not punishment. In a case where an offender has hidden stolen property, imprisonment might be seen as keeping him from enjoying his benefit; but in many cases, such as rape, punishment neither takes away nor prevents the enjoyment of an undeserved benefit.

Wasserstrom concludes that no theory has been worked out which fills the need to justify the institution of punishment; that more philosophical work has yet to be done.

There is indeed more philosophical work to be done concerning punishment. As one reviews the studies as a whole, a few major problems in particular come into focus.

Wasserstrom's criticisms of Herbert Morris' retributivist theory point up one major problem. This is the problem of providing a more fundamental principle on which to base the retributivist practice of fitting punishments to crimes. The difficulty may be seen from the fact that not just any answer to the question, "Why punish?" is compatible with the retributivist's answer to the question "Who should be punished, and how much?" This is essentially Hospers' point when he argues that if the rationale for passing laws which assign penalties to offenses is to be the maximization of social good, then this will not necessarily be compatible with punishing particular individuals in the amount they deserve. If the answer to the question, "Why punish?" is, for example, "To get people to obey the law," then there will be a tension between this answer and the retributivist's answer to the question "How much should an offender be punished?"

If the object of the *institution* of punishment is deterrence, then this in itself dictates the amount of punishment that is appropriate for particular offenses, and this is *not* necessarily the amount of punishment that is deserved for the crime. In Herbert Morris' theory we have at least an attempt to provide an underlying basis for the retributivist dictum that the punishment fit the crime. On his account, it would be an underlying principle of equality which would dictate that a person receive a burden of the same approximate magnitude as the undeserved benefit he took. This principle would be like a principle of distributive justice dictating that certain burdens and benefits be shared equally. The answer to the question "Why punish?" might, on this theory, be put: "To keep this distribution equal," and this answer would support the retributivist answer to the question "Who should be punished and how much?"

But if Wasserstrom's criticisms of this attempt to justify retributivism are telling, then we are left with the problem of finding some other underlying support for fitting punishments to crimes.

It might be replied that our moral intuition concerning the appropriateness of punishments being equal in gravity to offenses, is strong enough that there is no need for a more fundamental principle to support it. But this raises a second major problem: What exactly do we mean by a punishment "fitting" an offense? If we can not say precisely what the *content* of this principle is, can we be certain that it is a principle to be followed? This problem has already been mentioned in reference to Bedau and Pincoffs, but one point might be worth making here to remind us of the magnitude of the difficulties we face.

The problem of fitting punishments to crimes seems sorted out in a helpful way by Pincoffs when he divides it into (1) anchoring the scale of crimes to the scale of punishments at some point, and (2) determining the intervals between crimes according to seriousness. What seems encouraging here is the prospect that once we anchor the scales at some point, all the other coordinates will fall into line. However, as Pincoffs acknowledges, the spacing of crimes does not admit of exact measurement, and Bedau's analysis makes it appear even less hopeful that anything like measurement can be performed, if in fact we must gauge seriousness in terms of such incommensurate components as guilt and harm. The consequence of this is that we are really left with an anchoring problem at every point of the crime scale. Variations in culpability might even produce the result that the appropriate punishment for a particular offense be less than that assigned to a crime that is ordinarily placed lower on the scale. This and related problems of fitting punishments to offenses, are ones on which there is a great deal of work yet to be done.

One final problem seems particularly worth mentioning. There is a considerable gap between the context in which writers such as James Q. Wilson, David Fogel, and Norval Morris attempt to deal with the questions of what kind of system of punishment can be made workable and defensible in our society as it exists, and the context in which philosophers attempt to determine the justifiability of punishment. Much of the philosophical work on the problems of punishment involves determining what kind of system of punishment would be called for in an ideally just society. This raises the question: "What about a society that is considerably less than just; a society such as our own?" In determining the kind of system of punishment which would characterize an ideally just society, are we necessarily also determining the kind of system of punishment which should be adopted here and now?

It seems that there are two possibilities here. The first is the more simple. It could be that after a society reaches a certain point of injustice, it then becomes incumbent upon citizens to oppose the laws and system of punishment of the society and attempt to change them; but that until this point of injustice is reached, the same general *kind* of system of punishment which is appropriate to the ideally just society, is also the kind which is appropriate to a less than just society. For example, if retributivism would in fact characterize a just society, then it would not be the case that a rehabilitative system should characterize a less than just society.

The other alternative is more complicated. It *could* be the case that certain defects in a society such as inequitable distribution of wealth and opportunities would dictate also a change in the way in which offenders should be treated. It is at least possible that it would be illegitimate to punish according to retributivist principles if persons in a society did not live in a context of equal opportunity.

There are reasons for believing that the less advantaged members of a less than just society who become offenders would fare worse in a system of treatment or rehabilitation than in a retributive system of punishment. Some of these reasons are presented in the criticisms of rehabilitation which occur in this book. But it is not clear that *as a general rule* whatever kinds of institutions characterize an ideally just society are also the kinds of institutions which should be brought about in a less-than-just society. It is particularly in the discussion of punishment that this issue is of pressing importance, since those who are punished have often been victims of injustice.

The impression with which one is left after reading this book is not only that there are many unanswered questions concerning the justification of punishment, but also that the deeper one delves into these questions, the more they multiply and the more complicated they become. There seems to be progress of a sort in the elimination of faulty theories. But knowing what is not a good reason for punishment provides little comfort as we face the dilemma of feeling compelled to punish without knowing our justification for doing so.

NOTES TO CHAPTER ONE

1. John Rawls, "Two Concepts of Rules," *The Philosophical Review*, v. 64, n. 1 (January, 1955), pp. 3-32.
2. Herbert Morris, "Persons and Punishment," *The Monist* v. 52, n. 4 (October, 1968), pp. 475-501.

✳ *Chapter Two*

Punishment, Protection, and Retaliation
John Hospers

Who should be punished, why, and by whom? These questions have been argued for two thousand years, with some clarification of the issues but no great measure of agreement. No issue in ethical theory has been more extensively studied, and the chances of coming up with something novel are small indeed. I shall avoid the strong temptation to discuss what classes of offenses should be legally punishable and concentrate on (1) the justification of punishment and (2) who should administer it. In doing so I shall have to go over once again, though briefly, some well trodden ground regarding classical theories of punishment. I want primarily to discuss four views that could be called "theories of punishment," beginning with the two "classical" theories.

I shall follow Flew's five-fold definition of punishment: punishment (1) must involve an unpleasantness to the victim; (2) must be for an offense; (3) must be of an offender; (4) must be the work of personal agencies (natural evils will not do); and (5) must be imposed by virtue of some special authority, conferred through or by the institutions against the laws or rules of which the offense has been committed. I shall leave the definition undiscussed not because no objections could be made to it, but because no contrary opinion will turn on it and it serves to isolate neatly the central concept of our discussion.

I

What has traditionally been called the *retributive* theory, but would be less confusing if it were called the *deserts* theory, is very straightforward: a person who is guilty of an offense should be punished in proportion to the penalty he *deserves* for the crime. The degree of punishment should depend on the degree of the offender's desert. Punishment should not be in excess of what is deserved. (But it may be less, depending on various circumstances to be discussed shortly.) At any rate, the justification of punishment lies in the commission of *past* acts, not in any *future* good effects which the punishment may produce. Punishment is strictly because-of, not in-order-to. It is possible, even desirable, for a prisoner to be improved and rehabilitated during his term, but this is a fringe-benefit, not the purpose of punishing him—just as, in the opposite case from punishment (reward), the justification for giving a worker wages is the work he *has* done, not the stimulation of future efforts, though this may be one of its effects.

The deserts theory, then, claims that guilt is a *necessary* condition for punishment: if no guilt, then no punishment, no matter what goods might be achieved by imprisoning the innocent, such as rehabilitating the prisoner or increasing the public's sense of reassurance or stopping a crime-wave. It does not claim that guilt is a *sufficient* condition for punishment: that if there is guilt, there must be punishment. (a) If guilt simply means having committed the crime, then there are circumstances under which the guilty person should not be punished, or need not: e.g., insanity, senility, coercion. (b) And if guilt means moral guilt, so as to exonerate these classes of offenders, there still might be conditions that would mitigate or even rule out punishment, e.g., if the defendant's physician has given him three months to live.

The deserts theory is often misunderstood in several ways:

It is said that the theory is simply an attempt to sanctify the lust for vengeance, and that its proponents desire punishment for punishment's sake.[1] But this is sheer confusion. The conviction that the wrongdoer should be punished is not to be confused with the desire for vengeance; if the desire for vengeance is the primary emotion present, the retributivist would disapprove of this, and wish to see it replaced by a desire for justice. "Revenge is the deliberate production of evil, evil that can neither undo what has been done, nor create some mystical atonement in which evil cancels evil."[2] It is not punishment for punishment's sake, nor the infliction of pain for pain's sake, that is the justification for punishing (on the deserts theory); it is rather punishment for the sake of justice. Motives other than the desire for justice are irrelevant.

It is said that punishment is simply a device by the retributivist to 'restore the moral balance.' Again, we have here a metaphor; there are scales, of which one is depressed when a crime is committed and the other is depressed to an equal depth when that crime is punished. But I do not see to what facts this metaphor corresponds. Who is to say how much punishment is required to make the scale balance again? or what kind? or even that there was something that could be called 'balance' prior to the commission of the crime? or why once disturbed it should be restored? or why imprisoning some would restore it? Baier says that "the moral balance is preserved when everyone is 'strictly minding his own business,' "[3] but no reason is given for holding this view.

It is often assumed that the punishment must "fit the crime"; and this may be true, depending on what the metaphor of "fit" is construed to mean. If it means only that more serious punishments should be attached to more serious crimes, the retributivist would offer no objection. But if it means that punishment should *resemble* the crime, in being a mirror-image of the crime, then it is not true; at least, this would be a special *version* of the deserts theory, not held by most of its proponents. And this version has not much to recommend it. It is committed, for example, to capital punishment, which the deserts theory in general is not: if a person takes a life, says the mirror-image theory, then his life should be taken. But from the fact that the punishment *resembles* the crime, it does not follow that this is the punishment that the offender *deserves*. Nor is the mirror-image theory very feasible to apply in many cases: if A has stolen from B, should B's punishment be to be stolen from? Since most thieves lack money and that is why they steal, the prospect of extracting money from them is not a very hopeful one. Besides, the theory is not always possible to apply. If being killed is the proper punishment for killing someone, what is the proper punishment for rape? And what punishment should be assigned to a blind man who has blinded someone else?[4]

But the temptation to say "he deserves to get what he gave others" is a strong one. After his capture Adolf Eichmann said, "I will leap into my grave laughing because the feeling that I have five million human beings on my conscience is for me a source of extraordinary satisfaction." And *Time* magazine commented, "Remembering the stinking holes of Poland's Auschwitz, the smoking crematoriums of Germany, the boneyards and mass graves of the Ukraine, vengeful Israelis are not disposed to argue the fine points of the law. Instead, they debate what punishment could possibly fit the crime. Hanging, most agree, is too easy. Said one survivor of Eichmann's camps: 'He should be made to live under the very same conditions that we lived in in the camps, eat the same crumbs of dried bread, work the same, smell the same putrid odors from the furnaces. Let's see how long he would last!' "[5] Now it is possible that just such a punishment is what Eichmann deserved, but the deserts theory in general does not assert it. Even the mirror-image theory cannot really assert it, for one man cannot die 5 million deaths.

There are other distinctions that should be made:

We should distinguish "He deserves to be punished" from "He ought to be punished." If jailing a man would endanger his life, and other alternatives were available, he should not be punished even though he deserved it. If the punishment of a convicted spy triggered off a nuclear war, we would have reason to say he should not be punished, even though he deserved it.[6]

To say that a person deserves a certain punishment is not to say that someone is justified in inflicting it. This is partly because the person inflicting it may not be the person empowered to inflict it—e.g., the enemy or victim of the aggrieved person; and partly because of a change in circumstances. If a Nazi war criminal finds his way to an uninhabited island[7] where he carves out an idyllic existence for himself, and is discovered 30 years later, with no desire to leave or cause more trouble, he would (says the desert theory) not be justified in complaining about any suffering imposed for his misdeeds; yet it does not follow that he should be taken in and punished: from the fact that he deserves it, it does not follow that he should be given it by just anyone or under any circumstances.

We should also distinguish desert from entitlement. The winning player may have had a bad day and yet won the meet because all the other players were even worse. He doesn't deserve the prize, but he is entitled to it because he did the best in this meet. The defeated presidential candidate who deserved to win is not by that token entitled to the office, nor does he have any right to it.[8]

The main problem for the deserts theory centers around the question: what punishment, if any, does a specific person deserve for a specific offense? How do you tell? If two people disagree on this, how is the issue to be resolved? There are two related problems here: (a) Whereas all retributivists agree that the more serious the offense, the more serious the punishment should be, not all will agree on which offenses are the most serious (nor which punishments are either). Some would say that rape is more serious than armed robbery; others not. So while agreeing on the general formula, there would be disagreement on which offenses are the most serious, and hence the most deserving of punishment. (b) Even if all retributivists agreed on which offenses are the most serious, there would still be disagreement on what the specific punishment for each should be.

Two persons might well agree that murder is the most serious of crimes, but disagree as to whether capital punishment, life imprisonment, or imprisonment with the possibility of parole would be the most deserved punishment for it in an individual case. There is no underestimating of the seriousness of these objections if the retributive theory is to be satisfactorily implemented in practice.

II

And so we turn to the *utilitarian* theory, which could well be called the *results* theory. Punishment here is not *because* a crime has been committed and the offender deserves to be punished for it; the punishment is *in order* to promote good (and/or prevent evil) in the future. What's past is finished; all one can hope to do is prevent similar occurrences in the future, and this should be the sole aim of punishing. Punishing is not because-of, but in-order-to; and if no good future end is served by inflicting it, it is immoral, merely the adding of one evil (punishing) to another (the crime).

If an offender against the law is imprisoned, this can serve three distinct utilitarian purposes: (a) to reform or rehabilitate the offender himself, so that he will not repeat his offense, and will emerge from the punishment situation a better person than before; (b) to deter others, who might otherwise see a crime going unpunished and thus commit one themselves; and (c) to protect society at large against people who are dangerous to the safety of others by isolating them, for a time at least, from the rest of society by imprisoning them.

It is improbable, of course, that all three of these aims will be fulfilled in any particular case of utilitarian punishment. Imprisonment very seldom rehabilitates law-breakers; if that were the sole purpose of imprisonment, prisons should close shop tomorrow; most prisoners learn about crime and are oriented toward crime more after imprisonment than before. The second aim, deterrence, is more effective: many people who would otherwise kill and pillage and steal are deterred from doing so by the consideration that they may get caught. Unfortunately, however, deterrence is only sporadically effective; it is much more effective for minor offenses, such as overparking and game-shooting out of season, than it is for a major crime like murder; most murders are committed "in the heat of passion" with no thought of possible consequences, and no amount of threatened punishment would be sufficient to deter them. Deterrence then is rather a mixed bag. But even if deterrence fails in a particular case, the third aim may be achieved: the protection of others. Even if the offender is not improved by punishment, and even if no one else is deterred from crime by his being imprisoned, at least during the period of his imprisonment other people are protected from further acts of aggression by him; and this is sufficient to justify his imprisonment even if the other two aims don't work. It is the *isolation* of the offender from the rest of society that is crucial here; and, the argument is, it is more important to protect innocent people than it is to protect the freedom of the offender to do what he wants. The protection of society against dangerous people is, then, the most important of the three types of good to be achieved by imprisonment according to the results theory.

(Even this is not achieved by the prison system. According to Maya Pines in her book *Cruel and Usual Punishment*, even the most hardened prison wardens agree that 80 to 85 percent of the people in prisons do not belong there; and that if the entire prison population of America were released tomorrow, the nation would be just as safe (or unsafe) as it is now, because the vast majority of dangerous people are loose and roaming the streets.)

It is quite possible for these three future-looking functions of punishment to *work against* one another. What deters others may not improve the criminal or protect society, and where protection is most needed deterrence or reformation may be least effective. And this fact places the utilitarian in a dilemma as to what should be done. For example, murder is the most heinous of crimes, yet murderers on the whole may be the most nearly ideal prisoners: most of them are one-time criminals, and are extremely unlikely to commit murder again. If they were let loose at once they would be no danger to society, not nearly as much at any rate as the petty thieves, who are much more likely to repeat their acts. Thus, society needs no protection from the typical prisoner who is in for murder, but other people do need to be deterred from murder—though murder is the crime least likely to be affected by techniques of deterrence. So the effects of one aim of punishment may be at odds with the effects of another. And in such a case, there is some problem of what the utilitarian is to recommend.

Long sentences of imprisonment might effactually stamp out car parking offenses, yet we think it wrong to employ them; *not* because there is for each crime a penalty 'naturally' fitted to its degree of iniquity . . . ; not because we are convinced that the misery caused by such sentences would be greater than that caused by the offenses unchecked . . . ; The guiding principle is that of a proportion within a system of penalties between those imposed for different offenses where these have a distinct place in a common-sense scale of gravity.[9]

But this guiding principle seems quite incompatible with utilitarianism.

The utilitarian says nothing at all about *just* punishment or what a criminal *deserves*; nothing is said about the seriousness of the crime committed, only about the probable future effects of punishing him. Murder, most people believe, is a more serious crime than robbery, and robbery more serious than a parking offense. And we tend to believe with the retributivist that the punishment should in some way be proportional to the seriousness of the offense. But the utilitarian will reject all this: if the crime is a very serious one, but he will commit no future offenses, so that others need no protection against him, and he needs no rehabilitation, then the only reason for leaving him in prison is to deter others; when more deterrence is needed, he is kept in prison for a longer period. And in that case *he is being used solely as a means* toward other people's end—toward giving others a lesson. And when deterrence is minimal, as it is with murder, then there remains no reason according to the utilitarian for leaving him in prison at all. It looks as if the utilitarian (sometimes at least) would have to recommend longer sentences for smaller crimes than for greater ones.

Nor is this the most serious consequence. Whether others are deterred by the incarceration of a lawbreaker depends not on the act of incarceration itself but on the *publicity* given it: it depends on others *knowing* that this man has been imprisoned for armed robbery, not on the fact that the robbery occurred. If the fact of his incarceration were kept a secret, and no one knew about it, it would deter no one. And this leads to the familiar nightmare consideration: why need the man be guilty at all? Suppose there is a crime wave, and crimes of a certain kind need badly to be deterred, and a man is arrested who at the time may be suspected of being guilty; he has probably been guilty of numerous previous offenses but has got off on a technicality, and now the authorities can really nail him and make it stick. But there is just one problem: the judge knows that the man is innocent, having seen him himself at another place at the time the crime of which the man is accused was committed. If the judge is a utilitarian, he may reason as follows: "Normally the sentencing of an innocent man is antiutilitarian, since the facts can come out and public confidence in the legal process plummets. But in this case, no one will ever know except the accused man and me. No one will believe *him*, and as for me, I shall keep my mouth shut. Sentencing him will have all kinds of good effects: it will deter others, it will stop or abort the crime wave, it will restore public confidence, people can rest secure in their beds believing that the culprit has been caught. So, balancing the bad consequences to the innocent man against the good consequences to society in general, the case is overwhelmingly in favor of the latter: so I'll sentence the man, even though I know he is innocent." And as a bit of utilitarian reasoning this is impeccable.[10] If one fears that the really guilty man will turn up and confess, one could counter that for every major crime there are lots of phony confessions, and this could easily be made to seem one of them; or we may even stipulate that the guilty man is dead, and that the judge knows this, so that the possibility of his turning up is now excluded. The question is, even if this is so, is it any the less unjust to sentence a man known to be innocent? The fact is simple: the question of what is *just* punishment and the question of what punishment will have *good effects*, are two distinct questions; and the answer to the first need not be the same as an answer to the second.[11]

This point has been made with remarkable clarity by Professor J.D. Mabbott in his essay "Punishment."[12] He considers two cases. "Suppose," he says "that it could be shown that a particular criminal had not been improved by a punishment and also that no other would-be criminal had been deterred by it, would that prove that the punishment was unjust?" The answer, he says, is clearly No. Secondly, "Suppose it were discovered that a particular criminal had lived a much better life after his release and that many would-be criminals believing him to have been guilty were influenced by his fate, but yet that the 'criminal' was punished for something he had never done, would these excellent results prove the punishment just?" And again, he says, the answer is obviously No. But if this is so, what happens to the utilitarian (results) theory of punishment? The least we could say is that it doesn't have much to do with justice.

Nor is this even the most serious consideration: there is another consequence of the results theory not yet considered: the utilitarian, geared as he is toward the achievement of future goods, is likely to be inclined against punishment and in favor of *treatment*. As a utilitarian he need not be so inclined in every case: a prisoner may be totally unresponsive to treatment, or no treatment may be known which will change his actions or his attitude; so the utilitarian will simply favor his incarceration for the specified period. But if the prisoner is responsive to suggestion at all, it is likely that the utilitarian in charge of prisoners will say, "Don't punish him—treat him, mould his personality so that he won't be inclined any longer to commit similar offenses in the future." It all sounds very attractive, very advanced, very humanitarian.

But there is a very ominous side to this practice of treatment: (1) By what standards will the treatment be conducted? What is to be the criterion of improvement? It is almost inevitable that the prisoner will be considered 'unimproved' or 'unrehabilitated' until he shares the values of the person treating him. (2) Will the treatment be compulsory? If it is, this is a very serious matter if the prisoner doesn't want to be changed in the direction prescribed by the therapist. Even if it isn't compulsory, great pressure can be brought to bear to make him engage in it, such as depriving him of access to facilities, or keeping him in solitary until he decides to "cooperate." There are horrendous true stories of what has happened in prisons when prisoners chose not to "cooperate" with the therapists in charge. (3) How long will it last? A prison sentence is for a definite maximum period of time, and then at least the person is out. But in view of the increasing popularity of treatment, the indefinite sentence is now the in thing. How long the sentence will last depends on the whim or wisdom of the therapists. If the prisoner doesn't cooperate, he can be made to remain incarcerated and 'treated' indefinitely. Even if he is in for a fairly trivial offense, that doesn't mean his treatment is short—the therapist may find so many things wrong with his personality (in the therapist's opinion) that it will take years and years to 'cure' him. The imprisoned man is the therapist's prisoner, and if he doesn't respond the way the therapist wants him to he can be in for good. This is already the case in Soviet Russia, where the fashion is to put dissenters into asylums for the 'mentally diseased,' and subject them to deprivation, shock, cold, and a variety of injected chemicals until "they see the error of their ways" or until the prisoner dies of the 'therapy.' In this respect American prisons are not many years behind. The British philosopher C.S. Lewis put the matter dramatically when he wrote:

> They are not punishing, not inflicting, only healing. But do not let us be deceived by a name. To be taken without consent from my home and friends; to lose my liberty; to undergo all those assaults on my personality which modern psychotherapy knows how to deliver; to be re-made after some pattern of 'normality' hatched in a Viennese laboratory to which I never professed allegiance; to know that this process will never end until either my captors have succeeded or I have grown wise enough to cheat

them with apparent success—who cares whether this is called Punishment or not? That it includes most of the elements for which any punishment is feared—shame, exile, bondage, and years eaten by the locust—is obvious. Only enormous, ill-desert could justify it; but ill-desert is the very conception which the Humanitarian theory has thrown overboard.

If we turn from the curative to the deterrent justification of punishment we shall find the new theory even more alarming. When you punish a man . . . , make of him an 'example' to others, you are admittedly using him as a means to an end: someone else's end. This, in itself, would be a very wicked thing to do. On the classical theory of punishment it was, of course, justified on the ground that the man deserved it. That was assumed to be established before any question of 'making him an example' arose. You then, as the saying is, killed two birds with one stone; in the process of giving him what he deserved, you set an example to others. But take away desert and the whole morality of the punishment disappears. Why, in heaven's name, am I to be sacrificed to the good of society in this way?—unless, of course, I deserve it. . . .[13]

It would seem, in fact, that we shouldn't call the utilitarian theory a theory of punishment at all. It is, like the retributive theory, a theory of *retaliation*—that is, the offender isn't ignored, something is done to him. On the deserts theory what is done to him is punishment; on the results theory what is done to him may be treatment and may simply be incarceration or isolation from society, whichever will promote the more total good; but in either case it is dubious whether this should be called punishment at all. What if the best effects on society as a whole are to be produced in a given case by not incarcerating the murderer at all (he is no apparent danger, his family depends on him for support, etc.) and keeping a compulsive purse-snatcher in for fifty years? If you consider all the millions of the population, as against the one prisoner, this could surely be the case. Is this kind of retaliation to be called punishment? In the extreme case, as we have seen, a person need not be guilty at all, as long as imprisoning him produces good consequences for society at large. In a case described by Solzhenitsyn, one prisoner asks another what his sentence was. "25 years," he says. "What for?" "For nothing. I didn't do anything at all." "That can't be," says the other prisoner. "The sentence for nothing at all is ten years."[14]

"The death penalty," writes Solzhenitsyn, "was rechristened 'the supreme measure'—no longer a punishment but a means of *social defense.*"[15] Under these new edicts, "more than sixteen thousand persons were shot (in 15 months)";[16] and if this did not get rid of people fast enough, the practice was begun of "sinking barges loaded with uncounted, unregistered hundreds, unidentified even by a roll call." Is there any possibility that the number of violations of the law multiplied so rapidly after the Revolution? One is tempted to say no—the charges, most of them, had to be manufactured. But if you make enough actions legal crimes, it is, of course, possible that the number of violations multiplied. For example, "Six collective farmers . . . were guilty of the following crime: After they had finished mowing the collective farm with their own hands, they had gone back and mowed a second time along the hummocks to get a little hay for their own cows. The All-Russian Central Executive Committee refused to pardon these six peasants, and the sentence of execution was carried out."[17] Reading these and a few thousand more similar incidents from Soviet history, one can hardly conclude that most of these acts constitute punishment; either there were no violations of law at all by the persons in question, or when there were the laws were dreamed up in order to be violated so that more people, unwanted by the new regime, could be killed or provide cheap labor in Siberia. "Just give us a person, and we'll create the case."[18] And "it was not what he had done that constituted the defendant's burden, but what he *might* do if he were not shot now."[19] In either case, there is no doubt that action is being taken against the prisoner, but is it punishment? It *may* have had certain utilitarian effects; I doubt this, but this at least is arguable; that the penalties were undeserved is not arguable. In the early years of the Revolution not all of the people condemned to death were shot; some were fed alive to the animals in the city zoos. "How else could they get food for the zoos in those famine years? Take it away from the working class? Those enemies were going to die anyway, so why couldn't their deaths support the zoo economy of the Republic and thereby assist our march into the future. Wasn't it expedient?"[20] The whole "utilitarian theory of punishment" should, I submit, be called not punishment at all, but social engineering.

III

There have been attempts to combine the two theories, to "skim off the best" of both of them and do justice to both sides.

1. It has been suggested that the retributive theory is acceptable in providing a *justification* for punishing at all: unless the person has committed a crime he should not be punished, no matter how socially therapeutic his imprisonment might be; the retributive theory *sets*

a limit on who may be punished. But once a person has been adjudged guilty, then the results theory takes over: the sole purpose of punishing anyone should be not to avenge past wrongs but to produce as much good, and prevent as much evil, as possible in the future. Thus, it is said, the "best" aspects of the two theories have been preserved. "The traditional opposition of retribution and prevention is meaningless," writes Alf Ross, "because the opposing answers are not concerned with the same question. To maintain that punishment is imposed *in order to* prevent crime is to offer an answer to the question of the *aim of penal legislation.* To say that punishment is imposed *because* the criminal has incurred guilt, is to offer an answer to the question of the *justification for imposing penalties.*"[21]

I am not so optimistic about this "solution." I intend my question to be about justification in both cases—i.e. how does one justify doing either? Granted that we are not supposed to incarcerate the innocent; but once guilt has been determined, we are supposed from there on not to consider the past offense but only the future welfare of the prisoner and that of society. To the extent that this is done, of course, considerations of desert must be abandoned. What if the offender is a perennial public nuisance of a minor sort and the welfare of society would be maximized in this case by keeping him in for fifty years—not because he personally deserves such a fate, but because he is one and society is many, and many individuals find him offensive and a nuisance, and moreover he is immune to any known psychiatric or other techniques of rehabilitation? If we are to consider future effects, the petty offender who is incurable should certainly receive a longer sentence than the model-prisoner murderer who will never do it again, and whose future incarceration (from the point of view of producing useful consequences) would be pointless.

Let me add that sometimes the results theory is suggested in preference to deserts, because it is so difficult (or impossible) to determine what a person deserves, that it seems more desirable to rely on what results can be obtained from punishing him. If that is the motive behind the switch, I would point out that the second is no less difficult to determine than the first. Whether what is recommended is imprisonment or treatment, it is simply impossible to predict with any pretense to accuracy the results of such procedures. One prisoner may be improved by imprisonment, another unchanged, and another rendered criminal for life—and there is no predicting who will be which. The very same treatment prescribed by therapist A will be held to be useless by therapist B and harmful by therapist C. Each person will be inclined to evaluate a proposed punishment or treatment by considering the effects it would have on *him*; and of course he is different from everyone else in countless thousands of crucial respects, including the prisoner, that the experiment in identification is virtually useless. If you leave it to individuals to produce what they believe will be the best consequences for *other* people, you usually produce prevailingly bad consequences rather than good ones—it seems to me that if history shows anything it shows this.

> If in these personal affairs, where all the conditions of the case were known to me, I have so often miscalculated, how much oftener shall I miscalculate in political affairs, where the conditions are too numerous, too widespread, too complex, too obscure to be understood. Here, doubtless, is a social evil and there a desideratum; and were I sure of doing no mischief I would forthwith try to cure the one and achieve the other. But when I remember how many of my private schemes have miscarried; how speculations have failed, agents proved dishonest, marriage been a disappointment; how I did but pauperize the relative I sought to help; how my carefully governed son has turned out worse than most children; how the thing I desperately strove against as a misfortune did me immense good; how while the object I ardently pursued brought me little happiness when gained, most of my pleasures have come from unexpected sources; when I recall these and hosts of like facts, I am struck with the incompetence of my intellect to prescribe for society. And as the evil is one under which society has not only lived but grown, while the desideratum is one it may be spontaneously obtain, as it has most others, in some unforeseen way, I question the propriety of meddling.[22]

Spencer was talking about the administration of public welfare benefits, but his remarks apply equally to the prescription of punishment and treatment for others.

2. It has also been suggested[23] by John Rawls that the retributive and utilitarian theory each has its place, but in a somewhat different way. When we ask what is the justification for punishing a particular person we are retributivists: we say, because you robbed a bank and were tried and found guilty. But when we ask what offenses should be punished, and what laws should be passed forbidding which types of acts, then we should be utilitarians, and consider only the consequences of prescribing, say for armed robbery, the death penalty, 10 years in prison, 5 years in prison, or no penalty at all, or some other alternative, and pass the law determining what punishment is to be prescribed, entirely on the basis of the probable consequences of passing the law.

The compromise theory is neat, and seems at first to give each party his due, as well as giving warring parties the impression that each of them was right all along. They each settle for a piece of the pie. But I do not believe that this compromise view is any more satisfactory than the previous one, partly for the same reasons as in the case of the other compromise view.

One is impelled to ask, why should the legislator, who in Rawls' view should be a utilitarian about punishment, actually be one, any more than the judge who according to Rawls should not be one? It has never been clear to me why the legislator's eye, as opposed to the judge's eye, should be solely on the results of punishing. Why shouldn't the legislator also have an eye on, and only on, what degree of punishment each category of offender *deserves*? Suppose that it is determined with a fairly high degree of probability that incarcerating the minor nuisance-maker (whose condition is incurable) for fifty years is highly desirable in its consequences, and that to punish a one-time murderer (the kind who'll make a model prisoner and doesn't need imprisonment for his own rehabilitation) is not. Is this consideration supposed to be decisive? is one then to pass a law incarcerating such nuisance-makers for years, or for indefinite sentences, and giving that kind of murderer a suspended sentence or no sentence at all? Surely if you consider what the results of punishing would be, you might very well come up with this result. It is popularly taken for granted, that the worse the crime (the more deserving of punishment) the more severe will be the sentence, since there's that much more we need to protect ourselves against; but as we have already seen, this is not so—there is just *no correlation* between the gravity of offense A vs. offense B and the good consequences of punishing offense A vs. offense B. Once this lack of correlation is clearly perceived, and we *then* ask, Why should we punish a less serious offense more severely even though doing so does have better consequences?—now our question stands out naked, as it were, shorn of its utilitarian trappings; and now it is by no means obvious that we should still answer, "We should assign the severest punishments to those offenses the heavy punishment of which would have the best consequences." In fact, it may now seem obvious to many people that legislators should *not* go about passing laws with utilitarian consequences exclusively in mind.

I feel that I have still not communicated the full force of my objection. The retributive and utilitarian theories represent irreconcilable positions; the gulf between them is unbridgeable. The one looks for a justification to the past, the other to the future, and never the twain shall meet. To combine one aspect or one view with another may not be strictly inconsistent (internally contradictory), but it is an unstable compound which had no business coming into being in the first place. Consider: The deserts theory is individualistic/distributive, the utilitarian theory is aggregative/collective. Aggregative concepts such as the production of maximum good results (the general welfare, the public interest, etc.) are concerned with a total benefit to be produced. They are not concerned the way in which such benefits are to be distributed.[24] On the other hand, justice, fairness, and equity are concerned with the *apportioning* of benefits rather than with the *totaling* of them. To consider desert, then, is not the same as to consider public benefit; not only are they entirely different things, but the first may clash with the second. The question, What happens when they clash? which must give way? cannot plausibly be answered by saying that the two can't clash, or that when they do we should take desert into due consideration but then we should also consider results too . . . and so on. It may be that sometimes a punishment recommended by the one theory is also recommended by the other, but never for the same reason.

IV

Before turning to alternative theories of punishment, let us stop to consider the question, Who should administer the punishment—or treatment, or retaliation, as the case may be? There are three possibilities here: first, the victim; second, the State; third, private enforcers.

First, the victim (or in the case of murder, the victim's family or heirs). The trouble with this is that the victim almost always overestimates the gravity of the offense. An ultrasensitive person might believe that having the aggressor boiled in oil would be a well-deserved punishment for the crime of stepping on the victim's toe. The family of a murdered son will often want to see the presumed killer hanged or tortured to death without even stopping to make certain that he really did the deed. The problem with such individual retaliation is that there are *no rules*—it all depends on the whims of the aggrieved party whether the burglar will be let go, shot, tortured, or bound and gagged for a month. This is such a well known fact that almost no society leaves retaliation to the victim itself.

And so it is placed in the hands of the State. The State is supposed to be an impartial arbiter. The State's judges do not know the plaintiff or defendant personally, and if in some particular case the judge does, he does not rule on that case.

One of the troubles with the State is that it doesn't do anything well. If the State can't even run the postoffice, and is an utter disaster in running the school system, how in the world (it could be argued) could it run the judicial system well? And it doesn't, of course. We all know thousands of cases of miscarriages of justice in courts, in police departments, and in prisons. Still, there are judicial systems and judicial systems. If trials are conducted by prescribed rules, if persons are assumed innocent till proven guilty, if both sides can be fairly heard, if the rights of defendants are carefully safeguarded, then it is possible to have a good system of penal justice, even if it is run by the State. Who runs it counts less than (a) what the procedural and substantive rules are and (b) whether they are impartially observed.

One could be either a utilitarian or a retributivist and still hold that the State should not be in charge of the administration of justice. A retributivist, for example, could well say, "Justice demands that each person receive what he deserves (reward or punishment, as the case may be). But no one, save God, knows what each person deserves; so let us not leave such a vital matter to an inefficient and corruptible organization like the State. The State will dispose of the lives and liberties of others without full knowledge of the facts, or in the face of the facts, and from motives such as power which are inimical to justice." It is one thing to say that people should receive what they deserve, and quite another to say that the State should preside over the administration of this desert. A retributivist might agree to the first part, but not to the second.

Similarly, a utilitarian might not want the State to have charge of the offender. Are the State's representatives, subject to all kinds of political pressures, so wise and so impartial that they know what imprisonment or what psychiatric treatment will have the best consequences on the whole for every person whom they take into custody? Do they really know more about the probable consequences of various techniques, and are they in a better position to prescribe for all of society, than other people are? Isn't what distinguishes the State's representatives from other people that they have the other people's tax money with which to impose their ideas of justice upon others?

Indeed, if one asked either retributivists or utilitarians *by what right* the State apprehends, tries, passes sentence on, and imprisons people suspected of violating the State's law, it will be difficult to come up with an answer. One answer that could be given is, "The State alone has the power to enforce its decrees," but power is hardly synonymous with right. If you asked most people why the

State of all organizations should be entrusted with such a job I suspect that the most usual answer would be "Well, who else would (could or should) do it?" And this, if true, would explain why the State steps into the situation and takes over the job, but it is a very lame answer to the question, what gives the State the authority or the *right* to take on the job? And yet, in virtually 100 percent of the extant writings on punishment, it is assumed without question that the State has the right to apprehend, try, and punish.

The State's role in the administration of penal justice, then, is both difficult to justify and easy to criticize in practice. But what is the alternative? Doubtless pathological liars, minor nuisance-makers, and just plain screwballs need be punished only in the court of public opinion and the esteem of their fellow men; but the same can hardly be said of rapists, embezzlers, and murderers. And if the State isn't the one to do it, then who should? And here *anarchists* have an answer to suggest: *private agencies*, to which people will voluntarily subscribe as paying customers, should do it.

This procedure has been worked out in some detail by various political writers. Most people probably don't wish to take on the onerous task of their own protection, so they hire others (or a whole neighborhood does) who will, for a fee, protect them. If Pinkerton Defense Agency doesn't do a satisfactory job of protecting their life and property, then a competing agency such as Acme or Ace may do so; at any rate, one can choose among competing defenders just as one can choose among competing cars and laundry soaps, and competition always makes the suppliers of goods and services "shape up or ship out." The defense agency would have a tie-in with the (privately hired) arbitration agency (court), of which there would be many from which to choose, as with any other product or service on a free market with no State monopoly. Thus, if I belonged to defense agency A, and someone stole from me, a member of Agency A would go to the residence of the suspect, charge him and apprehend him if he did not come along willingly. He would then be tried in A's courts. If he were unjustly found guilty A would be likely to be sued for false arrest by the defendant's agency B. There is much more to it than this, and it has all been rather thoroughly worked out, but space does not permit a more extended description of it here.[25]

It is almost certain that a private agency will do a job more efficiently than a government one will; the government agency, whether it be the postoffice department or the department of motor vehicles or the police department, has no competition and thus fear no loss of business; they know that you have to get the service from them, so they can afford to make you wait, and to charge you insane prices from their services. There is nothing like competition to weed out the inefficient suppliers of goods and services. Still, here are features of private agencies in the case of "law-enforcement" which do not characterize private competition in the economic sphere. (1) The members of agencies are human and fallible, and would probably apprehend, judge, and sentence on the basis of as incomplete a knowledge of facts of the case as the State's judges and attorneys now do. (2) What would ensure that their decisions were impartial? Wouldn't they be likely to inflict whatever punishments were most popular among their own clients? Wouldn't their main motive be to increase their own revenue through subscriptions from members, than to pay for expensive trials (and even more expensive prisons) for nonmembers? Their own paying members will be their first concern, not the protection of nonmembers whom their agents apprehend on the members' behalf. (3) Indeed, the agencies might in effect become privately owned and operated vigilante groups, and if feelings ran high—for example if one agency were to arrest (kidnap?) a member of another agency for a crime of which he was suspected— armed conflict might break out at any time. Bad as the State may be as an arbiter of disputes, there is a distinct advantage in having one organization for apprehending (police) and trying (courts) rather than numerous competing organizations, with each group attempting to impose its will upon those outsiders who violate its rules.[26]

V

Where then do we go from here? It is with some relief that we discover that there is still another theory of punishments which is quite distinct from the previous two.

This view is the *restitution* theory. In both preceding views the person most lost sight of is the *victim* (or victims) of the criminal act, and it is the victim to whom restitution is owed. Under present legal systems, when your house is burglarized, you lose your valuables, and when the thief is caught, your tax money is used to sustain him in prison—so in a way you pay double; and in the meanwhile, his imprisonment, for which you help to pay, does *you* little if any good. According to the restitution theory, the chief aim of the penal system should be, not to give offenders what they deserve, nor what is best for society, but to make restitution to the victim. Let the guilty party (for example) work for the person he has robbed, until the stolen amount is restored, plus some more for pain and suffering inflicted. Let the murderer do work for the widow of the man he killed—and if she doesn't want him to do this in her home (as is very likely), let him do it in a work farm, or in prison, and surrender half or more of his weekly pay, perhaps for years, until he has paid restitution—not to society in general, but to the family of the man he killed, so that at least the death of the family breadwinner won't be a total loss to them. Here, then, is another theory of punishment; it is not punishment in accordance with desert, but it is an attempt to "make amends." And very often the amount of the loss for which restitution is to be made *can* be determined with some accuracy.

This is hardly a new concept. It is already operative in the civil law, particularly in tort (damage or injury) cases. Indeed, many scholars believe that the earliest views of punishment were restitution-type views. "In the earliest legal system of which we have record, that of Hammurabi, there is a lot about penalties, but these are considered as *damages* which a malefactor must pay to an aggrieved party. . . . It has been maintained . . . that there was at first no special criminal law, since all cases of wrongdoing were treated in the same way as those special cases which are called in modern legal parlance torts or civil wrongs, that is to say, cases where damages are payable."[2] [7]

Some have suggested today that the concept of restitution, now used only for some offenses, be extended to include all offenses, just as the same concept, once used for all offenses, became limited to tort cases. The suggestion is tempting, and the emphasis upon the victim of the offense is surely salutary. Nevertheless, there are questions that need to be put to the proponent of such a theory:

1. The major crime of all, murder, is one for which no restitution is possible; you can't bring the dead back to life. This of course must be admitted; but the restitutionist might say, "You can't undo the past, but you can still try to do the best that anybody can do, make some kind of restitution to the victim's family. Years of income would certainly be more welcome to the widow than nothing at all, even though there is no way of ever restoring the status quo."

2. If the offender "works out" his crime, by whose authority? Who sets the amount, and the time to be spent? Traditionally this is done by the judge as representative of the State; and no matter how conscientious he may be, we have the old problem of one person, with less than total knowledge, coercively determining the fate of another, and to determine it via laws the victim never consented to.

But if, with anarchists, we have no State at all, but private defense and arbitration agencies, the same problem arises: by what right does a group of men from Agency A, representing the plaintiff, have to decide the fate of someone who doesn't belong to the agency, who never consented to its rules or to be tried by them? What right has Agency A to arrest (kidnap?) the man it thinks guilty, try him, and imprison him or whatever? The problem of who has the right to determine who should make restitution, and in what amount, especially when the different parties to the dispute disagree on the amount or extent of restitution that is proper, is left unsolved.

3. The use of restitution to determine damages seems fair, in principle, in tort cases, but less obviously so in criminal cases. The gravity of the offense seems to bear no clear correlation with the amount of restitution that would be required. For example, if the guilty person is disabled or elderly, it is not likely that he is in a position to earn enough while he lives to provide anyone much restitution at all; and the victim of a robber who dies two weeks later would simply be out of luck.

Specifically, it would seem that all reference to *intent* would disappear if the restitution theory were put into practice. And the law as it now exists does consider intent, and, it seems, quite rightly so. A person who kills someone through an unlucky accident surely doesn't deserve the punishment that another person does who does so from malice aforethought. Shouldn't the law consider this difference in the assignment of penalties, even though it makes no difference in the amount of restitution (the victim is equally dead both ways)?

Here is a person who has no malicious intent at all, but his brakes suddenly give out while he is driving (although he had them checked the day before, so he can't be accused of negligence), and he runs down a pedestrian, who is seriously injured or killed. The amount he would have to pay for this inadvertent act could well be enormous; to pay for months of expensive hospitalization he might have to give up 90 percent of his paycheck for the next thirty years, if indeed he lives that long. One might say he doesn't deserve all this for what was really a stroke of bad luck; but then, the restitution theory pays no attention to desert, it only tries to assess the damage and make the person who caused it pay for it. On the other hand, here is a man who is out to murder me: but he is a bad shot and he misses—or let's say that the hairs on the top of my head are singed but that's all, except that I'm also scared to death. I suppose that he would go free—his intent was murderous, he may yet carry out his intent in the future, but aside from a possible recompense for frightening me, goes free; there is no real damage to be rectified, and on the restitution theory there could hardly be much restitution for an attempt that failed. This does not seem to be a very happy kind of arrangement. I would not rest secure as long as I suspected that he was still on the warpath against me, although until he has actually done something there is nothing for which restitution can be paid.

The actual outcome of an act is largely a matter of chance.

(1) One may pull the trigger and the gun doesn't go off, so no damage is done and no restitution required. Or one may fire it accidentally and kill someone, which may require years of restitution. A man may aim to kill me, but being a bad shot he misses, and I am unscathed, with nothing (except perhaps a bad case of fright) to receive restitution for. Another person means no harm, but shoots me by accident during target practice, and has to pay me or my family restitution for years. (2) An elderly woman may trip and fall on a banana peel, breaking her hip, and requiring months of painful and expensive hospital care, although the person who dropped the banana peel is unknown and will never be found. (Or is the owner of the property on which this occurs to be held liable? Surely not! But in that case the person will never be recompensed.) (3) In the classic Palsgraf vs. Lond Island Railroad Case, a man, carrying a package, jumps aboard an already moving train; the package is dislodged and falls on the rails. Unknown to the bearer, the package contains fireworks, which explode when they fall. The shock of the explosion upsets a scale at the other end of the platform, which strikes a woman and causes her injuries. This causal chain of events is a million-to-one shot: it would probably never happen again if one tried repeatedly. But the simple falling of a box is the act that initiated the whole series of events which ended in injury and damage. Who is supposed to make restitution for the damage? (4) An arsonist who purposely starts a fire may have very little damage to pay by way of restitution if the fire doesn't catch; on the other hand, a woman who has a candle lighted in the dark to see the cow she's milking may find that a sudden gust of wind spreads the flame of the candle to a pile of combustible material in the corner, with the result that the building burns down, and since the direction of the wind is just right, the entire city of Chicago is set in flames—this supposedly happened in Chicago in the 1870s. Knowing how capricious and complex the chains of cause-and-effect may be, many cities have statutes to the effect that a person can be held liable only for the damage to the building in which the initiatory act occurs. This is done so that the unfortunate initiator won't have to spend five lifetimes paying millions of dollars in damages for a series of events he inadvertently set into motion. But on the restitution theory, it would seem that the unfortunate initiator of the causal chain would have to spend the rest of his life working out the debt. (For hundreds of cases of this kind, see Hart and Honore, *Causation in the Law.*)

As if this weren't enough, what about *threat* of harm not yet done? What if a person is clearly dangerous? Shall a person be permitted to run through the streets with an axe threatening to kill the first person he meets whose initials are R.L.? A colleague of mine who lived in an apartment in New York City was confronted nightly by a mad woman who came down the fire escape from the floor above with a knife threatening to kill him and his entire family. Of course, she hadn't done anything yet, must one only wait until she kills the family before anything may be done about it?

If one says yes, then there are problems; many more people are going to get killed, since no preventive measures can be taken. If one says no, and the person may be incarcerated (in prison rather than committed to a mental institution) if he or she is demonstrably dangerous to the lives of others, then we are doing one very evil thing (as well as setting a very dangerous precedent), that of incarcerating someone for what he hasn't done yet but what we think that he may do. And surely on the restitution theory this would presumably be outlawed: before an act has been committed, there is nothing to make restitution for.

Even the term "demonstrably dangerous" is very elastic, and just as difficult to apply to individual cases as is the retributive theory of punishment. A few years ago a patient was released from a mental hospital in New York City, having been there for a dozen years and having been tranquil and pleasant during that period. But there was a difference between the artificial conditions of hospital life and the great wide world outside: people took trouble not to cross him in the hospital, because his ego was easily offended; but on the same day he was released into the outside world, somebody made an offhand remark to him and he knifed four people to death in five minutes on a street in Brooklyn. What stupidity on the part of the doctors in releasing him, we say. Perhaps; but it often isn't possible to tell what a patient will do under new and different conditions. Of a thousand patients thus released, no more than one might act in this way. As a result of this incident, and the unfavorable publicity it evoked, New York hospitals became much more cautious in releasing patients; when in doubt, they didn't release. The result of this was that many thousands of mental patients are today rotting away in these institutions although they would be perfectly capable of conducting themselves peaceably in the outside world to which they wish to be returned. Is it better to keep an entire thousand incarcerated, for what they *might* do, than to release them knowing that one of the thousand may become a murderer when he's on the outside?

The dilemma is this: (1) If everyone, no matter how dangerous to the safety of others, is to remain at large until he has actually committed a crime, then many preventible crimes are going to get committed, and the safety of all will be greatly reduced. You yourself may be the next victim of such a policy; and neither you nor anyone else can feel safe. (2) On the other hand, if the psychotic woman who comes down the fire-escape with a knife is to be incarcerated because of this threat, then an awful lot of people are going to be unjustly incarcerated. In many cases, the threat will turn out to be idle; and it will be hard to prevent a situation in which any indignant parent or disturbed neighbor can have you locked up because he says you are "dangerous to society," and so indeed you may be; but how is anyone, even a trained psychiatrist, to know this for sure? And even if he is, has he or anyone the right to have you incarcerated for crimes not yet committed? Borderline cases are always bothersome, but in this kind of case, where human nature is so complex and our knowledge still in its infancy, we are in the unfortunate situation of finding the majority of cases to be borderline. And yet we cannot suspend action until our knowledge is complete; even if we decide to do nothing, this too is an action, and it too has consequences.

To summarize then: there is a very wide disparity between the amount of restitution and the amount of desert. A man may be not at all to blame, or only very little to blame, and the amount of restitution required may be immense; and he may be very much to blame, and no restitution be required at all because no damage was inflicted. And if one goes in for things like "preventive detention," one may alleviate the danger to others, but only at the cost of doing a terrible injustice to the incarcerated person himself.

The extreme case, which is the ultimate test of any penal theory, occurs when there is an enormous danger to others and yet the person who constitutes the danger is guilty of nothing. At the turn of the century and after, there were "typhoid Mary" cases: the women in question were not sick with typhoid, but they were carriers of it; whenever they were in contact with other persons they would spread the disease to these others—and in those days the fatality rate from typhoid fever (before the days of vaccine) was extremely high. Should the typhoid Marys then be incarcerated for life? But that is unjust, since they have done nothing for which they were personally responsible—they had not committed one single aggressive act. Should they then be left free to move about in society? But if that was permitted, many people would catch the plague and die of it. Here the hazard to others (one of the utilitarian criteria for incarceration) was at a maximum, but the amount of guilt (the retributive criterion) was zero. Danger to others doesn't always go along with criminality. What should one do in such a case? Nor does the restitution theory really help: let's suppose that typhoid Mary infects someone else, and does restitution to him (or his family).

What wrongful *act* of hers makes it morally permissible for others to exact restitution from her? Here is a kind of case which tests any theory of retaliation to its utmost—and serves to remind us that no theory that has yet been worked out is satisfactory in covering all possible cases.

VI

It is against this background that still another view has been presented: the extreme and somewhat surprising view that no retaliation of any kind is ever justified—not retribution, not rehabilitation or deterrence, not restitution. (Only the first of these, retribution, is properly a theory of *punishment*; but all three of them recommend forms of *retaliation* against others for their initiation of a crime against others.) Protection against aggression is justified, according to this view, but no retaliation once aggression has been committed. This view has been set forth by Dr. Robert Lefevre.

According to Dr. Lefevre, the problem in both views of who should exercise the retaliatory use of force is much the same. When government does it, it jails people on suspicion of some crime and sentences them if convicted. Anarchists, believing that no government at all is legitimate, believe that defense agency A has a right to invade the home of a member of defense agency B and arrest him (kidnap him?) on suspicion that he has violated the rights of a member of agency A. Aside from the fact that there is only one organization doing this in the first case and a multiplicity of such organizations in the second, what is the difference?

> Instead of having a constabulary, the sheriff, the police force, the national guard, the army, et al., we are to have the Acme Protection Company, the Benign Protection Company, and the Conservation Protection Company. But each of these private firms, financed only by earnings from voluntary customer support and patronage, is to have the *sanction* of violating the wills, wishes, property boundaries, or lives, of those upon whom the *suspicion* of wrong-doing falls. Without that sanctioned power, private-company retaliation would become no more than vigilante action.[28]

What is the answer? According to Dr. Lefevre, there should be no retaliatory use of force at all. There can and should be *protection* against the use of force, but no *retaliation* once force has been initiated. You may protect yourself by having the latest technological devices for keeping the burglar from entering your house (including electrified fences, etc.) but not seek recourse in law (or through private agencies or even oneself) to apprehend him after he has committed his crime.

One argument against retaliation is that it is locking the barn door after the horse is stolen. The injury has already been inflicted; the thing to do is try to *prevent* the injury rather than to go after the injurer afterwards. "What is to be done when, despite the protection one has voluntarily paid for, he is victimized? The answer almost invariably is: "Then I have a *right* to get back what was taken. This entails *sanctioned* retaliation, forced restitution, and in some cases the infliction of punishment upon the wrong-doer. *But that is what we have.* ... And again we are back to the debate about how to violate the boundaries, properties, liberties, and lives of others *by right.* While a different method of invoking force may provide a service desired by some, it leaves intact the power of one group of men to violate the boundaries of other men with the approval of the collective."[2 9]

We must, then, "concentrate on protecting ourselves, and abandon retaliation *by right.* Retaliation and protection are opposite concepts. If you are protected, in fact, retaliation is impossible. If you believe you must rely on retaliation, it can only mean that you were not protected. As governments are organized and as the protection companies are envisioned, *you must first be injured* before you can be protected. ... If you believed for a moment that you could be protected, you wouldn't be so worried about retaliating."[3 0]

The second argument against retaliation is that it is wasteful, an expensive and dangerous luxury. "Many men in business have long realized that it is folly to throw good money after bad. If an employee is guilty of willful and negligent actions which result in company losses, the employee is fired. But the police are not called. Trying to retaliate is a waste of time and money. Even where an employee is caught stealing inside the firm, he usually gets a pink slip and the matter is dropped. Why? Because the employer cannot afford the luxury of vengeance. He simply moves to reduce the factor of continuing risk."

How is protection, as opposed to retaliation with all its problems, to be supplied? By the marketplace. Private protection companies (not retaliatory agencies) can operate very efficiently. "They do so now. Given a free market with no government taxation to erode purchasing ability, their successes could become monumental ... The market must operate with as high a level of efficiency as possible or the units in it go bankrupt." "The cost in a free society from occasional losses, when you are purchasing protection rather than retaliation, is minimal. The cost of paying for retaliation, by legal action, war, or any other method which requires further violence has become prohibitive." Besides, "retaliation is the modus vivendi of bandits, of legalized governments, and of vigilante groups. It is the standard of Big Daddy and of Godfather I and II. It is the tool of barbarism and must be abandoned if we are to be civilized."[3][1]

The high cost of retaliation cannot easily be disputed. The moral problems about the *right* to retaliation, especially on suspicion of a crime, and of disposing of the lives of others by putting people away for having committed it, are also enormous and well known. Thus to get rid of retaliation entirely (and retaliation includes not merely punishment but restitution) strikes us then as a welcome relief. It short-circuits all the thorny problems about punishment and retaliation by insisting all the while, "Protection, yes; retaliation, no."

But this theory too has its problems—severe enough to keep most people from buying it: it is all very well to emphasize preventing a crime rather than doing something about if afterwards. But no matter how great the precautions we may take to *prevent* crime, it is humanly impossible for all of it to be prevented. And when we try to prevent it and it happens anyway, then what do we do then? Just ignore it?

Consider the consequences of such a position. The thief, the mugger, the murderer, the rapist, will redouble their attempts to circumvent your protective devices, knowing that if they do elude these devices there will be no retaliation. Any counsel of wisdom would seem to be to let them know that if they do commit the crime, there will be retaliation against their act. If someone has murdered your wife, should you have no recourse whatever against the murderer? Should the killer be free to kill again? or the thief, emboldened by getting away with it this time, be free to inflict a similar loss upon others? Doesn't he deserve, if not retributory punishment, at least to be made to do restitution to the injured party or his family? It is true that this isn't easy to do, and very expensive (particularly if a trial is held and prepared for, to make certain who is guilty), but does this really matter if a dangerous killer is on the loose?

The distinction between prevention and retaliation, so emphasized by Dr. Lefevre, is somewhat fuzzy at the edges, enough to make the distinction in some cases "academic." Let's say that you don't believe in retaliation after a crime is committed, but you do believe in taking whatever measures you can to prevent it from occurring. And so to prevent unwelcome visitors from entering your property, you could have an electrified fence, which would kill anyone trying to climb it; or you can surround it with a moat full of water containing piranhas; and the moment the trespasser comes, you take out your trusty bow and arrow with poison tips and strike him down, leaving him to fall to his fate. Now, first: did he deserve this fate for a minor and perhaps inadvertent trespass? Second, how is this really different from retaliating against him? isn't it rather like retaliating in advance? The effects on him are certainly as bad as any retaliation that anyone could concoct. Third: are you entitled to take *any* measures you wish to prevent someone from doing something to your person or property, such as rigging up a device which will tear his hand off if he touches you? Are your property rights so superior to the rights of others to their lives that you may do anything you wish, including murder, to keep uninvited guests away? Fourth: who or what is to make the determination as to what your rights and the rights of others are in the matter? Mustn't someone decide whether attractive nuisances like the moat full of piranhas are to be permitted? For that matter, in the absence of a State (Lefevre is an anarchist), who is to determine what the limits to your property are, or whether it is yours at all? Fifth: it's true that in Lefevre's system there is no retaliation (though others could well believe that retaliation is quite proper), but there is a similar problem about prevention: there is no *system of rules* to determine *who is entitled to prevent what and to whom*. If you are paranoid and kill someone in order to prevent him from killing you, even though in fact he has no designs against you at all, is this all right? (You wouldn't dream of retaliating, of course—that would be immoral; you are only *preventing* him from doing something which he has no intentions of doing except only in the vagaries of your disordered brain.) What the whole system or nonsystem seems to be crying out for is a context of rules, law, to set forth the fundamental rules of permitted and prohibited action in human relationships. The Lefevre system or nonsystem seems capable of handling nothing more advanced than Robinson Crusoe-type cases.

In this world prevention isn't always possible; nor is it always justified. Retaliation against aggression—which includes all the previous three theories—is indeed troublesome, expensive, and cumbersome, especially if it involves courts, lawyers, trials, and prisons, with no guarantee of justice done even after all these complex steps have been undertaken. All the same, I think we are stuck with it. For the fundamental question we must face in connection with this issue is this: when prevention has not worked, and a crime has been committed in spite of it (or perhaps because of it), what is to be done about it—*nothing* or *something*? To most people the answer seems obvious.

A pure prevention theory, then, is surely unsatisfactory. Retaliation of some sort is called for if the world is not to be populated with dangerous aggressors. But this still leaves us with the other three theories: retributive, utilitarian, and restitutive. There are problems with every one of them, and I am not completely satisfied with even one of them, though I think that the retributive view has the most to be said for it. In any case, there is a further difficulty that cuts across all these theories: who is entitled to administer a system of penal justice in accordance with any of them—the State, or private agencies? And here again we have difficulties on both sides, but fewer, I suspect, with the State. I conclude, however, that there is *no* totally satisfactory theory, either of what constitutes penal justice or of who should be empowered to administer it. This unfortunately is a rather negative conclusion, but at least it is not one which makes wildly exaggerated claims.

Let me indicate where I think the trouble lies. (1) In other issues, we can "live and let live:" we can say, you live according to your life-style, and I'll live according to mine. If you are generous and I am niggardly, fine, we each have the right to be so. If you want to take out insurance policies and I prefer to take my chances with the future, fine, we can each act in accordance with our own judgment on the matter, or flip a coin if judgment fails us. In these and countless other cases we can each decide as we choose, without interfering with the choice of the other. (2) But in the case of forcible *interference* by one person with the freedom of another, we cannot do this—or at least we can't do it without paying the inordinate price of being prey to any aggressor who comes along. If I let the killer live when he comes to my door, he will kill me. (3) But once we've admitted this, we have the problem of how these aggressors should be dealt with, by what criteria, and who is to be empowered to pass judgment upon them.

Now all this is very discomfiting; we don't want to be put in the position of using coercion against others; we don't want to give orders to other people and penalize them if the orders aren't obeyed; we don't want to manage the lives of others, we only want to manage our own. And yet reality puts us in a position where we have to: for reality is such that there are people who would exterminate us if they had the chance, and we can survive only by not giving them that chance. And that's the problem: we want to live and let live, but some other people don't want to extend this same privilege to us—and reality forces us into a corner, requiring us to use retaliatory coercion upon others if we are to survive at all.

If we don't use it, or threat of it, we ourselves will likely become the next victims of aggression by others. So we decide to use it; but when we do use it, we realize that there are different views about what should be done by way of retaliation, as well as different views about who should be in charge of it. And what can we do then? Can we say "You be a retributivist against me, and I'll be a restitutionist against you"? And if we did, we would still be inflicting our view forcibly on others, even if others thought our view erroneous or immoral. And this more than anything else is hard to swallow—not only that retaliatory coercion has to be used, but that it has to be used in putting into practice a theory of penal justice which was not agreed to by the person against whom we used it. He is being forced to play a game with rules he never consented to. We have the feeling that we are doing something terribly wrong here—using force, even retaliatory force, in implementation of a view which the one on the receiving end of that force never approved or consented to. But this would be the case with *any* theory of punishment we attempted to put into practice, there being no one which everyone agrees to. Yet if we don't practice any, and leave aggression intact without moving against it, civilization goes down the tubes and we are dead. This is the tragic dilemma which makes the problem of punishment one of the most intractable problems in all of moral philosophy. And this, I daresay, helps to explain why no theory of retaliation has yet been worked out which can satisfy us—at least satisfy us enough to enable us to sleep with a clear conscience after we have implemented our view in practice, in the only way a theory of retaliation *can* be implemented in practice, by imposing it on others.

NOTES TO CHAPTER TWO

1. Antony Flew, "The Justification of Punishment," in *Philosophy*, XXIX, October 1954, pp. 291-307. Reprinted in W. Sellars and J. Hospers, *Readings in Ethical Theory* (Appleton-Century-Crofts, 2nd ed. 1970), p. 621.

2. Brand Blanshard, "Retribution Revisited," in *Philosophical Perspectives on Punishment*, ed. Edward Madden, Rollo Handy, and Marvin Farber (Springfield, Ill.: Charles C. Thomas, 1968), p. 80.

3. Kurt Baier, *The Moral Point of View*, Chapter 7, Section 5 (Ithaca: Cornell University Press, 1958).

4. John Kleinig, *Punishment and Desert* (The Hague: Martin Nijhoff, 1973).

5. *Time*, June 6, 1960.

6. Kleinig, *op. cit.*, p. 63.

7. Kleinig, *op. cit.*, p. 67.

8. Joel Feinberg, "Justice and Personal Desert," *Nomos VI: Justice* (New York: Atherton Press, 1963), ed. C.J. Friedrich and J.W. Chapman, p. 96.

9. H.L.A. Hart, "Principles of Punishment," in *Punishment and Responsibility* (Oxford University Press, 1968), p. 25.

10. Cf. a similar case in Brand Blanshard, "The Impasse in Ethics and a Way Out," Howison Lecture 1954, University of California Press; reprinted in W.

Sellars and J. Hospers, *Readings in Ethical Theory* (Appleton-Century-Crofts, 2nd ed. 1970), p. 290.

11. I do not believe that rule-utilitarianism offers any improvement on act-utilitarianism in this regard. Act-utilitarianism considers the consequences of this act of sentencing an innocent person (which may sometimes be good), and rule-utilitarianism considers the consequences of adopting the rule that an innocent person may sometimes be sentenced (and such consequences may also sometimes be good). Both views consider only the future consequences of punishing, not the desert of the punished.

12. J.D. Mabbott, "Punishment," in *Mind*, 1939.

13. C.S. Lewis, "The Humanitarian Theory of Punishment," in *Res Judicatae*, VI, 1953, pp. 224-30. (In Sellars and Hospers, *op cit.*, pp. 646-50.)

14. Aleksandr Solzhenitsyn, *The Gulag Archipelago, 1* (Harper & Row, 1974).

15. *Ibid.*, p. 436.

16. *Ibid.*, p. 435.

17. *Ibid.*, p. 437.

18. *Ibid.*, p. 146.

19. *Ibid.*, p. 309.

20. *Ibid.*, p. 174.

21. See Alf Ross, *On Guilt, Responsibility and Punishment* (London: Stevens, 1975), p. 44.

22. Herbert Spencer, *The Man vs. the State*, p. 122. (Originally published 1884. Reprinted 1940 by the Caxton Press, Caldwell, Idaho.)

23. John Rawls, "Two Concepts of Rules," *Philosophical Review*, 64, 1955.

24. John Kleinig, *op. cit.*, p. 79. See also John Rawls, *A Theory of Justice*, pp. 26-7.

25. See Morris and Linda Tannehill, *The Market for Liberty* (1971); *Patterns of Anarchy*, ed. Leonard Krimerman and Lewis Perry (Anchor Books, 1966); David Friedman, *The Machinery of Freedom* (Harper, Colophon Books, 1973).

26. See Chapter 11 of John Hospers, *Libertarianism* (Plainview, New York: Nash Publishing Co., 1971).

27. William Kneale, *The Responsibility of Criminals*, The Clarendon Press; partially reprinted in H.B. Acton, ed., *The Philosophy of Punishment* (St. Martin's Press, 1969), pp. 178-79.

28. Robert Lefevre, "The Free Society: Practical Considerations," *Lefevre's Journal*, Fall 1975, Vol. 2, No. 4, p. 2. See also Lefevre's *Nature of Man and His Government* (Caxton Press, Caldwell, Idaho, 1963).

29. *Ibid.*, pp. 2-3.

30. *Ibid.*, p. 3.

31. *Ibid.*, p. 3.

※ *Chapter Three*

Concessions to Retribution in Punishment

Hugo Adam Bedau

After decades of official neglect, the role of retribution in the theory of punishment has staged a remarkable revival in recent years. The many advocates for an augmented and indispensable role for retributive ideas include philosophers[1] as well as jurists[2] and penologists.[3] Despite the flurry of renewed interest, we are still far from solving the major problem: What do retributive ideas contribute to the theory of punishment? It is my purpose to try to answer this question.

I

Before we can discuss this question, we need some provisional clarity on the nature of retribution itself. Among classic writers, Locke, for instance, held that "the right to punish," which he also called the power to "retribute," consists in the right to inflict "what is proportionate to [the] . . . transgression, which is so much as may serve for Reparation and Restraint."[4] On this view, retribution in punishment consists of two things: making adequate reparation to the victim and making sure the offender commits no further crimes. No doubt there is an etymological tie among 'retribution,' 'restitution,' and 'reparation.' But there is no other general connection between putting the victim back on his feet (restitution or reparation) and inflicting a deprivation on the offender (punishment),[5] and so there is no way in general to explain the latter even in part by reference to the former. As for restraint, even if it may be justifiably exacted from an offender as (or as part of) his punishment, this is not a reason for thinking of restraint as a component in just retribution. I shall have more to say about restraint (or deterrence) and reparation, but not because either is truly part of retribution.

Among current theorists, there are different difficulties. H.L.A. Hart, in his useful sketch of a retributive theory of punishment, incorporates into his model the doctrine that punishment is justified only if the offender "has voluntarily done something that is morally wrong . . . "[6] On this view, a retributivist must hold that it is not harm as such to the innocent, but fault in the offender that constitutes the criminality of an act. Historically, this seems a dubious view, even if the retributivism of Kant and his successors cannot be understood without such a doctrine.[7] The biblical doctrine of "a life for a life"—surely the paradigm of retribution in punishment—has no such tacit distinction built into it between harm done and fault incurred. Likewise, the distinction in the law between murder and manslaughter and the belief that the latter is a lesser crime (because it involves less or no fault in the offender even though the harm done is the same) probably postdates the notion of retribution in punishment and, in any case, shows that the harm/ fault distinction is logically independent of the idea of retribution itself. Below, I shall examine in greater detail the connection between retributivism in punishment and the idea of criminal fault, but it seems to me unnecessary and unwise to insist on the centrality of this connection at the onset.

Probably the most widely held assumption about retribution in punishment is the idea that it makes desert the central feature of just punishment.[8] On this view, a retributivist holds that a punishment is just if and only if the offender deserves it. It seems not to be noticed how essentially trivial this doctrine is; it cannot be central or unique to the theory of retributive punishment. Any theory of the distribution of benefits and burdens, rewards and punishments, can incorporate a notion of desert if it wants to; whatever is said to be properly allocated to (or withheld from) a person under the theory can be said to be therewith deserved (or not deserved) by that person. In all cases, the ultimate question will be what the principles are in terms of which allocations are to be justified, because they are the criteria in terms of which deserving one thing rather than another is established. Since this is no more true of retributive than of nonretributive theories, there is no reason for, and good reason against, making it appear that desert is a creature of retributive theories alone. Accordingly, I shall have little to say about desert.

What, then, is central to the doctrine of retribution in punishment? It is simply the belief that *justice in punishment requires the features of a punishment to be shaped by reference to the features of the offense for which it is meted out.*

Thus, a retributive theory is necessarily backward-looking in its orientation to punishment. Its focus is on the offense and nothing else, especially not any social cost/benefit or individual eugenics that can be calculated to result from punishments. These, the typical concerns of forward-looking, consequentialist theories of punishment, have no place in a retributive theory. Hence, retribution in punishment ignores all features of the offender's character, the victim's situation, all the effects (for the offender, the victim, and the rest of society) of the threat or infliction of punishment (or the remission or omission thereof), insofar as these are distinct from the nature and gravity of the offense and whatever else is central to characterizing the offense itself. These are the fundamental ideas of any theory of retributive punishment and will suffice to focus the topic of this investigation.

II

Let us begin by asking why it is rational to want to have a system of punishment. The answer is to be found by reference to the rather abstract notion of a *just society*, the idea of which underlies most of the influential recent writing in the theory of punishment.[9] Here we can only sketch the idea of a just society; what it took John Rawls six hundred pages to state cannot be re-stated in three pages, much less three paragraphs. Roughly, for our purposes, a just society can be characterized by three fundamental features.

First, a just society is a society whose social, legal, political, and economic institutions are themselves just. Their procedures, and so their results, are fair. Whatever our criteria for distributive justice may be, the institutions of a just society are designed to insure that everybody gets the rights, benefits, privileges, liberties, and duties, burdens, and responsibilities he or she deserves. It follows from this fact about the institutions of society that many kinds of *justification* for illegal (and *a fortiori* of criminal) conduct are absent. In the real world, one of the kinds of considerations that justifies illegal conduct is the immorality, injustice, corruption of our social institutions. The whole theory of civil disobedience, for example, traditionally proceeds by reference to precisely this feature of actual societies. Hence, in the real world, individual noncompliance with social institutional requirements is not only not invariably wrong, it may even be morally required. Some would advance a similar line of reasoning on behalf of violence (e.g., terrorism), as distinct from civil disobedience, in at least some circumstances. All this is ruled out by definition in a just society.

The second important feature of a just society is that its members will be moral, rational persons. That is to say, they will be persons not unlike ourselves, except for those respects in which you and I are characteristically immoral and irrational. The significant consequence of this consideration for our purposes is that many of the usual kinds of *excuses* for illegal and criminal conduct will be missing. An excuse, after all, typically brings forward some feature of ignorance, incapacity, or lack of intention to account for a person's wrong-doing.[10] Ideally rational persons would lack most such excuses for their wrongful act.

The third and final feature of a just society is that its ruling idea is to *maximize freedom for all equally*.[11] Accordingly, the rules and practices that are embodied in the institutions of society are recognized as systematic limitations on conduct, and are to be understood as self-imposed limitations on persons otherwise equally free to do as they like. The point of the restrictions is, of course, to maximize opportunities that cannot flourish without such rules. The chief consequence is that these self-imposed restrictions give rise to a *right of compliance*. As Rawls (paraphrasing Hart) has expressed it, "The main idea is that when a number of persons engage in a mutually advantageous cooperative venture according to rules [i.e., construct the institutions of a just society], and thus restrict their liberty in ways necessary to yield advantage for all, those who have submitted to these restrictions have a right to similar acquiescence on the part of those who have benefitted from their submission."[12]

III

This brings us to the problem of compliance, and it is precisely this problem that connects the theory of a just society with the theory of punishment.[13] Given the nature of persons, it is a fact that in any conceivable society, some kinds of conduct will be harmful (even lethal), and everyone (that is, everyone who is rational) will want to be free of these harms whatever else he wants. These fundamental facts about ourselves tell us that the initial answer to the question, "What sort of conduct is it reasonable to want to punish?" is: The sort of conduct that is *harmful to persons*. Reflection on the value of freedom will promptly lead us to revise this answer so as to confine punishment to *intentionally* harmful conduct. Even in an ideally just society, the possibility arises that any person at any time could be a victim of intentional harmful conduct by another. Any informed rational member of society knows he or she is a potential victim of crime. In addition, the less a society is perfectly just, the more probable this potentiality will be. Similarly, to the degree that persons are not just but selfish, self-absorbed, and self-centered, it will be reasonable from their point of view to harm others as long as they expect to gain more than they risk. Considerations need to be introduced as a supplement to the love of justice to provide a further selfish motive against harming others out of a prospect for selfish gain. Sanctions against harmful conduct—its authoritative prohibition—are not enough. The threat of something unpleasant as standing liability upon wrongdoing—in short, the threat of and liability to punishment—is also necessary. If we ignore the situation in an ideally just society, and consider a nearly just society (i.e., one in which the institutions are nearly just and the members of society largely motivated by a sense of justice), it will be reasonable to provide in advance of any wrongdoing a system of sanctions and punishments as a direct disincentive to wrong-doing, and thus indirectly as a reason to conform individual conduct to social rules.

Must we have a further reason for wanting a system of punishment beyond the desire to secure compliance with rules? I think not. The basic idea on which we rely is that it is just, or justified, or at any rate not unjust, to threaten deprivations to secure compliance with just rules. To put it in a syllogism, individual compliance with rules is a necessary condition of having a just society, the threat of punishment is a necessary condition of securing individual compliance, therefore, a system of punishment is a necessary condition of having a just society in an imperfect world; and what is a necessary condition of justice cannot itself be unjust.

It is crucial to realize that this basic idea is not retributive. Our reason for a system of punishment has nothing to do with features of offenses, although it has much to do with preserving social justice. Our reason for introducing punishment into the world is the forward-looking concern for compliance with just rules. Also, nothing has been said about actually inflicting punishment on anyone. Only the threat of and the liability to punishment have been explained. Ideally, there would be no actual infliction of punishment upon anyone, because ideally the threat of and liability to punishment would suffice to keep the qualifying condition of eligibility for punishment from occurring. No one would commit a crime and, therefore, no one would be found guilty of a crime. All theories of punishment should be in agreement on this point.

From the legislative point of view, however, we can see a concession to retributivism, not usually noticed, already implicit in this first consideration. Even if our basic reason for having a system of punishment is not retribution, retributive reasons do require us *not* to punish some things. If, as it is often alleged, there are statutory offenses making punishable conduct that in fact harms no one—so-called "victimless crimes"—a retributivist would want all such statutes repealed. Since, by definition, a victimless crime does not harm the victim, retributive justice tells us that there cannot be anything appropriate as a punishment for such conduct, and it should not be deemed criminally offensive. It is, of course, disputable whether anything is a victimless crime, and whether any or all of the statutory offenses often classified in this way (e.g., prostitution, gambling, public homosexuality, nudity, after-hours sales) are truly victimless and harmless.[14] But if anything is, then the reasoning of the retributivist is perhaps the clearest and most direct in explaining why such conduct should never have been made criminal and subject to punitive sanction in the first place.

Thus, one might say that the first concession to retributivism in a theory of criminal justice is that nothing should be made subject to punishment unless it intentionally harms someone.

We are now at the threshold of a second concession to retributivism. When we ask, "What sort of thing is it appropriate to threaten and, should the occasion arise, impose as a punishment?", the answer is bound to be: Suffering or deprivation. Inflicting suffering and deprivation are essentially what an offender does in committing an offense against a person's life, limbs, or property. They are harms to anyone who undergoes them. Things that persons generally like, or are indifferent to, or which it is believed they like or are indifferent to, cannot serve as suitable candidates for punishment. Roughly, in order to punish somebody we have to pay him back in coin like that he spent on his victim. A system of punishment, therefore, is a system for inflicting threatened suffering or deprivation upon certain persons under certain circumstances. This is an unmistakably retributivist idea, and it is a feature of any possible theory of punishment.[15]

However, it is not a feature of punishment that only a retributive theory can provide. Since, as we have seen, the point of a system of punishment is to secure compliance with just rules, threatened punishments are to be seen as providing a disincentive to prohibited conduct. That can be done only if the threatened event or experience is viewed in general as suffering or a deprivation—and this in no way depends on a retributive outlook. Thus, if we define the role of retributivism in punishment in terms of the number of features of an adequate theory of punishment that *only* retributivism can supply (or can best and most plausibly supply), then our second concession to retributivism fails this test. The same is also true of our first concession to retributivism. If there are victimless crimes, statutory offenses in which no harm befalls the nominal victim, then there are ample utilitarian reasons for the repeal or nonenforcement of such laws. It is not only retributivists who have a good reason for confining punishment to the intentional violation of laws that cause innocent persons harm. From the standpoint of trying to determine exactly what features of punishment we owe to the role of retribution in punishment, it is obviously important to distinguish (a) those features that retribution alone introduces into the theory of punishment, from (b) those features that either retribution or some nonretributive theories can supply. Whether there are any features of the former sort remains to be seen.

IV

Probably the most widely acknowledged concession to retributivism in theories of punishment in recent years is the notion that the guilty (or, more precisely, those who have been found guilty by some authoritative tribunal) deserve to be punished.[16] Just as a liability for punishment derives from rules prohibiting certain conduct, eligibility for punishment derives from having been found guilty of such conduct. This is an indisputably retributivist idea: No notion of good (or avoidance of harm) for the offender, for the victim, or for the rest of society enters into the considerations relevant to answering, "Whom should we punish?" Whether 'the guilty deserve to be punished' is an implicit tautology on any theory of punishment, or only for retributivists, or whether it is a tautology at all, is a point on which philosophers have disagreed.[17] What is true in any case is that to punish the innocent, or to punish those not found or not even believed to be guilty, is a travesty of justice and of just punishment.

Difficulties immediately arise when we ask whether we are

logically required out of considerations of retributive justice to
punish *all and only* those authoritatively found guilty of an offense.
Prosecutorial discretion, rehabilitative considerations for youthful
and first offenders, victimless crimes better left unpunished, all are
considerations that in actual life play a role in defeating the idea that
all the guilty ought to be punished. Different considerations defeat
the idea that *only* the guilty should be punished.

Vicarious and strict liability, which insure that persons not at fault
and not the cause of criminal harms will nonetheless have to answer
for criminal offenses, continue to maintain a firm grip on some
portions of the criminal law, despite the fact that from a retributive
point of view these modes of liability seem to require that persons
with valid excuses (notably, those of non-negligent ignorance, incapacity, or lack of intention) are nevertheless subject to criminal
punishment. Punishment without guilt, based on punitive liability
without fault, is a feature of actual criminal justice systems, and so is
the converse.

Must the retributivist think that it is unjust for administrative
considerations to outweigh retributive considerations in the operation of a criminal justice system? We can imagine a more and a less
comprehensive retributivism, the former of which does and the latter
of which does not insist that every social choice where crime and
punishment are involved must be resolved in conformity with the
requirements of retributivism. A single-minded retributivist of the
former sort is bound to appear arbitrary and fanatic. How does the
retributivist know that we should try to secure retribution at any
cost? How does he know, for instance, that it is better to spend a
given tax dollar to pay for prosecution of the guilty than to spend it
either on preventive policing or on compensation for the injured
innocent victim? In the real world of criminal justice, we do not
believe that we should sacrifice whatever it takes to secure retribution, and it is not clear that we are morally wrong to believe this. In
the real world, no matter how much weight we attach to retributive
justice, given a sufficiently large volume of criminal activity and a
sufficiently large volume of other claims on social resources, we will
have to underfinance the criminal justice system in those respects
where its perfect operation is a necessary condition of securing
retributive justice. This will guarantee that prosecutorial and judicial
choice will often leave some convictable guilty persons untried, some
convicted guilty persons underpunished or unpunished, and still
other guilty persons unapprehended or unconvicted, and so unpunished. The retributivist may look upon such a society and judge it
retributively unjust. Everyone else will look on the same society with

varying degrees of dissatisfaction, but with the understanding that retribution is not the only (and not even always the first) claim upon our allegiance and our resources. It is ironic, but not impertinent, to add that if the actual distribution of property in the real world is itself unjust by the principles of distributive justice, then the failure to support a more efficient criminal justice establishment capable of achieving more retribution begins to look less unreasonable.

V

Given that society is confronted with a person found guilty of an offense, to ask why such a person should then be punished (apart from administrative considerations like those reviewed above) is a bit odd. About all one can reply is that we punish such persons because we meant what we said. That is, by enacting rules with penalties for their violation, society in effect declares that anyone whose conduct violates such rules is liable for punishment. Confronted with a convicted law-breaker, and thus in theory a person with flawless eligibility for punishment, society has to show that it meant what it said when it established sanctions against such conduct. (It is not that society *promised* the offender he would be punished if he committed a crime. The imposition of a system of punishment is analogous to promising, if at all, to the extent that the system can be seen as an implicit promise to the law abiding that law-breakers will not be treated with impunity.) "Because we meant what we said," therefore, is a kind of further reason for punishing those eligible for punishment. Is it a retributive reason?[18] I think not. If it is laid down as a general policy that all classes with over a hundred students are liable to be moved from an ordinary classroom to the auditorium, and my class enrolls over a hundred students, it is hardly 'retributive' of the administration to switch my class to the auditorium. Yet, the ground for inflicting a punishment on a person given a system of punishment and a finding of his guilt is no different from the ground for switching my class.

We punish particular persons, therefore, not because we believe in retribution as a sacred or central requirement of social justice, but because as long as there is crime committed by persons now in our society, we cannot with consistency prohibit their conduct and then refuse to punish them for noncompliance.

This brings us to the threshold of what is both the most perplexing and potentially the most significant feature of retribution in punishment. According to most advocates of retributivism, punitive liability is supposed to be a consequence of one's own choice.[19] This sounds rather like saying that the question, 'Why am I being punished?' is to be answered by saying, 'Because you asked for it: you made the rules and you knowingly broke them, so you bring the unpleasant punitive consequences of that violation upon yourself.' This is an echo of the classic views of Kant and Hegel and other retributivists that the guilty have a 'right' to be punished, and that the criminal 'draws upon himself' his punishment. This is truly a retributivist idea, because it relies upon a symmetry between the criminal act and the punitive response. Retributivists believe that criminal acts meet for punishment are all and only the acts harmful to others that are 'willed' or chosen by the offender. By the same token, in a just society, the punishment that befalls the offender is nothing but the application to him of sanctions he in concert with others has 'rationally willed' to impose for the violation of just rules.

Critics have always thought this feature of retributivism one of its more laughable eccentricities.[20] Even defenders of retributivism have conceded that it is "exaggerated" to claim that "in choosing to do an act violative of the rules an individual has chosen to be punished."[21] The question is whether there is any truth in it at all.

Taken in any straight-forwardly empirical fashion, the whole idea is wildly implausible. (1) Rarely does anyone who commits an offense choose to be punished. The exceptions are of two sorts. First, there are the clinically pathological cases of persons who commit crimes in order to be punished, and thus in that sense "choose" to be punished. Secondly, there are the contrite guilty who want to cancel, expiate, or annul their guilt and view (rightly or wrongly) their punishment as necessary to that end. They, too, may be said to "choose" their punishment. Retributivism has no interest in either of these classes of cases. (2) Occasionally, sentencing authorities allow the convicted offender to choose his punishment—from among a small range of possibilities (enormous fines, mutilation, life-long banishment, etc.). But offering such a choice to the offender is an adventitious, not an essential, feature of punishing. There is no reason to believe that a punishment is unjust, or even retributively unjust, whenever the convicted offender is denied such a choice. (3) There are good grounds for insisting that much of what passes for criminal choice—the decision to commit a crime (including what crime to commit, where and when to commit it, etc.)—is in fact pathological to such an extent that the offender cannot be said to have really or freely chosen to commit the crime that he did commit.

On retributivist principles, it follows in such cases that the offender cannot have chosen to be punished. Hence, if he is to be forcibly detained as a consequence of victimizing others, it cannot be as punishment or for punishment; it can only be for such nonretributive reasons as his own good or the good of others. (4) Few of those who commit criminal acts ever in fact play any direct role in determining either that such conduct shall be punished or that it should be punished in the particular way it is or that they should be punished as they are.

If, therefore, any of (1)-(4) above were what is meant by the criminal's "choosing" his punishment, we could say with considerable assurance that criminals hardly ever choose their punishment and even more rarely choose their punishment in choosing to commit a crime.

Of course, retributivists know all this. Their idea that a criminal chooses to be punished in choosing to violate just rules is the telescoped expression of an entirely different viewpoint. Perhaps it can be put more clearly like this. A criminal act is the intentional, informed act of a free agent, a person who understands what he is doing and could do otherwise, and would if he wanted to. In a just society, criminal conduct is necessarily the expression of selfish preferences, of someone who wants more than his fair share, regardless of the cost to the innocent victim. Since even a criminal, insofar as he is a person, is a member of society, he must know that society is inconceivable without rules to govern its members. He cannot rationally regard himself as an exception to the rules that sanction punishment for intentionally harming the innocent (as though, somehow, when *he* commits a crime, no one is harmed, or when *he* harms someone, no crime is committed). He must know, therefore, that he is liable to punishment when he violates the criminal law. Hence, a person in choosing to commit a crime in effect chooses to be punished for it (provided, of course, he is caught, tried, and convicted). Indeed, society must punish such a person in order to treat him as a rational being, a person, a free agent worthy of moral respect.[22]

This argument is not intended to give a special sense to "choice" or "intention," as these concepts figure in the notion of a normal person's commission of a crime. Instead, it is intended to lay the basis for claiming that there is a logical connection ("a priori," Kantians would say) between criminal conduct and the deserved imposition of punishment, which is a completely different thing. What is retributively based about the idea of punishing a criminal in order to treat him as a person is simply that there is no other way to respect his rationality. For it is his rationality that is manifest in his intentional commission of a harmful act upon an innocent person; it is also his rationality that makes him a member of a society with punitive sanctions for violating rules against intentionally harming the innocent. Thus, it is one and the same feature in a crime that determines the criminality of the act and the deserved imposition of the punishment for it: the criminal's rationality. This is how I reconstruct the argument, so familiar since Kant, that in punishing a person for his crime, we regard the person as a morally worthy creature ("end in itself"). The epigram that in choosing to commit a crime a person chooses to be punished turns out, consequently, not to be false or perhaps even exaggerated, but only obscure and even misleading because of the complex argument it condenses.

No doubt we have here a feature of the theory of punishment that is not likely to be derived except on a retributive theory. But it is not necessary to derive it on a retributive theory, unless that theory, like Kant's and Hegel's, elevates what today we would call *mens rea*—the criminal mind—to the essential factor that makes an act criminal. Not every retributive conception of just punishment does this, which is not to deny that a retributive theory may be both more subtle and morally impressive if it does.

Once it is done, however, then at least two important concessions to retributivism are likely to ensue. One is that retributivism explains why the ordinary criminal, insofar as he really is a normal, rational agent, is not to be rehabilitated or treated except as these are involved in or result from punishing him.[23] This concession is, moreover, a significant one because it is extremely difficult to identify any other conception of punishment on which this important constraint is likely to be forthcoming so directly. Moral principles from which this same conclusion can be derived no doubt abound, but they are not principles distinctive of the theory of punishment.

The second concession to retributivism is that it explains why punishment is never to be imposed on anyone with an excuse; and anyone who acts without *mens rea* has an excuse. If not only harm to the innocent but harmful intention in the offender is necessary before a person deserves to be punished, then the absence of the harmful intention must negate the justice of any imposed punishment. No matter how harmful the act may be, on this theory of retribution, there is nothing *of* the agent as a rational person *in* the act, and therefore, no legitimacy in punishing *him* for it.

It has often been noticed, though rarely by retributivists, that given this feature of their theory, it may well be that few if any persons who actually have caused harm to others truly "deserve" to be punished. What is more surprising is that classic as well as recent retributivists seem to have shown no great interest in developing the theory of excuses that their own doctrine of just punishment elevates to such importance. (Perhaps they think that few if any of those who cause harm to the innocent really ever have an excuse!) In any case, there is more to be learned about excuses in a few lucid paragraphs of Hobbes or Bentham than in all the tortured pages of Kant and Hegel put together.

Here again, however, we must note that not only retributivism can provide the needed theory of excuses arising from absence of "the mental element" (intention, *mens rea*) in a crime. For this was guaranteed already by our initial conception of a just society and the confinement of punishment to intentionally harmful conduct. At most, the appeal to retributivism may improve our understanding of why it is unfair to punish certain kinds of conduct, because it widens and deepens the range of acceptable excuses beyond what a non-retributive theory would allow.

VI

Classical retributivism, like Gilbert and Sullivan's Mikado, is wedded to the idea that the punishment must fit the crime, or to put it less elliptically but more ponderously, that justice requires the severity of the punishment to be equivalent to the gravity of the offense. Hence, retributivism is often characterized in terms of the biblical doctrine of "a life for a life." As Kant or Hegel would have said, no lesser punishment (and no greater punishment, either) would properly "annul" the offense. Nothing else is fair both to the offender and to the victim. The problem, however, (as the Mikado's familiar song acknowledges) is to establish what such a punishment is for each kind of offense and for each offender.

The traditional answer of retributivists was *lex talionis*, the law of retaliation. No contemporary retributivist defends this view; the standard objections are familiar and they are at least as old as Blackstone's commentaries.[24] There is simply no mode of retaliation appropriate for a kidnapper who has no children of his own. The multiple murderer, the impoverished robber or thief, and many others, present comparable difficulties. So the challenge for the retributivist is to abandon *lex talionis* without abandoning retributive fairness.

There are two recent attempts to meet this challenge, and both are worth examination. One is to be found in the volume, *Doing Justice*, by Andrew von Hirsch. Von Hirsch proposed to supplant the old principle of retaliation with what he calls "the principle of commensurate deserts." According to this principle, "Severity of punishment should be commensurate with the seriousness of the wrong . . . Seriousness [what I call the gravity of the offense] depends both on harm done (or risked) by the act, and on the degree of the actor's culpability."[2][5] Justice in sentencing requires that we comply with the principle of commensurate deserts, and this principle stipulates that the severity of the sentence is commensurate with the gravity of the offense if and only if the severity of the punishment is equivalent to the degree of culpability of the offender plus the harm (or risk of harm) to others in the offense itself.

Before any parole board, judge, or legislature tries to implement von Hirsch's suggestions, there is much work to be done. First, the principle of commensurate deserts requires a mode of measurement for degrees of culpability in offenders. Even if we can agree that a malicious killer is morally and legally more culpable than an accidental killer, how are we to answer the question, "How much more culpable is he—twice as culpable? ten times? seven and one half times?" Second, the principle needs a mode of measurement for degrees of harm inflicted by different offenses. Granted that murder is more harmful than rape, how much worse is it in terms of harm to the victim (or to society)? Twice as harmful? Ten times as harmful? The concepts of culpability and harmfulness are not like the concepts of temperature or ductility because we lack standard units in terms of which to measure them, something we do not lack for the latter. Third, we need a way of combining the two concepts—culpability and harmfulness—into one common concept of gravity of offense. Without a common measure for these concepts, there is no way of telling, e.g., whether an offense that falls on the mid-point of the culpability scale and the bottom of the harmfulness scale is exactly as grave or half as grave, or twice as grave, as an offense that falls on the mid-point of the harmfulness scale but at the bottom of the culpability scale. Culpability and harmfulness seem to be not even as like each other as the proverbial apples and oranges; the latter are, after all, members of a common genus, whereas no genus subsumes both degrees of fault and degrees of harm.

Although von Hirsch shows that he is aware of these objections, the solution he offers is inadequate. He relies on the Sellin-Wolfgang measurements of degree of gravity of offenses to get around these problems.[2][6] What the Sellin-Wolfgang research seems to show is that there are statistically reliable judgments on the seriousness of most crimes. As a rejection of sceptical relativism, such consensus is very important. However, these judgments do not involve, implicitly or explicitly, any such principle as von Hirsch's principle of commensurate deserts. The doctrine that we can make sense of fitting punishments to crimes by analyzing the gravity of the latter into two components, culpability and harmfulness, is not even investigated, much less vindicated, by Sellin and Wolfgang. In addition, there is no objectivity in these measures comparable to those we have for temperature and other scalar properties of physical objects. At best, there is a cultural and population-relative aspect to all judgments of gravity of offenses reached by the Sellin-Wolfgang methods, and this relativity in turn may rest on biases for which no controls are known.

There are, then, these difficulties in taking seriously the retributivist's doctrine that we can fit punishments to crimes in some objective, reliable fashion. I do not wish to argue that justice in sentencing may flout "the principle of commensurate deserts," as though this principle were fraudulent or erroneous or trivial. No one disputes the claim that a slap on the wrist for murder is too lenient and that a month in prison for overparking is too severe. It is common sense judgments like these that inspire the search for a principle such as the principle of commensurate deserts. What I have been arguing is that the retributivist's principle of commensurate deserts is not at present an objective, reliable way of going beyond such common sense judgments, so that sentencing authorities may rely on the principle and be secure in the belief that with it they can achieve retributively just sentences in practice.

The other recent attempt to make punishments fit crimes is by Claudia Card, in what she calls "the penalty principle." This principle asserts that a punishment is retributively just if and only if it imposes on an offender a deprivation of rights to the extent of his "evident culpable failure to abide by a law" and "the hardship to which he is thus exposed ... does not exceed the worst that anyone could reasonably expect to suffer from the similar conduct of another if such conduct were to become general in the community ... "[27] This is akin to von Hirsch's principle of commensurate deserts in that it attempts to determine the appropriate severity of punishment by reference to a combination of culpability and harmfulness. However, Card's position has one notable improvement over von Hirsch's. She addresses directly the question of how in a punishment the degree of severity appropriate on retributive grounds is to be related to the degree of severity appropriate to provide the disincentive to law-breaking that underlies the whole point of a system of punishment.

Her answer is this: The penalty principle renders unjust any punishment the severity of which is greater than *"the least that is sufficient to maintain a reasonable mutual assurance of general obedience on the part of persons who might otherwise be suspected of the same fault as the offender."*[28] To develop a schedule of penalties governed by this principle, however, requires considerable empirical knowledge about what kinds and degrees of punitive deprivations are in fact sufficient to provide the incentives requisite to compliance. In this way, Card's retributivism makes a deep bow in the direction of nonretributive (deterrent) considerations and cannot serve as an example of a purely retributivist solution to the Mikado's problem.

The chief difficulties in Card's penalty principle arise, as she herself recognizes, over interpreting the second clause, or "Full Measure principle," as she calls it. "The Full Measure consists in a deprivation of rights exposing the offender to a hardship comparable in severity to the worst that anyone could reasonably be expected to suffer from the similar conduct of another if such conduct were to become general in the community."[29] The purpose behind this somewhat complex formulation is to approximate the intuitively sound requirement of retributivism that a just punishment consists in "a suspension or withdrawal of rights of the offender corresponding to his failure to respect such rights of others."[30] There are two main problems with such a principle. First, how can we be assured that this is *the* principle that retributive justice requires? There are two obvious alternatives to the full measure principle. One is that the appropriate severity in the punishment is determined by the *average* hardship that would result were such harmful conduct to become general. The other is that the appropriate severity is determined by the *actual* hardship that results from the offender's wrongful conduct. Card considers both these alternatives, and rejects them. I wish to reject them, too, but for different reasons. The chief objection to the latter is that it asks of a principle essentially intended to guide penal legislation the exactitude of a judicial judgment in a particular case, and therefore requires something that is totally unobtainable. The chief objection to the former (the more attractive alternative of the two under consideration) is that it is in fact incalculable what the total hardship is (except over arbitrary finite periods of time, and even this is very doubtful) and therefore incalculable what the average hardship is. There may be (as Card herself argues) retributivist reasons against these two alternatives. If my criticisms are correct, there are strong nonretributivist objections also.

Essentially the same criticisms apply to Card's full measure principle. Like von Hirsch's principle, we cannot apply it without having some way of measuring the hardship or loss of rights suffered by the victim. Consider the crime of rape. How much hardship does it involve for the victim? Is the hardship a function of (a) the victim's feelings, such as how much the assault hurts and how much embarrassment or numbness it causes? Or is it a function of (b) the victim's status, such as whether the victim is a virgin, a child, a prostitute, a spouse? Or is the hardship to be determined by some combination of (a) and (b)—and if so, what combination? Or does the hardship in question involve neither (a) nor (b)? Card does not tell us. Instead, she would have us speculate on the answer to such questions as these: What is the worst that any given person could expect to suffer were rape to become widespread in the community? What is the appropriate suffering to legislate for the generality of rapists that is equivalent to this worst suffering of victims? Card does not tell us the answer to these questions, and it is extremely difficult to see how we are to proceed to find their answers. Thus, her attempt to solve a problem essentially equivalent to the one von Hirsch faces is no more successful than his.

I conclude from this discussion that although justice does require us to concede to the retributivist that the punishment must fit the crime, and that a punishment fits the crime when it matches in its severity what the crime involved in offender fault and victim harm, there is not much content or rigor in this abstract concession because we do not have adequate measures for fault and harm. The new retributivism thus fails at precisely the same point where the old retributivism, wedded to *lex talionis* as it was, also failed. The same is true when we transform the doctrine that the punishment must fit the crime into the admonition that punishments are unfairly severe when they exceed the gravity of the offense and unfairly lenient when they are less than the gravity of the offense. These moral truisms are indisputable, but we are able to get a purchase on their meaning only at the extremes, e.g., the judgments that a $50 fine for murder or six months solitary confinement for double parking on a side street are retributively unfair. They provide little guidance of a practical sort in the difficult tasks of sentencing faced by judges and legislatures.

VII

Let us leave to one side the problem of fairness to the offender and turn to possible retributive concessions that originate in the need to be fair to the victim. Even if retributive justice requires the offender to suffer as the offender caused the victim to suffer, it is worth at least passing notice to realize that causing offenders to suffer does not improve the situation of the victim. Making the offender worse off by punishing him does not make the victim better off. The victim is still dead or maimed or bleeding or otherwise injured. The most that can be said is that victims of a vindictive turn of mind will take satisfaction in the knowledge that punishment of the offender will cause the offender to suffer something like the suffering caused the victim. Whether this should count as an improvement in the situation of the victim, however, is not so clear. One can, of course, imagine a world in which, miraculously, the wounds of the injured begin to heal the instant the offender is punished, and are healed more perfectly the more perfectly the offender's punishment fits the crime. Questions of maladministration of criminal justice to one side, if our world were such a world, it might seem difficult to reject the claims of retributive justice. Except that even in such a world, our interest in the quantum of punishment imposed for a given offense is determined by its *restorative* effects. But restitution for the victim is not the same thing at all as retribution for the offender. In any case, we live in no such fanciful world as the one just described. Nevertheless, the substitution of restoration for retribution in such a world has a lesson for us in our world. It is this: Fairness to victims of crime requires that their wounds be bound and their suffering assuaged; and if this can be done in part (as it can with some crimes against property) by depriving the offender of his unjust gains and returning them to the rightful owner, so much the better. Fairness does not require injuries to the guilty offender when they in no way alleviate the prior injuries of the innocent victim. In an ideally just world, everything is in the hands of its rightful owners, and therefore anyone who commits a crime upsets a just distribution. Fairness in such a world requires that the person who has suffered harm through being a victim of crime be restored through compensation, or restitution, preferably from the person who originally injured him. If this is so, then there is nothing we can do to offenders in the name of retributive justice that will do what justice to the victim requires. Why it should ever have been thought that justice to victims requires retribution for offenders I do not know. Perhaps, as some have suggested, it is owing to a deep confusion between retribution and restitution.[31]

As the foregoing discussion shows, retributivists, whether of the old or the new variety, are totally uninterested in binding up the wounds of the victims. The only fairness retributivists are interested in is the fairness of deserts to be visited upon the offender; as for the victim, retributivists seem quite willing to let him fend for himself. This is a strange as well as an incomplete theory of justice in the full context of crime in society. Similarly, just as retributivists have no reason to demand reparation for the innocent victim in the name of justice, retributivists can do nothing to cope with the character, incidence, and volume of crime itself. It is too rarely noticed that retributivists in principle are fundamentally indifferent between the state of the world in which there is no crime, and the state of the world in which there is a wide variety of horrible crimes each of which is punished fully and exactly as retribution requires. Depressing the crime rate is no concern of the retributivist; neither is avoiding recidivism; he willingly leaves these concerns to the utilitarian, thereby revealing just how narrow are his interests in the overall social problem of crime and punishment. If justice or other moral principles dictate a concern about innocent victims and the innocent public, it is not thanks to the views held by retributivists.

VIII

There are, no doubt, further considerations to be brought forward under the rubric of retributivism that bear on its adequacy as a penal philosophy. But they are, I believe, of distinctly secondary importance to the considerations already examined here. Let us, therefore, look at the tally sheet and draw some conclusions from it.

Fundamentally only these concessions have been made to retributivism: (1) punishment is to be imposed only for intentional harms, (2) a punishment must be a deprivation, (3) the guilty deserve to be punished, and (4) the severity of the punishment should match the gravity of the offense. If we add the distinctively Kantian doctrines that focus on the role of *mens rea* in establishing criminality, then we get two additional concessions; (5) a just society must punish criminals, not rehabilitate or treat them as such, in order to respect them as persons, and (6) no one may be punished who lacks a *mens rea* for his harmful act. It has not been argued that these six are the most important aspects of any possible theory of punishment; nor has it been claimed that only a retributivist outlook can accommodate these features of just punishment. On the contrary, what is evident is that several of these requirements can be provided by utilitarian reasoning, and taken together, they neither exhaust the relevance of ideas of justice to the tasks of coping with crime nor suffice to construct a theory of punishment. In sum, trying to pattern punishment entirely by reference to the nature of crime and in the name of justice yields distinctly meager results.

Moreover, only two or three of these concessions seem to be firmly and properly part of any system of punishment. Concession (2) is not disputed by any theorist of punishment, nor is there much dispute over what counts as a "deprivation." The same is true of concession (6), except that it contains little not already expressed in or implied in concession (1). Concession (1) can be expected to receive ever wider acceptance as moralizing through the criminal law proves ever wider acceptance of moralizing through the criminal law proves increasingly wasteful of social resources and constrictive of human liberty. Concession (3) in its weak form—only someone deemed guilty of an offense is a proper candidate for punishment—is, like concession (1), part of every theory and system of punishment. In its stronger forms—all and only the guilty (i.e., those with culpable participation in crime) must be punished—it is far from persuasive; justice for the guilty does not consist in their being punished, because facts about guilty persons other than their guilt and pertinent to their being punished cannot be wholly ignored. Concession (4), the Mikado's principle, is not only vague, but like concession (3), collides with other considerations of justice and morality that pull us in a different direction. Concession (5), for all that it may stay the hand of over-eager social reformers, does not tell us much as long as concession (4) remains vague and we do not live in a just society.

Nothing we have seen in this discussion shows why retributive considerations should always (or ever) prevail over other considerations of justice where there is a conflict of principles. To resolve issues of this sort would take us deeper into moral philosophy, a task better left for another occasion. I have also not tried to draw up the negative side of the ledger, that is, to identify those features of a theory of justice in punishment that retribution requires us to include but which, upon examination and reflection, we must reject as morally unacceptable. The final tally sheet on retribution in punishment cannot be drawn up until the entries on this side of the ledger are all in place.

NOTES TO CHAPTER THREE

1. See particularly Herbert Morris, "Persons and Punishment," *The Monist*, 52 (October 1968), pp. 475-501. A more recent and more popular source is

Ernest van den Haag, *Punishing Criminals* (New York: Basic Books, 1975). The growing interest in retributivism among philosophers can be most easily traced in H.B. Acton, ed., *The Philosophy of Punishment* (London: Macmillan, 1969).

2. See especially the decisions by the U.S. Supreme Court in the death penalty cases, *Furman* v. *Georgia* (1972) and *Gregg* v. *Georgia* (1976), and the briefs submitted by the Solicitor General as *amicus curiae* in *Fowler* v. *North Carolina* (1975) and in *Gregg*.

3. See, e.g., Norval Morris, *The Future of Imprisonment* (University of Chicago Press, 1974) and Andrew von Hirsch, *Doing Justice* (New York: Hill & Wang, 1976).

4. John Locke, *Two Treatises of Government* (1690), II, § 8.

5. Elsewhere I have discussed at somewhat greater length the contrast between compensatory and punitive justice; see "Compensatory Justice: Cases and Principles," *Anuario de filosofia del derecho* (1975), pp. 517-523, at 519-520. See also W.N. Kneale, "The Responsibility of Criminals" (1967), reprinted in Acton, ed., *op. cit.*, pp. 172-196, at pp. 176-184. For a vigorous argument to the effect that retaliation (retribution) and restitution are inseparably connected, at least historically, see David Daube, *"Lex Talionis,"* in his *Studies in Biblical Law* (Cambridge University Press, 1947), pp. 102-153.

6. H.L.A. Hart, *Punishment and Responsibility* (Oxford University Press, 1967), p. 231.

7. For a useful discussion of Kantian retributivism, see Edmund L. Pincoffs, *The Rationale of Legal Punishment* (New York: Humanities Press, 1966), pp. 2-16, reprinted as "Classical Retributivism" in Joel Feinberg and Hyman Gross, ed., *Punishment* (Encino, California: Dickenson Publ. Co., 1975), pp. 17-25.

8. E.g., K.G. Armstrong says, ". . . a retributive theory is . . . the only theory which connects punishment with desert, and so with justice . . . " "The Retributivist Hits Back" (1961), reprinted in Acton, ed., *op. cit.*, p. 155. Cf. the remark "I have in mind the appeal to a person's deserts when referring to retributive considerations." John Kleinig, *Punishment and Desert* (The Hague: Martinus Nijhoff, 1973), p. viii.

9. See especially Hart, *op. cit.*, and *The Concept of Law* (Oxford University Press, 1961); Herbert Morris, *op. cit.*; and John Rawls, *A Theory of Justice* (Cambridge, Mass.: Harvard University Press, 1971). A popular attempt in this direction will be found in the essay by the American Friends Service Committee, *Struggle for Justice* (New York: Hill & Wang, 1971).

10. For a general discussion of excuses and their place in the theory of punishment, see Herbert L. Packer, *The Limits of the Criminal Sanction* (Stanford University Press, 1968), pp. 103-135.

11. Some may complain that this emphasis on freedom shows that my conception of a just society is not neutral with respect to all social values other than justice. This is true; the notion of a just society on which I am relying is one familiar to the liberal tradition and to that extent not a neutral, ideologically pure notion.

12. Rawls, *op. cit.*, p. 112. He cites H.L.A. Hart, "Are There Any Natural Rights?" *The Philosophical Review*, 64 (1955), pp. 175-191. What Rawls calls "the right of compliance" is not to be identified with a right to punish noncompliance.

13. Since I have so frequently referred to Rawls' views, it is perhaps well to

point out that what I have called here "the problem of compliance" he calls "the assurance problem"; see Rawls, *op. cit.*, pp. 268-270. Rawls confines the term 'compliance' to the fit between the actual rules of social institutions and the ideal rules of just institutions.

14. For a general discussion, see the volume I have co-authored with Edwin M. Schur, *Victimless Crimes: Two Sides of a Controversy* (Englewood Cliffs, New Jersey: Prentice-Hall, 1974).

15. In "A World Without Punishment?", in Milton Goldinger, ed., *Punishment and Human Rights* (Cambridge, Mass.: Schenkman Publ. Co., 1974), pp. 141-162, at 152-153, I failed to mention this point.

16. The starting point for emphasis on this truth is Kurt Baier, "Is Punishment Retributive?" (1955), reprinted in Acton, ed., *op. cit.* pp. 130-137, especially at 132.

17. Some will want to insist that only retributivism can provide this feature of just punishment: it has been a stock objection against nonretributive (or utilitarian) theories of punishment that they countenance the punishment of the innocent. Some recent utilitarians also seem to think that they may, indeed, have to defend some such view. See, e.g., Rolf E. Sartorius, *Individual Conduct and Social Norms* (Encino, Calif.: Dickenson Pub. Co., 1975), pp. 134-135. I take it, however, that this controversy has been shown to rest upon misunderstandings about punishment as a social practice or institution. See John Rawls, "Two Concepts of Rules" (1955), reprinted in part in Acton, ed., *op. cit.*, pp. 109-114. If this is correct, then it is not only retributivism that secures us from thinking that punishing the innocent is morally wrong.

18. Van den Haag, *op. cit.*, p. 21, thinks it is.

19. See Claudia Card, "Retributive Penal Liability," *American Philosophical Quarterly Monographs*, No. 7 (1973), pp. 17-35, at 26.

20. Cf. the quip by A.M. Quinton, "It is an odd sort of right whose holders would strenuously resist its recognition," reprinted in Gertrude Ezorsky, ed., *Philosophical Perspectives on Punishment* (Albany, N.Y.: S.U.N.Y. Press, 1972), pp. 8-9.

21. Herbert Morris, *op. cit.*, p. 479.

22. I have considerably changed my tune in this and the next few paragraphs, owing to the prodding from my colleagues David Israel and Daniel Dennett, who criticized an earlier version.

23. I have discussed this point at somewhat greater length in "Physical Interventions to Alter Behavior in a Punitive Environment," *American Behavioral Scientist*, 18 (May-June 1975), pp. 675-678, at 674-676.

24. Blackstone, *Commentaries* (1765), Bk. IV, Ch. 1, sec. ii.3; cited in Hart, *Punishment and Responsibility* p. 161 note 3. Kant's views are bewildering when he gives examples of the punishments he believes satisfy *jus talionis*; e.g., slander he proposed should be punished by requiring retraction, apology, and "some meaner ordeal, as kissing the hand of the injured person" (reprinted in Ezorsky, ed., *op. cit.*, pp. 104-105); rape and pederasty should be punished by castration (Immanuel Kant, *Metaphysical Elements of Justice*, tr. John Ladd (1965), p. 132).

The recent alternative proposed by Kleinig, *op. cit.*, pp. 123-129, avoids the absurdities of *lex talionis* only because it yields no determinate results for most cases.

25. Von Hirsch, *op cit.*, pp. 66, 69.

26. Thorsten Sellin and Marvin E. Wolfgang, *The Measurement of Delinquency* (New York: John Wiley, 1964), discussed by von Hirsch, *op. cit.*, at pp. 78-79. Sellin and Wolfgang claim to be able to rank order criminal offenses according to the degree of "severity" (what I prefer to call 'gravity') of the crime. They do this by means of a scale with twenty-six equal intervals, such that at one end is the least serious crime (larceny in the amount of $1) and at the other the most serious crime (murder) (Table 69, p. 289). Armed robbery of $5 turns out to be five times as serious as the least serious crime, and forcible rape is two and a half times as serious as armed robbery of $5 (*loc. cit.*). Their rating scale implies the implausible consequence that the harm caused in a crime that costs the victim his one good eye is equivalent in seriousness to the harm that results in a crushed rib without accompanying lung puncture (because neither injury can be treated merely with first aid, neither results in death, and both require hospitalization; see p. 191). Also, their scales provide no way of discriminating among criminal homicides as to their seriousness, because the theory does not include a way to treat separate aggravating (or mitigating) factors numerically once it has been determined that the crime results in the victim's death. A fundamental criticism is that their theory collapses seriousness of an offense into the harm caused, thereby entirely leaving out of account any role for the culpability factor in the severity of crimes (see p. 306). Insofar as they address themselves to this feature of their theory at all, it is only in their insistence that they are measuring the properties of the criminal "act," and not the properties of the offender (see pp. 248, 252, 258).

27. Card, *op. cit.*, p. 22.

28. *Ibid.*, p. 25, italics in original. As Card notes, her view is less retributive than it might be because it does not ever allow retributive considerations to outweigh the severities needed to assure compliance.

29. *Ibid.*, p. 27 and cf. p. 31.

30. *Ibid.*, p. 31.

31. See Daube, *op. cit.*, and also Kneale, *op. cit.*

 *Chapter Four*

Are Questions of Desert Decidable?

Edmund L. Pincoffs

In the best of all possible worlds, our official and unofficial acts and activities would be justified by considerations so finely balanced that no critic could complain of their relative weightings. Justice and utility would nestle together like the lamb and the lion; the keystone of every institutional structure would fit so firmly into place that mortar would insult the architect. The innate wisdom and decency of the people would insure that not much weight need rest on those structures anyway, thus freeing judges, legislators and other such for useful and morally untroubled lives. But since one of my colleagues has recently raised the question whether the best of all possible worlds is itself *possible*, and since I have for some time suspected that it is not *actual*, I will approach our common topic, the criminal justice system, very much aware of the possibility that there is something fundamentally wrong with the moral rationale on which it rests.

To begin with, we don't know what to do about desert. Should the criminal justice system be concerned at all with what criminals deserve for what they have done? Or should considerations of desert be set aside as too prickly, difficult, vague, or emotion-laden for rational treatment? Does all talk of what criminals deserve rest on judicial hunch, legislative fiat, and general public vindictiveness and cussedness? Should probationary officers take desert into account in their recommendations? What, in fact, *is* desert? And *is* it? Does it really exist, or is it just a convention, useful, perhaps, but ultimately unfounded?

I will argue here that in any institution that imposes unwanted treatment, because it is unwanted, on normal, voluntary agents, in virtue of their acts, questions of desert necessarily arise. I will argue that debates about desert can be rational, and that the rationality of desert-talk is not a chimera. That is, it does not rest in turn on arbitrarily chosen social ends, nor on mere convention. It will *not* follow from these conclusions that there *should* be institutionally determined impositions on normal and voluntary individuals. That is another question. However, I should say that my own attitude toward that question, toward what is usually called the justification of punishment, has been qualified by the results of the study I have undertaken here.

WHAT DESERT-CLAIMS DO NOT CLAIM

If *A* claims that *B deserves C*, it always makes sense to ask *A* what it is *about B* that leads *A* to think he deserves *C*. To put the point another way, it would have no clear sense for *A* to say *B* deserves *C*, but there's absolutely nothing about *B*, nothing he has done or suffered, no quality of character, *in virtue of which* he deserves *C*. He just deserves *C*. People don't just deserve well or ill, they deserve *because of* some fact about or feature of themselves. Not only must there be reasons, then, for meaningful desert claims, but the reasons must have to do with some feature of the agent. For convenience, I will refer to these agent-directed reasons for desert claims as Desert-making Considerations (DMC's).

It might be felt that there are counterexamples against my contention that all meaningful desert claims imply backing by DMC's. For example, it might be argued that meaningful desert claims can be made on behalf of yet unborn generations, whose features are by hypothesis unknown, or on behalf of lottery winners whose features are irrelevant. We can meaningfully say, it might be argued, that future generations do not deserve to inherit an environment so polluted as to make life miserable. Or we can say that a person should not be deprived of his lottery winnings, that he deserves them since he holds the winning ticket. But these proposed counterexamples are instructive in bringing out further features of desert claims.

There is, as it turns out, one feature of the members of unborn generations that we do know, unless we accept an Old Testament theory of guilt. That is that they are not guilty of present pollution. The moral of this is that DMC's can be negative as well as positive. They can point to the absence of features that *would be* grounds for claims of ill desert to show that those claims are unwarranted.

They can do this either, as in the present example, by showing that for some reason the agent *cannot* have the feature in question, or by showing that he does not in fact have it. Reasons why the agent cannot have the feature can include, in addition to the rather odd one of present nonexistence just cited, infancy and insanity—in general the exceptions that we would ordinarily rank under the heading of incapacity. And there are many kinds of reasons why the agent may not in fact deserve *C*. There are in fact all of the exonerating considerations with which jurists are familiar, such as accident, coercion, and so on.

If meaningful desert claims must be backed by DMC's, which refer to some feature of the agent, what *feature of the agent* is relevant to the claim that he deserves to win the lottery? While it is difficult to say, *in abstracto*, what is to count as a feature, it surely seems that having purchased a ticket is not one. Perhaps the best we can say about the *kind* of feature that is in question is that it must be in some way *revelatory of* the agent, and revelatory in a certain way. Not revelatory of his aesthetic preferences, for example, as the pattern of his record-buying should be, or the novels on his shelves, or the patterns in his sitting room. Not revelatory merely of his affections, as a gift or a glance might be; nor of his social status or religious affiliation. Revelatory, rather, of what, in some morally fundamental sense, he *is*.

He might have been given the lottery ticket; he might have found it on the street. It might have been sent him by a mysterious stranger. For all sorts of accidental and extrinsic reasons he might have it, and his having it would have nothing to do with his desert because it has nothing to do with *him*; but it would have everything to do with his entitlement to the prize. He may claim it with his ticket but he may not deserve it. There are no DMC's to back the claim that he does. If he is old, poor, and honest, and has spent his life working for the benefit of others, and now needs something on which to retire, he will deserve the prize to which he is entitled. Those are desert-making considerations.

Failure to appreciate the implicit reference of desert claims to the DMC's that serve as their backing can lead to two different misconceptions of the nature of those claims. It can lead to a conception of desert as something just there or given, a rib of the universe or an inner revelation, not needing support. Or it can lead to conceptions of desert as requiring support, but of the wrong kind, of some kind other than DMC's.

That the first of these misconceptions *is* one can be seen, I have suggested, by noticing that it makes no sense both to claim that *B* deserves C and, in the same breath, to admit that one has no reason whatever for thinking B deserves C. But if the error is obvious when so baldly exposed, it is not so obvious when wrapped up in some otherwise plausible conception of desert. I will briefly mention three such conceptions: attitudinal or emotive theories of desert, intuitive theories, and authoritarian theories.

Anyone who reflects on the nature of desert must at some time be tempted to say that B's desert is simply a function of some A's attitude. If A detests B, or, more plausibly, what B has done, then B deserves ill; but if A likes what B has done, then B deserves well. This theory has, and has had, some appeal. Yet, more closely examined, it will not wash. On this theory, B's desert would have to fluctuate from good to ill and back again with A's likes and dislikes of B's actions. But, since there are other individuals, A_1, A_2, etc., who may like or dislike B's actions, his desert is going to fluctuate with their likes and dislikes too. But this analysis won't do, since B's desert might be embraced by the convinced attitudinal relativist, I shall have to assume that we are not ready to take so extreme a position. Obviously the price of accepting it is high. It would not be merely *difficult* to settle disputes concerning desert, it would be in principle *impossible*.

It is worth noting that there are more sophisticated versions of attitudinal theories, which allow a place for reasons but which still do not avoid the (assumed) unwanted consequence. Reasons would on such more sophisticated views be whatever sentences would be causally efficacious in changing the attitude of A_1, A_2, etc. toward B's act—changing it to accord with A's attitude. The difficulty here, well explored in the more general literature of ethics, is that there is no way of distinguishing, what most of us would say should be distinguished, the *relevance* of purported reasons from their causal efficacy. Whatever in fact changes an attitude concerning what a person deserves would be, on this theory, relevant to the question what he deserves. But, given the idiosyncracies of all of us, what may cause you to like B's action (perhaps that it reminds you of your Grandmother) may cause me to dislike it (perhaps that it reminds me of a former commanding officer). So that the introduction of 'reasons' that count only to the degree that they are causally effective in changing attitudes, succeeds only in introducing a new unwelcome consequence.

The intuitive and authoritarian theories of desert have little to recommend them either. On the intuitive theory, one simply appeals to one's intuition as ground for the claim that B deserves C. The intuitive theory says that, since we can directly intuit what a person deserves, no reasons need be given for our judgments (except that according to our intuition it is thus and so). It is a consequence of this theory, as of the attitudinal one, that a person can, on the same occasion, deserve both ill and well, since in principle A's intuition may always be at odds with the intuition of A_2, A_3, etc.

The authoritarian theory holds that B deserves whatever L, an Authoritative Desert Determiner holds that it is. But either L determines on the basis of DMC's what B deserves, or he doesn't. If he does, his desert claim rests, not on his authority, but on the DMC's. If he doesn't, the desert claim rests solely on his authority and is not so much a claim as a ruling. It is a consequence of this theory that, given the ruling, it makes no sense to raise the question whether A in fact deserves what L rules that he deserves. This takes care of the objections against the attitudinal and intuitive theories, since it will, on the authoritarian theory, be impossible for B both to deserve and not deserve C (given, what I take for granted, that there's only *one* L). But, of course, the authoritarian theory has formidable problems of its own. The rulings of L concerning desert are neither wise nor judicious, careful nor prudent, fair nor appropriate. To back any of *these* assessments of L's ruling we would need to appeal to DMC's, which are, by hypothesis, excluded from consideration. These difficulties will be familiar to devotees of Augustine's theology, where analogous problems arise over God's judgment of sinful man, or of Hobbes' political philosophy where rightness of action is determined by conformity with Leviathan's command. Despite the obvious difficulties of any such theory, whether theological or not, I suspect that it exerts a malign influence on discussions of desert. For it may well be that those persons who insist that desert is something more real or fundamental than can be captured by any 'merely conventional' analysis have at the back of their minds the notion that what desert *really* is can only finally be settled by a ruling which *cannot be appealed*. But the most obvious way to cut off all appeals is to decide that some L's decision takes precedence over *any* DMC that can be raised.

There are, I have been arguing, two main misconceptions of what desert claims are: the notion that they in some way reveal, or lay down, a truth that is beyond challenge, so that no reasons for the claim need be given; or the notion that reasons other than DMC's can serve to prove or anyway support desert claims. I turn now to the second of these misconceptions. In its most common form, it consists in confusing DMC's with considerations relevant to entitlement. A person is entitled to certain outcomes if he fulfills the requirements of the practice according to which distributions are made. Thus a person can be entitled to being declared winner of a race if he is first to breast the tape, to the prize for the best novel if the majority of the judges so vote, or to the Sweepstakes if he holds the ticket. There can also be negative entitlements. A person can, using the term broadly, be entitled to lose a (two-person) race if he is *not* the first to breast the tape, or he can be entitled to fines or imprisonment if he is duly sentenced according to appropriate procedures.

We sometimes use the language of desert in referring to entitlements, and this can be confusing.[1] Thus, we can say that, even though *C* may have won a race only because *D* and *E*, faster runners, way ahead, collided and fell, nevertheless he deserves the prize just because he was first at the finish line. He is entitled to the prize, that is; but we would typically not claim in those circumstances that he *deserved* to win, since his win was not attributable to his effort but to fortuitous circumstances over which he had no control. The point to bear in mind about entitlement is that the question can always meaningfully be raised whether a person deserves that to which he is entitled as the outcome of even a properly conducted procedure, a procedure which in the best of all worlds would always entitle people to what they *do* deserve. As we shall see, this ideal of matching procedural outcomes and desert presents peculiar problems for the practice of legal punishment.

An especially persistent and vexing confusion is that between DMC's and considerations tending to show that a given *outcome* would be for some reason desirable. This is not so much a confusion in practice as in theory. While we would seldom imagine that because a given sentence would have deterrent value it is therefore what the criminal deserves, still we might be inclined toward a theory that reduces DMC's to utilitarian considerations. We might believe that questions of desert can and should be settled on forward-looking grounds, that what a person deserves in a given situation is what is most likely to produce desirable consequences in the circumstances. The theory is an especially tempting one because of the neat way it apparently disposes of deterministic bothers. Thus, J.S. Mill, in *Hamilton*, reminds us that the 'necessitarian' (read, 'determinist') can perfectly well determine desert by reference to the deterrent value of this or that punishment. Yet it is simply wrong to identify DMC's with utilitarian considerations. Given any determination of desert made on purely utilitarian grounds, it will nevertheless make sense to ask whether the person deserves the outcome in question. Sometimes he will and sometimes not, but the relation is a contingent one. It is contingent, because it is not in virtue of what the agent is or has done that he deserves, but in virtue of what can, usefully, be done with or for him. Indeed, we may want to take what he has done into account, but that is not what is essential.

WHAT DESERT-CLAIMS CLAIM

If desert claims are essentially reason-invoking ones, and if the reasons they do invoke, explicitly but more often tacitly, are DMC's and not (merely) some other sort of reason, then what *are* DMC's? How do we set them off from other sorts of reasons? To answer, we must first have another look at what we are doing in claiming that someone deserves something. To speak of what a person deserves is to speak of what it is appropriate that he should receive, in virtue of what he has done or suffered. 'Deserves' is thus a relational term. *B* deserves *C* in virtue of *D*, where *B* is one or more persons, *C* something desirable or undesirable, and *D* what I earlier called a *feature* of *B*, that is, something attributable to *B*. *C* must be deserved in virtue of *B*'s act or what *B* has suffered. But we must insure that it is *B*'s *desert* we are talking about, not what will contingently come about as a result of *B*'s act, or what *B* is entitled to, or what will lead to good consequences if it is inflicted on *B*. Excuses help us make the distinction. What *B* did by mistake, by accident, or under coercion is not for our purposes a feature of *B*. It in no relevant way *reveals B*. The excuses qualify, in different ways, our judgment of desert; some remove ill desert, e.g., entirely, some merely mitigate it. So we should say that *B* deserves *C* in virtue of *D and in the absence of E*, where *E* are excuses that exonerate or mitigate. Of course, where *good* desert is in question, these same considerations (accident, mistake, etc.) tend to remove or reduce the claim to good desert as well.

In saying that *B* deserves something in virtue of what he has done, we are, I suggest, *appraising B's action* in a certain way. We make a claim concerning what is due *B* in consequence of the action. (We will speak here, for the time being, of desert for an action. There can be, as I have suggested, desert for what one has suffered as well as for what one has done. There can also be desert for what one is as the result of all one's actions, of one's life. I will not discuss those matters here.) What a person deserves for what he has done is a matter of judgment. There is no preexisting scale off which we can read an answer. In appraising a person's desert, we need to know the factual details of what he has done, and we need facts that help us determine the degree to which what he has done is a feature of the agent, reveals him, is *his*, and not merely something that has happened to (or through) him. But the facts do not entail an appraisal any more than the square-footage of a house and its location entails its value. Judgment is required; the facts are there to be used but are not themselves jointly constitutive of judgment.

Since desert claims are best understood as a kind of appraisal, an appraisal of what is due a person, such claims presuppose the belief that something *is* due people in virtue of their actions. If no one were due anything, desert claims would simply not be made. Since such claims are a kind of appraisal, they are better described as well-founded or ill-founded than as true or false. Entitlement claims, on the other hand, *are* true or false, since there are requirements of entitlement that may be fulfilled, or which one may fail to fulfill. Thus, in nearly every race there are winners and losers, only the winners being entitled to the purse or trophy. Judgments of desert, by contrast, seem, by the language appropriate to them, to be tacit or explicit appeals for the confirmation of the judgment of others. Conclusions from the considerations adduced are not entailed by those considerations but are claimed to follow from them.

If we think of desert claims as appraisals, then something more is revealed about the nature of the considerations that back desert claims (DMC's). They not only provide information about the agent himself, e.g., that he did whatever he did, wrote an essay or robbed a bank, *and* that what he did must be qualified in this way or that, e.g. that he had a collaborator in writing the novel, or that he was forced to participate in the robbery. They not only provide, that is, information about the deed and the degree to which the deed is fully the agent's and thus is revelatory of the agent. If there is to be an appraisal of desert, more is needed than these agent-revealing considerations, since appraisals are inherently comparative. Desert admits not only of good and ill, but of kind and degree. We can ask *what* a person deserves, and, if he deserves what admits of degrees, how much he deserves. We can ask these latter questions, that is, *given that appraisals are to be made.* Given the need to appraise, they can be forced upon us, *even when there seems to be no easy way of answering them*, or even when any answer given will be to some degree an arbitrary one.

Comparison with other types of appraisal may be illuminating here. In appraising a house, an appraiser must first establish a relevant description, both accurate and properly qualified. Not only must he determine the square-footage, damage, deterioration, and so on, but he must qualify his description in such a way that none of these facts will, taken alone, be misleading about the true state of the house. The qualifications are intended to make the description germane to the appraisal. Thus, a part of the square footage is in an unfinished wing, the tornado damage is superficial, or the deterioration of the foundation is serious. This qualified description establishes the groundwork for an appraisal, as does the qualified description of an act. The qualifications that are relevant to the appraisal to be made are, with respect to acts, qualifications that help us determine to what extent the (physical) act reveals the true nature of the agent's action. We are, thus, interested in questions of capacity, of excusing conditions, and of justification, so that matters like insanity, accident, and provocation hedge or cancel more purely descriptive matters, such as the presence or absence of a weapon. But given this hedged or qualified description, the appraisal remains to be made. Here, for all appraisals, including desert claims, a logically distinct type of consideration enters. For *an appraisal is a comparative judgment*, and a comparative basis must be established. The appraiser of houses must determine values of comparable houses by recent sales prices. But if there are no recent sales, he must use whatever evidence, however tangential, is available. Desert claims are, I suggest, appraisals, and, for them too, the basis of comparison may be difficult to establish. This is the fundamental problem in the setting of penalties for a criminal code, and of punishments for particular crimes.

PUNISHMENT: THE LEGISLATIVE AND JUDICIAL PROBLEMS

The two stages, legislative and judicial, of determining what the punishment should be for crime, are those of establishing, and of applying to particular cases, a pair of coordinated scales.[2] One scale, of crimes, reaches from the least to the most serious. It is an ordinal scale; any item on it should, ideally, be between a more and a less serious crime. The scale of punishments, on the other hand, is typically[3] (for fines and imprisonment) one that admits of regular intervals from very lenient to very severe. It is a cardinal scale, one that admits not merely of judgments of which item on it is lower and which higher, but of such judgments as that three years is half as many as six, and four years twice as many as two. I would like to make three preliminary remarks about the problem of relating these scales.

1. I will be speaking only of the question what a criminal deserves for a crime. I do not assume, and do not believe, that this is the only, or even the primary, legislative or judicial question in determining punishment. But I do believe that it is, within the limits I will mention, a meaningful question, and one that will inevitably arise,

given a system in which generally unwanted consequences are authoritatively imposed, because they are unwanted, on adult, normal persons who voluntarily commit crimes. It will inevitably arise because these unwanted consequences are not being imposed arbitrarily, or at least that is not the intention, but are being imposed according to a worked-out rationale and by means of comparative judgments made between cases. But if this is so, invidious arguments are sure to arise concerning the comparative judgments made, arguments that A has received a greater imposition than B, for equal crimes, or that A's punishment was out of proportion to the seriousness of his crime, given the judgments made concerning less or more serious crimes committed by B, or by others, or by A himself on another occasion. If impositions are to be made, then, and if they are to be made nonarbitrarily, but according to some scheme, then complaints can and will be made that A's deserts, under the scheme, are more or less than they should be.

2. The scheme according to which judgments concerning punishment are made can be more or less formal, thus leaving less or more leeway for individual judgments of desert. The most formal system, one that leaves no judicial discretion is, although the term is not entirely a happy one, a system of entitlements. Thus, if certain formally specified conditions are fulfilled, then the criminal is entitled to a certain punishment. The argument that he deserves the punishment to which he is entitled must then rest on an evaluation of the degree to which fulfillment of the requirements for entitlement approximates his desert. If, for example, given a legislatively determined penalty, it can be shown that a criminal is entitled to a three year sentence for robbery, the question whether he *deserves* three years will turn, first, on the justice of the legislative judgment that robbers should get three years, and secondly, on the DMC's relevant to the particular case. If, at the other extreme, no legislative determination is made, and the judge has full discretion, then there is no particular sentence to which the criminal is entitled, and DMC's may be, in principle, wholly or partially determinative of sentence.

3. Just as practical considerations may make it necessary to reach beyond the evidence in appraising a house, as, e.g., when there are no comparable sales, so it may be necessary, given a system of punishments, for a judge to decide what is deserved where there is no adequate comparative ground. DMC's tend to allow of degree, and finding a case comparable in degree on *all* counts may be impossible. This is to say nothing of the general problem of weighting one type of DMC, provocation say, against another, for example duress. Which is in general to count more in determining desert? Who is to say? But both do count.

The problems of determining *exactly* what a person deserves is one that arises only under a system that admits of indefinitely fine gradations of punishment. Imagine, for contrast, a system in which there were but two punishments: exile and confiscation of property. Then, the question of *exactly* what a person deserves would not be stage center, as it is in our system.

Back, then, to the interscalar problem, the legislative problem of relating the ordinal scale of crimes to the cardinal one of punishments. The problem is twofold. First, (the anchoring problem) even granting that an ordinal scale of crimes can be determined, there is the problem of establishing a relation between the scales. While we can know that first-degree murder should be higher than manslaughter, and that $x + 1$ years is a weightier punishment than x years, none of this tells us what we should substitute for x if punishment is to match desert. But this is not the only problem. There is a second problem, (the interval problem) often overlooked. It is that an ordinal scale, by nature, just establishes an order, but that if we rank crimes in order of their seriousness we still do not know anything about the intervals between crimes on the scale. Thus, if we have crimes ranked first through hundredth in ascending order of seriousness it may still be the case that, while the 50th crime is only slightly worse than the 49th, the 51st will be *far* worse than the 50th. The consequence is that, given this possible disparity of intervals, it seems simply arbitrary to move up the punishment scale by regular intervals in determining the punishment legislatively appropriate to the 49th, 50th, and 51st crimes. But, since the scale of crimes *is* an ordinal one only, there's no way of *calculating* that the 51st crime is, say, twice as bad as the 50th and that it therefore deserves twice as much punishment.

These problems for the legislative determination of a criminal code in which punishment matches desert are indeed troubling ones. Yet, if criminal codes are to be adopted, codes which to any degree specify punishment, the question cannot, as I have argued, be avoided whether crime x deserves the punishment apportioned to it, by inevitable comparison with the punishment apportioned to crime y. The interscalar problems are, by and large, problems that arise where the aim is *exact* determination of desert. But if the aim is the more modest one that there should be a reasonable proportion between what a man has done and what he suffers for it, the difficulties may prove more tractable. It may just be that while there are advantages in fine judgments concerning *punishments*, judgments of *desert* cannot be finely determined, at least not in the same way. If to judge desert is to make a kind of appraisal, it may be that desert appraisals, like appraisals of houses, must sometimes rest on less than satisfactory evidence.

The problem of anchoring the crime scale to the punishment scale is, in fact, not entirely intractable, for we do know *something* about where both scales begin. Or perhaps I should say that we know that certain beginning places are inappropriate. Thus, it is inappropriate to begin the ordinal scale of fines with three cents. These judgments are not merely blind intuitive ones on my part. We know what sort of consideration to appeal to in supporting them. We know, that is, *why* it is inappropriate to make tooth-picking criminal or to make three pennies a punishment. And we can approach, if never quite reach, a *reasoned* consensus on where each scale should begin.

Roughly, the rationale that sets the limits of the crime and punishment scales turns on the nature of the practice of punishment. It requires the threat of generally unwanted consequences of forbidden acts, the threat must be taken seriously, and three cents doesn't qualify; and it requires that the machinery of the law grind only for serious purposes, and the banning of tooth-picking is not a serious purpose. The anchoring problem, then, admits of rational, but not exact, solution.

The same may be said of the interval problem. We are not required to move up the punishment scale by just one regular interval corresponding to the possibly, irregular intervals on the crime scale. If the gap is greater between the 50th and 51st than between the 49th and 50th crimes, then the punishment interval should be greater too. Again, no more can be required than that a reasonable proportion should be maintained. The problem is one that does not admit of exact solution.

I have been speaking, for the time being, as if the legislative problem consists in setting definite (or 'flat') penalties for each crime. Obviously, there are other possibilities which will leave room for judicial discretion. The legislature may set minimum or maximum penalties, or both, and it may (or may authorize some agency to) set presumptive sentences from which the judge may depart for reasons given. The judge, then, may have more or less, and differently qualified discretion. And he may be more or less accountable for his sentence. Within the bounds of his discretion, then, the judge may make use of DMC's in determining and justifying sentences, and the criminal justice system will, finally, have ground out a sentence that is near to or far away from what the criminal deserves. It will always make sense to ask whether the criminal got the sentence he deserved, but it does not follow that he ought always to get just what he deserves, since other considerations than desert may be relevant too.

CONCLUSIONS

In this study, I have taken on the considerable task of showing that desert claims, once one understands what they are, are intelligible and *in principle* defensible by rationally acceptable considerations. I have held that the question what a person deserves is morally unavoidable under a system that intentionally imposes unwanted consequences, because they are unwanted, on normal agents in virtue of what they have, individually, done or failed to do. *Given* such a system, the question is what it would be *fair* to make him suffer. That question should not be confused with the question what, on balance, he *should* suffer, nor with the question what he is *entitled* to suffer under the procedure applicable to his case.

By identifying determination of desert as a kind of appraisal, I have tried to show how DMC's are relevant to such determinations. They are relevant primarily in establishing a comparative judgment. And I have been concerned to show that comparative judgments may be required under circumstances that do not necessarily allow of fine discrimination, of the kind of discrimination we are erroneously led to expect by an infinitely divisible cardinal scale. The comparisons in question are of the treatment persons receive under a system that purposely imposes unwanted treatment. The need for comparison arises only if there is such a system. Whether there should be such a system is a separate question.

The question whether there *should* be such a system has, I think, nothing to do with desert. Nothing, that is, unless one believes in all-embracing system of cosmic control. Given a controlled universe, questions are sure to arise whether men deserve their fates, and these judgments, too, must be comparative ones however vague the basis of comparison. But given no such assumption, it is far from clear what could be meant by the demand that men's fate should match their *real* deserts.

It does not follow that the justification of the practice of legal punishment should turn only on traditional utilitarian considerations. It can as well rest on contract theory or intuitive principles. But questions of *desert* arise only where the *possibility of distribution* of generally desirable and undesirable consequences is taken seriously.[4]

NOTES TO CHAPTER FOUR

1. Cf. John Kleinig, *Punishment and Desert*, The Hague, Martinus Nijhoff, 1973. I have found Kleinig useful, indeed the best available, on punishment as it relates to desert. On the concept of desert, one naturally turns to Joel Feinberg's well-wrought essays in *Doing and Deserving*, Princeton, Princeton University Press, 1970. Both writers distinguish between entitlement and nonentitlement uses of 'desert.'

2. Cf. Kleinig, *op. cit.*, ch. VII. For a helpful brief analysis of the problems of relating a cardinal to an ordinal scale, cf. W.S. Vickrey, 'Risk, Utility and Social

Policy,' in *Economic Justice*, E.S. Phelps, ed., Penguin Books, Harmondsworth, Middlesex, England, 1973, pp. 286-297.

3. But not necessarily. The following analysis does not apply to punishments (torture, mutilation), now abandoned, that do not admit of regular and infinite variation.

4. I should like to thank David Love and Marvin Henberg for criticism of the first draft of this study, and Alfred MacKay, Robert Grimm, Daniel Merrill, and Thomas Trelogan for points made in discussion of the issues.

Chapter Five

Criminal Sentencing: Some Philosophical Considerations
Martin P. Golding

I

Recent philosophical discussions of punishment in the English-speaking world have focused on three questions contained in this subject: (1) What is the general justification of punishment? (2) Who may justifiably be punished? And (3) how, or how much, may someone be punished? This way of dividing up the problem, which largely derives from the work of H.L.A. Hart, carries the suggestion that the three main traditional "theories" of punishment (deterrence, retribution, and reform or rehabilitation) differ in the relevance that they have to the stated questions.[1]

Thus, retributivism, for example, may be more relevant to the second question than to the first. To the question "On whom may punishment justifiably be imposed?" a relevant, and retributivist, answer would be "Only on deserving offenders." But retributivism may have little, and perhaps next to nothing, of relevance to say about the general justification of punishment. This particular question is concerned with why a society should have the *institution* of punishment in the first place, why it should have penal laws at all (i.e., laws that prescribe or forbid various kinds of conduct and that threaten punishment for violations). On this issue, a deterrence answer is clearly germane: a society has penal laws because it wants to deter people from doing, or not doing, certain things. Rehabilitation, on the other hand, does not seem very relevant here, for it would be both implausible and odd to maintain that penal laws are established in order to rehabilitate individuals who violate them. Finally, deterrence may have a lesser relevance to the question "Who may justifiably be punished?" than it has to the general justification of punishment.

In presenting the problem of punishment in this way I do not mean to imply that the above are necessarily the answers that Hart gives, or especially that Hart would regard himself as giving a retributivist answer to our second question. Nor do I necessarily agree that the lines between these questions are hard-and-fast. Moreover, whether deterrence is sufficient for the general justification of punishment might depend on what aspects of the institution are at issue. In any case, much will depend upon the kind of deterrence, retributive, or rehabilitative theory we are considering, for they occur in varieties. The point of Hart's suggestion is well-taken, nevertheless: if the problem is divided up in this way some of the standard difficulties and objections can be more easily dealt with; for example, the difficulty that a straightforward deterrence theory permits punishment of the innocent. In other words, the classical theories of punishment should be construed as answers to different questions rather than as rival answers to the same question.

The matter is less clear, however, in regard to the third question "How, or how much, may someone be punished?" On this issue it seems hard to deny the relevance of considerations of deterrence, retribution, and rehabilitation. In this study I want to explore a few of the ramifications that the classical theories have for this issue. I emphasize "a few" because there are many topics I shall not take up—for instance, capital punishment. The context of my discussion is the current debate over sentencing.

II

And there is a good deal of debate over this phase of the criminal justice process. It is difficult to open the pages of any major newspaper without finding an article about sentencing or a report on some proposal for change in this area. There is a tremendous amount of dissatisfaction with current practices, expressions of which come from the general public, criminal justice professionals, and academicians.

Probably the most obvious factor behind this dissatisfaction is the enormous increase in crime, a veritable crime explosion, and not just in the United States. Despite this increase, however, the prison population has been going down steadily (though there was a reversal of the trend last year). To illustrate the point, in 1975 over 25,000 arrests of juveniles were presented to Family Court in New York City alone. These included more than 6,700 arrests for murder, rape, armed robbery and felonious assault. No one need claim that these 6,700 were all guilty as charged. On the other hand, the 6,700 represented only a fraction of the total of such offenses committed. Yet in 1975 only 557 male and 25 female juvenile delinquents were in the custody of the state, and 330 males and 17 females were in homes run by private nonprofit agencies—under 1,000 altogether. Someone who finds this unsettling will not get much comfort from the situation of adult offenders. Out of 10 persons convicted of crimes in which guns were used only 4 served any time at all in prison. Little wonder, then, that dissatisfaction with sentencing is widespread. Too many offenders, it may be claimed, are punished for too short a time, if at all.

Expressions of dissatisfaction also came from the opposite corner. In 1968 Professor Herbert Morris published an article in which he criticized the rehabilitationist ideology and defended the proposition that a criminal has a right to be punished.[2] In 1972 the Iowa Parole Board disagreed with Morris. It released a Mr. Sweeney, who had been sentenced to 75 years in prison for killing a policeman, after Sweeney had served 2 years and 9 months of his sentence. The parole board reasoned that Sweeney was ready for release if a "complete rehabilitation" was to be achieved, and that the "only excuse for keeping him incarcerated any longer would be just to punish him." Apparently, then, Sweeney had a right not to be punished. Some writers, Judge Marvin Frankel is one, are also dissatisfied with sentencing because, they claim, too many offenders are punished for too long a time.[3] Of course, neither of the propositions "too many get too little" and "too many get too much" is very precise, and both may be true.

A second factor behind this dissatisfaction is the erosion of the rehabilitationist ideology that for so long has dominated sentencing and penology. Most rehabilitation programs, it is claimed, are sheer myth; they do not exist where they are supposed to exist, but sentencers continue to sentence on the assumption that they do. Many programs, where they do exist, are coercive and demeaning; they only serve to increase an offender's punishment, and they have not been successful in reducing recidivism.[4] More importantly, we do not know how to rehabilitate, which is a conclusion that can be drawn from a comprehensive survey.[5] At any rate, there seems to be no way of establishing that it was because of participation in a rehabilitation program that someone has not recidivated: maybe he has just gotten better at eluding arrest, maybe he has just grown too old for a life of crime. The treatment people, and the whole ideology of rehabilitation, are under attack. As might be expected they are not giving up without a fight. At an international conference on comparative criminal sanctions held in February of 1976 in Berlin, some French delegates argued that "the rehabilitative philosophy has not been given a fair trial." This answer will hardly satisfy the critics.

Finally, a third factor behind the current dissatisfaction is disparity in sentencing. Edward Levi, former Attorney General of the United States, concedes that sentencing in this country "has the attributes of a lottery" and is "unequal without reason."[6] In particular, disparity exists in decisions to grant probation or to imprison. Disparity is perceived by offenders as reflecting a fundamental unfairness in the criminal justice system, especially by minority and disadvantaged groups, who seem to receive the short end of the stick.

Disparity in sentencing, it should be noticed, is not unconnected with the rehabilitative ideal, for this requires individualization of disposition. And this in turn implies wide discretion for the sentencer and for the penal agency that determines a prisoner's release date. But it is not only the individualized sentence advocated by rehabilitationists that is responsible for disparity. We have individualized judges too, as Federal Judge Marvin Frankel calls them. Judges are subject to the same biases and prejudices as the rest of us, and a judge need not be an adherent of the rehabilitationist ideology to mete out unequal sentences for equivalent offenses if he has the power of discretionary sentencing. (Federal bank robbery, for instance, can get you anything from 0 to 20 years.) Disparity can also be expected as long as penal agencies have no clear criteria to go by in determining release. It is hardly surprising that the indeterminate and the semideterminate sentence are opposed by liberals and conservatives alike, though on different grounds. For liberals this opposition marks an about-face. In 1970 Ramsey Clark looked forward with welcome to the day when all sentences would be indeterminate. Recently, the Prisoner's Union, an organization which claims to represent 20,000 convicts and ex-convicts, has called for an end to the practice, and many liberals today would agree.[7]

These, I believe, are the principal factors behind dissatisfaction with current sentencing practices and the impetus for reform. There may be other ways of dealing with crime increase, for one. Bigger locks might reduce burglaries and bullet-proof vests murders. Staying off the streets at night might reduce muggings. We could also directly try to reduce the causes of crime. However, as Professor James Q. Wilson has maintained, we know little for certain about the causes of crime and even less about how to eliminate them.[8] Reform of sentencing at least merits our consideration.

III

What would be a "good" sentencing structure? What would be a "good" sentencing decision? What light do the traditional theories of punishment shed on the problem? This is clearly a crucial question, for our thinking on the matter must be *guided*, if not entirely determined, by fundamental considerations in the philosophy of punishment. If it be granted, for the sake of argument and for purposes of this discussion, that the rehabilitative ideal must be given up, then deterrence and retribution remain as the sources from which our fundamental considerations must be drawn. (This would mean that though rehabilitation is a relevant answer to the question "How, or how much, should someone be punished?", it is not a good answer. Obviously, more evidence than was presented here is necessary in order to establish this assertion.) The deterrence theory, in fact, would seem to be the place to go, if the reduction of crime is our prime worry. And retributivism, with its concern for justice and equality, is a natural starting point, if the indeterminate sentence and disparity are troublesome to us.

It is not that these philosophies of punishment provide quick solutions. I think it should be conceded at the outset that they do not. For the problem of formulating a good sentencing structure is in reality quite complex. It will be useful to see how complex it is before we turn to a discussion of the theories. Consider the following example, which I have taken from a standard text on criminal justice.[9] It will enable us to raise some of the main questions involved in sentencing:

> In a single term five defendants appear before the court charged with kidnapping. No. 1 is a woman whose baby died, and who took another woman's baby from the hospital. No. 2 is a young man whose girl-friend said she was breaking up with him. He put her in a car and drove her around for 24 hours trying to persuade her to change her mind, while her frantic parents tried to locate them and the girl did everything she could to get away. No. 3 is a divorced man who took his own child from its mother

who had legal custody and refused to tell the mother where the child was. No. 4 is a kidnapper for ransom who kept a young woman buried in a box fitted with air tubes for breathing in order to make it impossible for searchers to find her, and who demanded $200,000 from her wealthy father. No. 5 is a woman accomplice of the kidnapper for ransom. She assisted in the kidnapping because she was in love with the kidnapper and was also threatened by him. She did everything she could to keep the kidnapped girl alive when it was possible for her to do so.

The offenses charged are identical: kidnapping. How should they be disposed of? Should there be a "flat-rate" sentence, each convicted offender getting the exact same sentence? And what should that sentence be? Should it involve incarceration? For how long? Should the sentencer have authority entirely to suspend sentence? To parole? To set conditions of parole? May each offender receive a different sentence? To what extent should exempting or mitigating factors be taken into account? What role should the assessment of future behavior play in setting the sentence? What role should past conduct or prior record play? How should the issue of disparity of sentence be handled? Should there be a mandatory maximum? A mandatory minimum? Who should set the sentence: the trial judge, a group of judges, the penal agency, "treatment" people? Moving away from this set of cases, should these questions receive the same or different answers for different types of crimes? These are only some of the questions that need to be asked, but I think they are the main ones. They show the complexity of the issue of sentencing, and I think it is obvious that neither the deterrence theory nor retribution supplies an immediate answer to them. Perhaps the most we can expect is some inspiration along the lines *suggested* by one of these theories, a general attitude or approach.

Before we turn to these theories it is worth noting that many factors, "legal" and "extra-legal," currently enter into a sentencing decision. The legal factors include the nature of the offense (which some research has shown to be the most important variable), the number of counts with which the defendant is charged, previous criminal record; and such factors as representation by counsel, whether guilt has been determined by verdict or plea, and the sentencing alternatives available to the judge. A person's "real sentence" is a function of fixed legislative penalties, his individual sentence, the operation of good-time statutes, and of suspended sentence and probation and parole laws. The extra-legal factors include race, age, sex, financial condition, the defendant's status in the community, and the prejudices and ideology of the presiding judge or penal agency.

The British criminologist Nigel Walker points out that the sentencing system operates under a number of assumptions.[10] Two of them are of special interest to us: first, that a sentence must take one of the forms prescribed by law, and second, that the penal measure should be chosen with the offender's particular circumstances in mind. In a way all the questions asked above can be reduced to two: (1) How should sentencing be controlled by law? And (2), To what extent should there be provision for "individualization" of sentence? It is not easy to see how control by law and individualization of sentence are going to be reconciled. *Nulla poena sine lege*, no punishment without a law. So runs the principle of legality, and a state that violates it is not in conformity with the rule of law. This principle obviously excludes such egregious violations of the rule of law as was expressed in a statement of the Nazi Minister of Justice who in 1936 informed the German courts that if any judge finds that the prescribed penalty is "inadequate" in a given case, he should so inform the Minister—who will then supply him with a new law that would permit an adequate punishment. The principle of legality is also taken to rule out the less horrendous practice of discretionary sentencing and indeterminate sentences, as well. But are these really that much less horrendous?

IV

Let us turn to the deterrence theory.[11] It will receive the major part of our attention. This theory offers a general justification of the institution of punishment. The aim of a system of penal law is to announce that there are certain actions or forebearances that the state (or society) does not want to occur and it threatens punishment for their commission. In other words, its aim is reduction of the incidence of unwanted events (called crimes), and its means are the threats of evil we call punishment. A standard ojection to this theory is that punishment does not deter crime, as evidenced by the high rate of recidivism and by the fact that the offender now standing before the judge for sentencing was obviously not deterred by the prospect. This objection can be rebutted, however. We need to distinguish, first, between the threat of punishment and its actual imposition, and second, between general deterrence and special deterrence. The fact is that many people are deterred from committing many offenses because of the threat of punishment. Introspection is enough to show this. Who hasn't been deterred from committing the offense of overtime parking because of the prospect of a fine? The fact that we have at sometime committed this offense shows nothing against the point. And the same for other offenses. Most of us cheat only a little on our income taxes because we are afraid of what will happen if we cheat too much. If not for the threat of punishment and for the occasional carrying out of the threat, the incidence of crime might well be much greater.

How much we are deterred from committing offenses because of the imposition of punishment on others (general deterrence) is a difficult question to answer. Some recent studies tend to show that punishment does deter crimes,[1][2] but it would seem difficult to tell how much is due to the threat and how much to its imposition. I am content to take these studies as having some general validity. I do think that the public is not very well informed on the sentences that are meted out, yet the general deterrence value of punishment is dependent on the publicity it gets. What the public hears about is a few horrendous crimes and a few sensational trials. Perhaps the state should take out newspaper advertisements giving the names of convicted offenders, the type of offense, and the sentence received.

Special deterrence—the effectiveness of the punishment in preventing the individual on whom it is imposed from committing other crimes—is another matter. Whether a Mr. Sweeney is going to commit further offenses depends on the punishment he gets. If he is executed, he is completely deterred. If he is incarcerated, he is prevented while he is "inside." The Mr. Sweeney I mentioned earlier committed a burglary soon after his release, but he didn't commit any burglaries while in jail, and had he been kept longer he would not have committed the particular burglary he did. Had he been kept longer he might also have been deterred from committing other offenses, or at least fewer of them, after he got out. The real problem for the deterrence theorist, general or special (though general deterrence is the main aim), is not that punishment does not deter but rather how and how much to punish: what kinds and what amounts are necessary to reduce the incidence of crime in the desired degree, whatever that is.

In resolving this issue all the questions raised earlier must be faced: should incarceration be employed as a penal measure?, for what offenses?, for how long?, and so on. Nigel Walker maintains that where incarceration is necessary it must be for six months at a minimum in order to achieve any significant reduction in crime. From the point of view of general deterrence *mandatory minima* are indispensable whatever form they take: imprisonment, fine, or parole under stipulated conditions. The possibility of complete suspension of sentence seems to be ruled out by deterrence considerations, even for first offenders. And perhaps it is more correct that it should be ruled out especially for first offenders, for otherwise everyone would get one "free" crime of the given sort. (This appears to be the case with many juvenile offenders, who know they will be back on the street immediately—and they know this for more than the first offense, unfortunately.)

Should there be lower minima for first offenders? It is difficult to say, though the answer probably depends on the kind of offense. As far as present knowledge is concerned, perhaps the only reason that can be given for such lower minima is a common-sensical one: before you try something heavy, try something light. In the case of offenders with a prior record the matter seems otherwise; a higher minimum seems in order, as it would serve both general and special deterrence purposes. The general principle for setting minima was formulated by Jeremy Bentham, the leading classical exponent of the deterrence theory: the "lot" of punishment should be enough to overcome the potential offender's temptation to commit the given kind of offense.[13] (But is there such a one as "the potential offender," or will individualization get into the system somehow?)

This general principle is in need of qualification. We can see this by considering whether there should be maximum sentences. How tough can we get in trying to reduce the incidence of crime? Would it be permissible to execute double parkers? All of us, I think, would reject the mere thought. Double parking is a trivial offense, and trivial offenses should not be punished with severe penalties. Why not? Most of us, I think, would say that it is a matter of *desert*. A trivial offense does not merit a severe punishment—it would be unjust. This, however, is not the line taken by exponents of the deterrence view. Professor H.L.A. Hart asserts that the principle "severe penalties should not be meted out for trivial offenses" is a reflection of the utilitarian notion that we ought not to do more harm than good in reducing crime.[14] A similar position is expressed by Nigel Walker, though he calls it humanitarianism rather than utilitarianism.

Again, most people would find this rationale unsatisfactory. They would relate the principle in question to the retributivist idea that punishment ought to reflect the moral gravity of an offense, that is, proportional desert. But this idea of proportionality between the seriousness of an offense and the amount of punishment is said by Hart to have no fundamental connection with retributivism. Rather, according to Hart, it reflects a principle of justice or fairness

Fairness requires that some relationship be maintained between punishment and offense: it would be unfair to punish someone who has committed a trivial offense with the same harshness as someone who committed a grave crime. Now I must confess that I find this explanation unconvincing. It seems to me that the difference between Hart's rationale and that of the retributivist is the difference between Tweedledum and Tweedledee. We cannot escape the notion of desert, as perplexing as that notion is: a person who has committed a trivial offense does not deserve to be punished as harshly as a person who committed a grave one.

We see, at any rate, that deterrence theorists hold that the attempt to reduce the incidence of crime should be subject to certain limitations, basically that in pursuing this goal we ought not cause more suffering or do more harm than good. In setting the amount of punishment to be annexed to a crime we need a second general principle in addition to the one I referred to a few paragraphs ago. This principle, also from Bentham, runs: the lot of punishment should be no more than is necessary to overcome the temptation to commit the given kind of offense. We may take this as setting a maximum. Some potential offenders will be deterred by the amount of punishment threatened in virtue of the first general principle and others by the lot threatened in virtue of the second. Now I am not sure that this is a satisfactory way of handling the question of maxima and minima, although it is plain that what is enough to deter one person isn't enough to deter another. From the point of view of general deterrence it seems to me that punishments should be "flat-rate"—the same punishment meted out to all who commit a given offense, with the amount being set at the top.

But I shall pass this issue by, for there is a more fundamental difficulty that confronts the general deterrence theorist who accepts the proposition that the goal of crime reduction should be subject to the limitation I mentioned, limited reductionism as Walker calls it.

This difficulty arises from the fact that the deterrence theorist is going to have to decide, *before* he deals with the question of amounts of punishment, how much a reduction in the incidence of crime we should seek to bring about. Should we attempt to reduce the incidence of double parking to near zero? This might require truly draconian punishments, perhaps execution or life imprisonment. Or consider a more plausible example, the offense of grievous assault. Suppose it would take very heavy sentences to bring down the incidence of grievous assault in some significant degree, and that these sentences would have to be imposed on a sizable number of offenders. Would this be acceptable to the limited reductionist? In pursuit of the goal of crime reduction, he is committed to not causing more suffering than he eliminates. But now, I think, he is caught in a bind. He cannot cause more aggregate suffering to *offenders* than the aggregate he reduces for potential *victims*. His limiting principle involves the absurdity that the suffering of assaulters should be given a consideration equal to that of their potential victims! Furthermore, he cannot tell how much crime to reduce without first determining how much to punish for it; but he cannot tell how much to punish for it without first determining how much crime to reduce!

If I am correct in all this the theory of general deterrence is invalid. If I am not correct, there are difficulties enough, though of a lesser order. The main difficulties concern the problem of individualization of sentence and mitigation and excuse. I can only say a few words about these. Take mitigation and excuse first. The question here is whether mitigation of sentence and exemption from punishment (because the accused has an excuse) should be provided for in a system of penal law that aims solely at general deterrence, since such a provision might reduce the deterrent value of the threat of punishment. The case can be argued both ways. In my view, mitigation and excuse are matters of the culpability of the offender, which should be taken into account in sentencing. Despite Professor Hart's brilliant articles on the subject I find it hard to detach the notion of culpability from the retributivist concept of desert. But it would take us too far afield to treat this complicated issue here. Individualization of sentence comes into the picture as soon as the legislature presents the judge (or appropriate penal agency) with minima and maxima. Individualization leads to disparity in sentencing. However, this need not pose a very great problem for the deterrence theorist if the minimum and maximum set for a given offense are not spread too far apart. Nigel Walker, for one, is not bothered very much by disparity, though he admits it bothers offenders a great deal. As it should, in my opinion, so long as unequal sentences are meted out for apparently equivalent offenses with no evident rhyme or reason.

Finally, a few words should be said about special deterrence. There has been a noticeable shift in interest toward special deterrence in recent years. This point of view is more concerned with recidivism than anything else, the prevention of the *reoccurrence* of a crime. Special deterrence, however, is found in a number of varieties. Lady Barbara Wooton's approach leans heavily in the direction of rehabilitation, individualization and indeterminate sentencing all of which she associates with the abolition of punishment.[15] Nigel

Walker is skeptical of psychotherapeutic methods but he remains a "correctionist," nevertheless. Both he and Lady Wooton would let responsibility (culpability) "whither away," though Walker perhaps less so than Wooton. If people commit offenses due to "accident proneness" or other predisposition, they obviously are in need of correction of some kind, these writers maintain.

Professor James Q. Wilson has a rather different, and more classical, special deterrence approach.[16] For certain offenses at least (e.g., "mugging"), Wilson would have us reduce the incidence of their reoccurrence by simply keeping malefactors in prison and off the streets. This approach requires either flat-time sentencing or mandatory minima, about which I want merely to comment that both have their problems. In the case of flat-time the problem is mainly one of principle: how shall we deal with mitigation and excuse, with extenuating circumstances? Without some flexibility in sentencing, it will be hard to achieve justice in sentencing. Or, on the other side, should we be willing to sacrifice a bit of justice in order to protect the public by seeing to it that offenders are kept off the streets for a fixed time? We seem, in fact, to be caught on the horns of a dilemma, for the introduction of flexibility means individualization in some degree; and individualization opens the door to disparity, which gives the appearance of injustice in sentencing, at least.

Mandatory minima face a practical difficulty given the way the criminal justice system currently operates. I am here referring to plea-bargaining. Almost any minimum can be bargained down to a lower minimum, which of course may be better than nothing. Setting a minimum leaves us with the problem of setting the maximum, too, and given a range of discretion for the sentence, punishments are still going to have to be individualized in some fashion. Again, we are back to square one: individualization of sentence is a major source of current dissatisfaction with the criminal justice system.

V

Can retributivism help us move on to square two? As with the case of the deterrence theory, retributivism can function only as a *guide*, a general attitude or approach, to the problems of sentencing. It, too, has no quick answers to the questions we raised in section III. I do not intend, here, to enter into a full-scale discussion of retributivism, especially since it exists in a number of varieties. In the remaining space I want to develop the thought that retributivism might have something significant to contribute on the problems of individualization and disparity in sentencing.[17]

The retributive theory is well-known for its emphasis on such concepts as justice, desert, culpability and guilt. Anyone who has read the great works of literature is familiar with retributivism. A constant theme of these works (for instance, the *Oedipus* cycle or *Crime and Punishment*) is that the sinner must atone for his sin through suffering. Similarly, on the socio-political level, the criminal has injured the social fabric, which is a fabric of duties and rights, and he must in turn suffer some deprivation of rights. It is through this that justice and rights are vindicated and affirmed as principles of social existence. (Vindication of rights should not be confused with vengefulness.) But in order for this deprivation of rights to be justly inflicted on the offender, he must be culpably guilty of his crime, for justice and rights as principles of social existence are defamed only by a culpable wrongdoer. This does not mean that the retributivist overlooks the deterrent functions of punishment, as is sometimes believed. It is quite consistent with retributivism to recognize that the institution of penal laws aims at deterring individuals by means of threats of punishment. The retributivist, however, is mainly interested in the conditions under which the *imposition* of punishment is just. I think it is also arguable that the retributivist may concede, without inconsistency, that for certain types of offense the retributive element is less predominant than in others. The main purpose of punishing for tax evasion, perhaps, is general deterrence, and if incarceration is called for, the sentence should be short but inexorable. But there must always be a retributive element in punishment; punishment should never be meted out unless the offender deserves it.

It appears that retributivism and the rehabilitation theory, though they seem poles apart, have a genuine affinity for each other. Both focus upon the *wrongdoer* as well as upon the *wrong* done. (Admittedly, some and perhaps all rehabilitationists refuse to use these terms.) There is, in fact, an interesting historical relationship between these theories. Individualization of punishment seems to have been introduced in the 19th century in France and Germany by penologists of a retributivist bent who believed that many penal sentences failed to take excusing and mitigating factors sufficiently into account. The wrongdoer may not always be such a wrongdoer, after all. Let the punishment fit the criminal as well as the crime. It is easy to see how, with the rise of a social-science oriented penology toward the end of the 19th century, this doctrine should get transformed into: Let the punishment fit the rehabilitative "needs" of the offender. Retributivism thus prepared the ground for the rehabilitationist principle of individualization of sentence.

It should be clear, however, that the retributivist's view on the wrongdoer is quite far from that of the rehabilitationist's. (As I parenthetically mentioned above, rehabilitationists are anxious not to think of the offender as a "wrongdoer." This attitude is most explicitly to be found in Karl Menninger's *The Crime of Punishment.*) The distinctive outlook of retributivism may be seen by considering one of the main problems this theory has to confront.

How should society deal with dangerous individuals who have not committed any offense (not yet, anyway)? For the protection of society, a protection that the citizenry is entitled to, dangerous individuals may have to be deprived of their rights and be held in custody. The same applies to the individual who has committed an offense but who, because of his mental condition, isn't culpable. In neither case is the deprivation of rights deserved. There is no problem here at all for the rehabilitation theory, but there plainly is one for retributivism. How can the retributivist handle it? What he must do, it seems to me, is to prescind from regarding such deprivations as being any kind of punishment. The wrong that might be done, or the wrong that was done, *is* a wrong—but the individuals in question are not wrongdoers and there is no denunciation of them expressed by our putting them into confinement. The trouble with this line of reply, however, is that it looks perilously close to the double-think of the rehabilitationist who believes that punishment is abolished because it has been re-named "treatment."

In any event, I think we can begin to see why retributivism must make some allowance for individualization of sentence, for a sentence condemns not only the wrong done, the offending act, but also the wrongdoer, the offender. Just this year the Judicial Council of the Second Circuit approved new sentencing procedures which include a rule requiring judges to give the reasons for each sentence. This stipulation has clear retributivist overtones: a sentence should be imposed in such a way that the criminal is enabled to appreciate the wrongfulness of his conduct and the justness of his punishment. (Pronouncement of sentence and, on this view, explanation of the sentence to the offender are parts of the ritual of condemnation.)[18] Since not every offender is the same, individualization is not only appropriate but also indispensible in order for this to be possible. The penal law, therefore, should provide for mitigation and excuse, and ideally it should give the judge flexibility so that the sentence can be geared to the wickedness of the offender. Given such a retributivist framework, *disparity* of sentences, unequal sentences of seemingly equivalent offenses, need not have the appearance of systemic injustice.

While this approach has the advantage of relieving a bit of the sting of disparity, some potential difficulties should nevertheless be noted. The flexibility given to the judge may easily degenerate into the very arbitrariness from which retributivism is supposed to supply an escape. One of the problems with individualization of sentence, as mentioned earlier, is how to control it by law. Requiring the judge to give the rationale of the sentence—perhaps along the lines of Judge Marvin Frankel's suggestion in his *Criminal Sentences* that the judge should state the basis for each aspect of the sentence, and how it all adds up to the given amount of time or fine—may be just the way that this control can be exercized.[19] In any case, one would not want the judge to have too much flexibility, and the kind of flexibility being proposed, here, is very far from the indeterminate or semideterminate sentence favored by rehabilitationists, which is bound to seem arbitrary in its operation. Still, whether or not this more restricted kind of individualization will seem unarbitrary to the offender is going to depend on his attitude and intelligence: he may be too recalcitrant or too stupid to appreciate the reasons for his sentence and, therefore, its justness.

A good deal also will depend on the attitude of the sentencing judge. An aberrant retributivist judge might fail to make the fine discriminations among offenders that this approach presupposes. Mr. Justice Stephen may be a case in point, as described by his brother and biographer, Leslie Stephen, in the *Life of James Fitzjames Stephen:* "His mode of passing sentence showed that his hatred of brutality included the hatred of brutes. He did not affect to be reluctant to do his duty. He did not explain that he was acting for the moral good of the prisoner or apologize for being himself an erring mortal. He showed rather the stern satisfaction of a man suppressing a noxious human reptile." So much for the awesome and agonizing task of pronouncing sentence! Stephen's attitude contrasts with that of Immanuel Kant, the paragon of retributivism, who asserts that punishment should never be administered in the spirit of hatred.[20]

Perhaps the major difficulty, however, concerns these fine discriminations that the judge must make in order to gear the sentence to the wickedness of the offender. It is often remarked, in criticism of the retributive theory, that an assessement of wickedness is precisely what cannot be given. This seems correct, but it can be pressed too far. We do distinguish between degrees of culpability and we do grade them. Yet it must be conceded that these gradiations are very rough and, in the end, very few. But this disadvantage might be turned into a benefit, to an extent, if it puts a further limitation on the flexibility given to the judge. Related to this issue, of course, are the sentencing alternatives available to the judge—our battery of questions in section III.

How should the question of sentencing alternatives be handled by retributivists? This is clearly an important matter, for retributivism has a double focus: the wrong done as well as the wrongdoer. The sentencing alternatives that allow the culpability of the offender to be taken into account must also allow the gravity of the offense to be taken into account. It is well known that retributivists traditionally have held that the punishment should *equal* the offense. There are difficulties enough with this view, as was pointed out by Hegel, who was himself a retributivist, and there are even earlier allusions to the problem in retributivist writings.[2 1] The best that a retributivist can say, and perhaps all he can say, is that the punishment should be proportionally appropriate to the offense. A full discussion of this subject, which is in fact complicated by the double focus, would require a separate study.

But I shall permit myself a final remark. Obeisance towards the idea of the gravity of the offense is often made by exponents of rehabilitation. The American Bar Association Sentencing Standards issued in 1967 asserted as its general principle that an offender should receive the minimum sentence of custody or confinement consistent with the protection of the public, the gravity of the offense, and his rehabilitative needs. Reference to the gravity of the offense, however, is a retributivistic note that gets lost in the subsequent exposition of the standards, and rehabilitation emerges as the key idea. As matters currently stand, the ideology of rehabilitation has been exploded. But if it can be put on a solid basis again, we should clearly want to consider its ramifications for the problems of sentencing. Nor can deterrence be ignored either. For a criminal sentence has a social meaning that includes the deterrence of crime. Nor should retribution be ignored either, if the arguments presented here have any validity. But whether it is possible to fashion out of these three approaches a sentencing structure that will reflect anything more than a crazy-quilt of inconsistent considerations is very doubtful. Perhaps this shows how difficult a problem criminal sentencing really is.

NOTES TO CHAPTER FIVE

1. See "Prolegomenon to the Principles of Punishment," in H.L.A. Hart, *Punishment and Responsibility* (Oxford: Clarendon Press, 1968).

2. "Persons and Punishment," *The Monist*, vol. 52 (1968), 475-501.

3. See his *Criminal Sentences* (New York: Hill and Wang, 1973).

4. See the report of the American Friends Service Committee, *Struggle for Justice* (New York: Hil' and Wang, 1971).

5. See Robert Martinson, "What Works—Questions and Answers about Prison Reform," *The Public Interest* (Spring, 1974), 22-54.

6. Reported in *The New York Post*, May 5, 1976, p. 13, col. 1.

7. See the article by Alan Dershowitz, "Let the Punishment Fit the Crime," *New York Times Magazine*, Dec. 28, 1975, beginning on p. 7; and also Andrew von Hirsch, *Doing Justice* (New York: Hill and Wang, 1975).

8. *Thinking about Crime* (New York: Basic Books, 1975).

9. Hazel B. Kerper, *Introduction to the Criminal Justice System* (St. Paul, Minn.: West Publ. Co., 1972), p. 334.

10. *Sentencing in a Rational Society* (1971), pp. 113ff.

11. For a more complete discussion, see my *Philosophy of Law* (Englewood Cliffs, N.J.: Prentice-Hall, 1975), Chapter 4.

12. See Gordon Tullock, "Does Punishment Deter Crime?," *The Public Interest* (Summer, 1974), 103-111.

13. See Bentham's *An Introduction to the Principles of Morals and Legislation* (first published in 1789), Chapters 13-15.

14. *Op. cit.*, *supra*, no. 1, p. 173.

15. *Crime and the Criminal Law* (London: Stevens and Sons, 1963).

16. *Op. cit.*, *supra*, no. 8.

17. For a discussion of other aspects of retributivism, see my *Philosophy of Law*, Chapter 5.

18. See Joel Feinberg, *Doing and Deserving* (Princeton: Princeton Univ. Press, 1970), Chapter 5 ("The Expressive Function of Punishment").

19. But cf. the critique of Frankel in von Hirsch, *op. cit.*, *supra*, no. 7.

20. *The Doctrine of Virtue: Part II of the Metaphysics of Morals*, trans. M.J. Gregor (New York: Harper Torchbooks), p. 130.

21. *Philosophy of Right*, trans. T.M. Knox (Oxford University Press paperback, 1967), sec. 101.

Chapter Six

The Political Feasibility
of Punishment

James Q. Wilson

There has occurred within the last few years—indeed, to a substantial degree, within the last year—a revival of the concept of punishment (or, as it is sometimes called, just deserts) as the principle that ought to guide the sentencing of convicted offenders. This revival can be found in three books published within a year or so of each other: *Punishing Criminals*, by Ernest van den Haag[1] (popularly regarded as a "conservative"), *Doing Justice* by Andrew von Hirsch and the Committee for the Study of Incarceration[2] (most of whose members are generally regarded as "liberals"), and *The Future of Imprisonment* by Norval Morris[3] (generally, and rightly, regarded as a distinguished legal scholar).

The views of these authors are by no means identical (some of the differences will be explored in a moment) but they are striking in the extent to which they rely frankly on the concept of punishment as a major—in some cases as the only—rationale for imposing sanctions on offenders. Each rejects the contrary principle—rehabilitation—and each adduces a similar set of arguments and facts to support that rejection. Indeed, it is in large part because of substantial evidence as to the inefficiency and unfairness of the rehabilitative mode that punishment, or just deserts, has gained in favor.

This apparent agreement on a principle for sentencing ought to clear away the ideological differences that in the past have kept liberals and conservatives from joining in support of any important changes in the criminal justice system. "Liberals" will be defined for the purpose of this study as those whose interest in criminal justice has been chiefly directed at enlarging the range of procedural and substantive protections afforded those suspected of, charged with, and penalized for a crime. "Conservatives" I define as those who have chiefly sought to enhance the powers of order-maintenance and penalty-imposing institutions in order to protect society.

These two views, the suspect-centered and the victim-centered, have been the source of very different criticisms of the law and the criminal justice system. The *suspect-centered* view (which I label, a bit simplistically, the liberal view) has made the following arguments:[4]

1. Much "crime" is a self-fulfilling prophecy owing to the tendency of police, prosecutors, and judges selectively to impose sanctions on those who have already been caught up in the system. That is, a person once suspected of or charged with an offense is "labeled" as a "criminal" which leads to changes in the behavior of both the suspect and the system. The suspect, owing to the stigma of this label, loses access to legitimate opportunities (for jobs, friends, and respect) and thus is forced to accept illegitimate jobs and depend on the respect of other offenders. The system at the same time will place the person it has labeled as criminal under special or undue surveillance, arrest him more frequently than his behavior would warrant, and charge him on evidence less compelling than would be required to proceed against an ordinary citizen.

2. Persons concerned about crime are unreasonably preoccupied with offenses committed by lower-status persons and neglectful of "white collar crime" committed by upper-status persons, the dollar amount of which may be far larger than the dollar value of so-called street crime.

3. Accused persons are highly vulnerable to unfair treatment by police, prosecutors, judges, and wardens both in general (i.e., their essential rights will be violated in the name of crime control) and in relation to specific categories of offenders (i.e., blacks and other minorities will be treated more harshly than whites who have committed like offenses).

4. There are large and indefensible disparities in the sentencing of offenders that are caused by the personal predilection of judges and facilitated by the great discretionary authority given judges by penal codes. Even apart from whatever systematic biases result from racially selective sentencing, there are substantial random variations that are inconsistent with justice defined as fairness.

5. Parole boards, in the exercise of their authority to determine the time and conditions of release from prison, and judges and sentencing boards, in the exercise of their right to determine initially

the length of the sentence, rely in many cases on predictions that are invalid and biased toward falsely predicting recidivism. The result is that persons are often given long sentences, or denied release on parole, who if set free would not commit additional crimes.

6. The indeterminate sentence permits judges and sentencing authorities to set penalties too high. The maximum penalty allowed for most offenses is too severe and, though many judges and sentencing authorities actually give penalties well below the maximum, too many award excessively long prison terms. These severe sentences are purely vindictive, as little additional deterrent effect is achieved by the additional years of incarceration.

7. The rehabilitative ideal as actually carried out is corrupted by the correctional system. Rehabilitation personnel—psychiatrists, counsellors, teachers, parole and probation officers—use the goal of rehabilitation as a way of increasing their power over offenders. Prison guards manipulate access to rehabilitative programs as privileges which can be given or withheld in order to reward or punish various offenders and thus serve both the personal goals of the guards and enhance their collective interest in maintaining security.

8. Prisons and jails are inhumane institutions that degrade and brutalize their inmates and that, by operating as "schools of crime," increase rather than decrease the chances that a released inmate will commit more crimes.

The *victim-centered* or conservative view of crime, by contrast, makes the following arguments:

1. The stigma that attaches to crime does not increase the number of offenders by the labeling process; rather, it decreases the number of offenders because the fear of stigma is an important deterrent for would-be offenders. Reducing the stigmatizing effect of involvement in the criminal justice system would facilitate the entry of new offenders who no longer would fear disgrace or the loss of legitimate opportunities.

2. Though white collar crime is a problem, its relative importance cannot be measured by dollar losses. Street crime inspires fear, the psychic costs of which are far graver than the monetary ones. Furthermore, street crime victimizes specific individuals, often the poorest ones, while much white collar crime victimizes other large organizations (as in industrial price-fixing or bank fraud) or spreads the losses over such large numbers of individuals so that each person's cost is trivial (as in price-fixing or antitrust violations). Finally, street crime more commonly than white collar crime violates deeply held moral convictions the vindication of which is essential to the maintenance of a strong sense of community.

3. There is little empirical evidence that racial or other minorities are systematically discriminated against in law enforcement. As far as the rights of the accused generally are concerned, these are now weighted unfairly in their favor, making the probability of arrest, punishment, and conviction unduly low. The rights of victims, and of society generally, have been neglected in the vain search for what Judge Macklin Fleming calls "perfect justice."

4. There are, indeed, wide disparities in the sentencing practices of judges, the net effect of which has been leniency as well as unfairness. A large proportion of convicted offenders are given little or no punishment, thus obviating both the deterrent and incapacitative effects of prison.

5. Judges, sentencing boards, and parole boards have relied on predictions about likely future criminality which are invalid and which are biased toward falsely predicting *non*recidivism. As a result, persons are often given excessively short sentences, or premature parole, enabling them to commit crimes that could have been prevented.

6. The indeterminate sentence contributes to judicial leniency by providing little or no legislative guidance as to the appropriate penalty for various offenses. Judges and others take advantage of indeterminancy to set penalties too low, failing thereby to deter crime, incapacitate offenders, or vindicate communal moral sentiments.

7. Rehabilitation has failed. We do not have, and in a free society cannot have, any proven techniques that will systematically reduce the probability of recidivism for large numbers of offenders for long periods of time. Funds spent on rehabilitative programs are wasted; sentencing policies based on a belief in such programs are mistaken.

8. Prisons and jails are not intended to be pleasant places. They are primarily institutions for punishment and, though conditions in them could no doubt be improved, the level of amenity there must always be less than its level in society at large else people outside will envy those inside and perhaps even try to break into prison.

The convergence which has developed of late between liberals and conservatives around the concept of "just deserts" has profound implications for some of these issues—primarily for those bearing on sentencing policy. In addition, as I will argue, agreement on a standard of justice that ought to govern sentences has important, and I believe necessary, implications for the nature and quality of penal institutions. Despite this convergence, we are as a nation still some distance from taking action on the basis of this agreement. There are, I believe, two reasons for this apparent inability to convert intellectual agreement into public policy: First, the issues on which liberals and conservatives continue to disagree lead each to suspect the motives and wisdoms of the other and thus to avoid entering into any explicit coalition. Second, the political process, and the governmental institutions concerned with crime that are part of that process, operates to impede or frustrate the conversion of even an agreed-upon philosophy into practice.

Though the convergence of views on punishment among scholars and politically-active spokesmen is of quite recent origin, the philosophical analyses that would support such a consensus have long been understood and frequently been debated in the more technical journals. J.D. Mabbott's seminal essay, "Punishment," was published in 1939. In it, he brings to an elegant completion the demolition of utilitarian theories of criminal justice begun by James Fitzjames Stephens in the nineteenth century. Mabbott's central argument is that it is manifestly unjust to deprive a person of his liberty as a consequence of committing a criminal act for any reason other than the fact that he committed the crime—in short, that he "deserved" the punishment. Other considerations (criminal deterrence, social reform, prisoner rehabilitation) that are justified because of their presumed social advantage—that is, because of their utility—can be shown to lead, if strictly applied, to absurd conclusions. For example, both deterrence and reform would both on occasion "justify the punishment of an innocent man, the deterrent theory if he were believed to have been guilty by those likely to commit crimes in the future, and the reformatory theory if he were a bad man though not a criminal."[5]

Though such philosophical considerations have of late been rediscovered, it was not from reading back issues of *Mind* that the renewed respectability (one is tempted to say, the rehabilitation) of the concept of punishment derives. It comes rather from various empirical inquiries, the results of which have been so consistent and the implications of which so clear that they could no longer be neglected (though they were neglected for the better part of half a century). One line of inquiry has established beyond much doubt our inability to reduce the recidivism rate by planned efforts at criminal rehabilitation. Robert Martinson has supplied the best-known statement of this conclusion, but the essential facts have been familiar to specialists for the better part of a decade.[6] The last gasp of the rehabilitative ideal was probably to be found in the report of the President's Commission on Law Enforcement and Administration of Justice which pointed in 1967 with unquenchable optimism to the one example it could then find of a rehabilitative program that seemed to work—the California Treatment Program.[7] Within a year or two, the conclusions of that experiment were found to have been erroneously stated and now we have in Paul Lerman's account a book-length analysis of the failure of CTP to achieve either its rehabilitative or cost-reduction objectives.[8]

At the same time, others were writing about the extent to which the therapeutic efforts led, out of the best of intentions, to an increase in the extent to which offenders were placed under control in ways that to them were indistinguishable from punishment and to manifest inequities in the treatment of persons who had committed similar offenses. Jessica Mitford's *Kind and Usual Punishment*[9] was not only a conventional attack on the unpleasant conditions of prisons, but more significantly a radical critique of efforts to improve prisons by making them more therapeutic. Indeed, the five years preceding the appearance of the Mitford book were a watershed: in 1968, Karl Menninger had written, in *The Crime of Punishment*,[10] that crime is an illness that can be cured in a majority of cases; by 1973, Mitford denied that criminals were ill and scathingly indicted psychiatrists specifically and the reformist tradition in general for even trying to cure them. Both books were sympathetically received by liberals.

Neither Menninger nor Mitford had written a profound book. And each could have been dismissed by serious persons on the grounds that they were merely polemical critiques of criminal justice, albeit ones that revealed how far the content of a liberal position had changed. Not so easily dismissed, however, were the views of Marvin Frankel, federal judge for the southern district of New York. His book, *Criminal Sentences*,[11] published almost concurrently with the Mitford volume, was a devastating attack on disparities in sentences and the almost unconstrained and often badly-used discretion conferred by law on criminal court judges. A distinguished jurist criticized his colleagues in the strongest possible terms, not because they were lenient or because they were severe, but because they were incompetent, as would be any person, to administer justice when the legislature provided no guidance for the disposition of offenders other than such empty phrases as "imprisonment for any term of years" (the actual federal statute governing rape and kidnapping). Judge Frankel subsequently chaired an experimental test of the sentencing policies of his colleagues on the federal bench that confirmed his worst fears.

The changes in elite views on criminal justice, particularly among liberals, were contemporaneous with and no doubt linked to a generalized liberal disenchantment with the efficacy of planned social change. The recognition that we were not "curing" criminals was part and parcel of the awareness that we were not "curing" alcoholism, drug addiction, broken homes, or low school achievement scores either. But there was an added dimension to our failures in criminal justice that converted what otherwise would have been merely despair into active rage: our efforts to "cure" delinquents and criminals were creating profound injustices.

But liberals were not the only ones to change. Conservatives who might once have believed that putting more police on the street would reduce crime were having to cope with a mounting body of evidence that the numbers of police available, within any feasible range, seemed to have little effect on crime rates. The police, who had benefitted substantially from the financial largesse of a nation that, in the 1960s, looked to them to reduce crime, were belatedly discovered to be an organization that had not yet learned how to convert increased resources into less crime.[1][2]

Out of this range of discoveries, reflections, and reconsiderations arose a new interest in justice. If the discretion of judges was more narrowly bounded, if the penalties for various offenses were more certainly known, if the power of parole boards was more sharply curtailed, if the rehabilitative ideal was abandoned, *then:*

1. disparities in sentences could be reduced so that liberals need not fear excessive severity and conservatives need not fear excessive leniency;
2. penalties need not be based on predictions about future criminality, presumably pleasing liberals who fear "false positives" and conservatives who fear "false negatives";
3. resources need not be diverted to rehabilitative programs that are (to liberals) manipulative and (to conservatives) inefficacious;
4. sentences could become more certain so that liberals need not fear inequity and discrimination and conservatives could hope for greater deterrence and incapacitation.

This convergence depends crucially, of course, on whether liberals and conservatives can agree on an appropriate range of penalties which judges shall issue. Obviously, making just deserts the principle on which sentences are based leaves unanswered the question of the allocation of penalties among various offenses. What is the minimum penalty to be? The maximum? The relative costliness of rape, robbery, and auto theft?

There is no principle from which the answers to these questions can be deduced. A political body, such as a legislature, must make a political and moral judgment. But being political, legislators and those seeking to influence them are likely to note an obvious basis for coalition-building: perhaps agreement could be reached if liberals were willing to increase the probability of a significant penalty being imposed on less serious but still commonplace offenders, and if conservatives were willing to place relatively low ceilings on the maximum penalty that such offenders might face. In short, raise the minima and lower the maxima.

And there are utilitarian reasons for suspecting that such a tradeoff would have desirable social effects. If the studies purporting to show that the lower crime rates are associated with a higher probability of imprisonment are correct, then having some minimum penalty might exercise a deterrent effect on would-be offenders.[13] Furthermore, if it is the certainty rather than the severity of the penalty that principally explains its deterrent effect, then one would assume that lengthening the sentence beyond a certain point would be subject to the law of decreasing marginal productivity such that additional years added to the sentence would have only slight incremental value in deterring crime. Even the effect on crime from incapacitating offenders so that they can victimize persons outside prison should also be subject to diminishing returns.[14] We know that the average criminal career is relatively short—depending on when it begins, perhaps no more than five or ten years. Some professional criminals and some pathologically assaultive personalities will, to be sure, continue to commit crimes for as long as they are able to hold a jimmy or wield a knife, but they are a minority of all offenders. Thus, ignoring whatever deterrent effect a long sentence might have, its incapacitative effect will be no greater than the length of the average criminal career.

A policy of raising the minima and lowering the maxima would not satisfy those for whom certain offenses are so heinous that a very severe sentence is required by their sense of justice, whatever its deterrent or incapacitative effects. Clearly, Charles Manson could not with justice have been given only a five year sentence. Nor would it satisfy law enforcement officers for whom the ability to threaten a very severe sentence creates important bargaining power in attempting to persuade a charged offender to implicate other persons in a criminal conspiracy in exchange for more lenient treatment. But the proportion of all offenders who would meet these criteria is small, and thus for most offenses the policy of increased minima and decreased maxima is possible.

But only possible. There remain several intellectual and political difficulties in the path of agreeing on a just deserts concept of punishment. One is to be found in the amount of discretion judges are to have in imposing the minimum penalty. Liberals resist making a minimum penalty mandatory, as proposed by both President Gerald Ford and Senator Edward M. Kennedy (in itself a striking example of liberal-conservative convergence!) for several reasons. One is that their commitment to the justice model is incomplete: they wish to see benevolence served as well as justice by allowing judges to impose less than the minimum penalty, or no penalty at all, in "deserving" cases. But of course it was precisely a concern for benevolence—a desire to treat each person on the basis of what is best for him—that led in the first place to the expansion of judicial discretion, the promotion of the indeterminate sentence, and the development of the rehabilitative model. It is conceivable that a repetition of these past abuses could be prevented by specifying precise guidelines for the exercise of benevolence. Judge Frankel has proposed, for example, a "Sentencing Commission" that would formulate and enforce, subject to legislative review, rules governing sentencing.[15] (The judge is acutely aware that no voluntary arrangements have so far worked.) Whether such a specification is possible is unclear. If any consideration is taken into account other than the nature and circumstances of the offense, and perhaps the prior record of the offender (and even that can be a treacherous exception), it is hard to decide what should *not* be taken into account. And distressingly, the things that might be taken into account that are most determinative of criminality—the age, sex and race of the offender—are precisely those factors that society, for perfectly commendable reasons, often wishes not to take into account.

Another reason for liberal resistance to mandatory minima derives from their suspicions about how discretion is exercised in the criminal justice system. In this view, a decline in judicial discretion will lead to a rise in prosecutorial or police discretion. If judges no longer choose the penalty and thus manage the arena in which bargains are made, the police will choose who to arrest and the prosecutors who to charge and these bargains will be less visible, less subject to correction or appeal, and thus more pernicious. To accept this view, one must believe in the "zero-sum" theory of discretion: what judges lose, the police gain, and vice versa. At the extremes, there is without much doubt truth to this theory. If the penalty for drunken driving is a mandatory one-year revocation of a driver's license, the police will arrest fewer people for drunken driving. If the penalty for carrying an unlicensed gun is one year in jail (as it is in Massachusetts), prosecutors will not charge people arrested for having broken that law. If the penalty for murder is death (as it was, without exception, in England before 1965), the executive authority will discover that a large fraction of those condemned to death were "mentally ill" when they murdered and hence their sentence should be commuted. I would argue, however, that short of the extremes—that is to say, when the mandatory penalty seems correctly proportioned to the magnitude of the offense—a reduction in judicial discretion will not lead to a rise in discretion elsewhere in the system.

The history thus far of the New York State drug laws, requiring severe penalties for certain classes of heroin traffickers, seems to refute the view that with the reduction in judicial discretion there will be a corresponding increase in discretionary choices elsewhere. The police continue to make arrests and the prosecutors to prefer charges at about the same rate as before the law. Trials are more common than before and of course more costly than guilty pleas, but not unbearably so. The willingness to see more stringent penalties imposed, rather than to reassert the previous equilibrium, apparently stems from the view of all concerned that the penalties are just.

Despite these concerns, there has been a noticeable movement in liberal opinion in the direction of more certain sentences. The report of the Committee for the Study of Incarceration gingerly suggests that the "presumptive sentence" for "lower-range serious offenses" (such as theft involving the threat but not the use of force) should be something less than eighteen months unless the person is a repeater, that for "upper-range serious offenses" (such as unprovoked or deliberate violence) it should be something between eighteen months and three years, and that no sentence should be longer than five years except for certain heinous murders. The exact presumptive sentence would be set by a special rule-making body under the aegis of the courts.[16] Limited and strictly defined exceptions from these presumptive sentences would be allowed. Indeterminacy in sentencing would be eliminated.

Even these modest proposals by no means commanded the unanimous or enthusiastic support of the committee: there were four opinions of dissent or exception appended to the report. The reasons for some of these dissents, and for the general political difficulty in obtaining agreement on the principle of just deserts as a basis for punishment, can be found in those issues which continue to divide liberals and conservatives and on which there has been little convergence.

One of these is the problem of free will and the extent to which crime is "caused" by social forces. Herman Schwartz, a member of the Committee for the Study of Incarceration and later proposed for appointment as the chief correctional officer for the state of New

York, wrote that the deserts principle should not serve as a basis for punishment because it is not possible to say a person "deserves" punishment if he was hooked on heroin, confronted with racism or poverty, grew up in a broken home, went to substandard schools, and had no honest way to make a living.[17] Obviously, one's compassion and concern can and should be aroused for those whose personality has been shaped by destructive social conditions. But it is difficult to see how this principle could be made the basis for a criminal justice system. The chief *victims* of predatory crime are also persons who disproportionately have suffered from racism and poverty, have attended substandard schools, and have found decent jobs scarce. To excuse the predators, because of their exposure to adverse social conditions, is to condemn the victims even though they overcame these same conditions, a policy that is both unjust (differences in rewards do not correspond to differences in behavior) and socially disadvantageous (the incentive to overcome adversity is replaced by an incentive to yield to it). Mr. Schwartz does not carry his concern about free will to its logical conclusion, but let me suggest what it is: How can we say a president of the United States should be punished for violating the Constitution and federal statutes when he had been raised in a family on welfare, victimized by a failure at college athletics, defeated in several elections, hounded by a hostile press, surrounded by wicked companions, and scandalized by the prospect of youthful revolutionaries and black militants carrying out campus disruptions and street fighting?

The causes of crime, like the causes of political corruption or official malfeasance, should be addressed to the extent we are able, but one cannot base a system of justice on the prospects for the success of such social changes. For one thing, eliminating poverty and racism is difficult, time-consuming, and uncertain. For another, it may turn out that in the short run, reductions in poverty will be accompanied by increases in crime, as seemed to be the case in the 1960s. But surely it would be as foolish to say that we should ignore poverty because its reduction increases crime as to say that we should ignore crime because it is produced by poverty.

A second issue is that of stigma and labeling. The concept, which has been part of criminology at least since 1938, is too large a matter fully to be dealt with here. Certain versions of labeling theory, indeed, have few policy implications at all; they merely assert the commonplace that the perceptions and reactions of others are important factors in our own definition of self. But other versions, and I think the mood of labeling theorists generally, support some dubious policy implications insofar as we are concerned with predatory crime. Put oversimply, labeling theory suggests that crime is the result of what society does, not of what criminals do. Society "labels" certain acts as criminal and thus certain persons as criminals, and does so, it is implied, in an arbitrary manner. Persons arrested for breaking a law ("primary deviance") are treated in such a way ("labeled" or "stigmatized") as to make it likely that he will commit additional acts of which society will disapprove ("secondary deviance").[18]

There may be some virtue in thinking this way in order to understand how, for example, certain children come to be regarded as first stubborn, then truant, then delinquent, and finally criminal. The labeling perspective may also focus our attention on ways in which our criminal laws undesirably depart from generally shared notions of morality—with respect, for example, to certain consensual crimes such as sexual deviation or drug use. But it is difficult to take labeling theory seriously as a basis for making policy judgments about predatory crime, to say nothing of white collar crime. It requires a heroic commitment to moral relativism to maintain that armed robbery, or premeditated murder, or professional thievery are criminal—which is to say, wrong—merely because society chooses to label them as such. The absurdity of the view is clear if one tries to imagine a society that ignored murder, robbery, or thieving. Punishing certain kinds of lawbreakers is essential to the existence of society; it is a matter, not of convention, but of nature.

Nor is there compelling evidence that much crime is the result of persons being labeled criminals. Indeed, much of the evidence is consistent with the contrary. Wolfgang and colleagues studied ten thousand boys growing up in Philadelphia before 1963. Though well over a third committed one act that led to an arrest or similar intervention, about half of these boys committed no further criminal acts and only a tiny handful became persistent offenders. Whether the majority were deterred by the stigma of the initial contact with the police we cannot say; what we can say is that they were not recruited into crime by that contact.[19] We can make an even stronger statement: even those persons sent to jails and prisons (a small fraction of those arrested) are not more likely to commit more offenses (or to be "re-labeled" as a criminal) than persons who have committed the same initial act with the same background characteristics but who are placed on probation. Prisons on the whole neither reform nor deform.[20]

Despite the weak theoretical and nonexistent empirical basis for labeling theory, its grasp on the popular mind is tenacious. It leads some to argue against arrest, prosecution, or punishment, on the mistaken grounds that this will increase crime. It leads others to argue against punishment by changing the subject: a proposal to treat armed robbers severely is met by the demand that we decriminalize marijuana.

Finally, there is the issue of white collar crime. This is a puzzle to me, for I see no reason why it should be an issue at all. If a person steals, defrauds, or otherwise victimizes an innocent party in some nontrivial way, he should be punished whatever the color of his collar. Furthermore, the demand that white collar crime be taken seriously cannot consistently be urged by those who also believe in the labeling theory—surely we do not regard bank fraud, financial swindles, and official corruption of the electoral process to be undesirable "merely" because society has chosen to "label" them as such; surely we do not draw back from punishing embezzlers or Watergate burglars because we fear that the resulting "stigma" will confirm them in a real life of fraud and deceit.

I suspect what actually troubles persons concerned with white collar crime is the belief that it is treated by police and judges far more leniently than ordinary street crime. Indeed, the very punishment of an executive-suite conspiracy, far from assuaging this fear, inflames it by leading the onlooker to suppose that the detection of one such crime is good evidence of the existence of countless others being covered up. Unfortunately, the matter resists analysis because so much of what we call "white collar crime"—price-fixing, official corruption, large-scale financial swindles—produces no outraged victim and hence no report that the crime took place. Much of white-collar crime is consensual in ways little different from prostitution. As a result, it is harder to find out how much "white collar," as opposed to street, crime occurs, and therefore impossible to find out whether it is treated more or less leniently. My general impression is that, whether or not it is treated as severely as it should be, official corruption is more vigorously investigated and more sharply punished in this country than in Europe or Japan. Lockheed, after all, did not bribe the Pentagon or the White House—it bribed leading officials *abroad*, perhaps because abroad it was not only encouraged to do so, it was assured that there it could get away with it.

These intellectual issues—the ambivalent attitude toward discretion, the problem of causality, the belief in labeling and the concern for white collar crime—impede the formation of an explicit coalition to make just deserts the central rationale for punishment. I have suggested that two of these issues are spurious, one is important but irrelevant, and the fourth, the uses of discretion, can only be answered by experience and testing. But beyond these matters lie the frankly political and organizational, as opposed to theoretical, barriers to change.

Chief among these is the determination on the part of those now having discretion—which is to say, power—not to surrender it. Judges, like college professors, have wide authority and certain tenure. They are understandably reluctant to give up either. But the concept of just deserts requires that they give up a great deal of discretion; the security of their position makes the prospect of achieving this by persuasion or organizational leadership slim. It will require changes in the law, in the form of either more narrowly prescribed sentencing statutes or the creation of a new institution, such as a sentencing board, with powers that can override judicial preference. As one surveys the contemporary discussion of punishment, one is struck by the extent to which scholars, public officials, the police, and correctional officers are moving into closer agreement and by the absence from the consensus of large segments of the bar and bench. Attorneys like discretion because it can be manipulated to the advantage of their clients or their careers; judges like it because they genuinely believe, in the face of evidence to the contrary, that they are sufficiently wise and well-informed to use that discretion reasonably.

A second political obstacle involves matters of cost and allocation. A major consequence of the philosophy of just deserts is that many new, smaller, and better correctional facilities of varying kinds will have to be built. This may sound harsh; it is not. It is the necessary implication of the position adopted by even the most liberal adherents of the just deserts philosophy. We shall require more facilities because any sentencing policy with a mandatory, or presumptive, minimum penalty will overtax existing facilities. Even without a change in sentencing policy, existing facilities are too large to be orderly or safe, too few to permit the essential classification and segregation of offenders by age, prior record, tendency toward violence, or length of sentence, and too lacking in amenity to enable many judges in good conscience to send offenders there. For decades we have allowed our sentencing policies to be dictated in large measure by our supply of correctional facilities so that, except for periods (such as the 1960s) of undercrowding and periods (such as today) of some overcrowding, the number of persons in prison has been rather constant despite enormous changes in the crime rate. Finally, the range of facilities for incarceration has been too small to permit the implementation of a complete array of sentencing alternatives, ranging from confinement in the community only during evenings or on weekends for minor offenders to maximum security facilities with adequate medical care for the most violent or pathological offenders.

A set of institutions adequate to almost any reasonable sentencing policy will require committing new resources—which, obviously, states and cities find in short supply—and making difficult locational decisions. This is not to say that citizens oppose expenditures on, or decisions to build, prisons. Quite to the contrary. It is only that with respect to expenditures their preferences are overwhelmed by the opposition of organized groups who prefer spending the marginal dollar for other purposes and with respect to locational decisions they often prefer that prisoners be located in "somebody else's" community. Governors are struggling to bring their budgets under control. Though citizen fear of crime is real, citizen organization in support of crime reduction methods is almost nonexistent. The few organizations that do operate in this area are, disproportionately, those that retain their ideological commitment to the interests of the offender rather than to those of society and that trend, as a consequence, to press for closing institutions rather than opening new ones. And even where these groups do not operate, the unorganized citizen hoping for more funds spent on the judicial and correctional system will find himself competing, at a hopeless disadvantage, with well-organized groups fighting to enlarge expenditures on Medicare payments, on construction contracts, and civil service pay raises. The political problem of the citizen concerned about crime is a classic example of what economists call the "free rider" problem: individual citizens benefit so little, and are so many in number, that they have no incentive to organize. And if a small number of highly-motivated persons do band together, and even if they win the competition for the marginal dollar with antiprison associations, labor unions, or public employee groups, they still must overcome community resistance—greatest in urban areas—to the location of new facilities.

These intellectual and political considerations help explain an otherwise striking paradox: in a nation beset with crime, in which a dominant concern of the great majority of citizens is a fear of victimization, in which public officials must win elections, and in which intellectual and liberal resistance to thinking about crime and taking seriously the punitive aspects of the criminal justice system has lessened, little happens that might affect crime rates or at least satisfy the popular desire for justice. It is another example, and a sad one, of the fact that shared popular attitudes are not always a necessary, and are rarely a sufficient, condition for political action. But some progress is being made. Since our current crime wave began in about 1963, popular opinion has been receptive to policies that elite and intellectual opinion is only now coming to accept. The signs of policy change that we can detect seem to be caused by what the few now think rather than what the many long believed. But we should be thankful for progress, whatever its source.

NOTES TO CHAPTER SIX

1. New York: Basic Books, 1975.

2. New York: Hill and Wang, 1976.

3. Chicago: University of Chicago Press, 1974.

4. A helpful analysis of the nature and sources of competing ideologies about criminal justice is Walter B. Miller, "Ideology and Criminal Justice: Some Current Issues," *Journal of Criminal Law and Criminology*, vol. 64, no. 2 (1973), pp. 141-162.

5. J.D. Mabbott, "Punishment," *Mind*, vol. 49 (1939), reprinted in Frederick A. Olafson, *Justice and Social Policy* (Englewood Cliffs, N.J.: Prentice-Hall/ Spectrum, 1961), p. 39.

6. Robert Martinson, "What Works? Questions and Answers About Prison Reform," *The Public Interest*, no. 35 (Spring, 1974) pp. 22-54.

7. President's Commission on Law Enforcement and Administration of Justice, *The Challenge of Crime in a Free Society* (Washington, D.C.: U.S. Government Printing Office, 1967), p. 170.

8. Paul Lerman, *Community Treatment and Social Control* (Chicago: University of Chicago Press, 1975). Lerman first published evidence suggesting the inefficacy of CTP in 1968: "Evaluating Institutions for Delinquents," *Social Work*, vol. 13 (1968), pp. 55-64.

9. New York: Alfred A. Knopf, 1973.

10. New York: Viking Press, 1968.

11. New York: Hill and Wang, 1973.

12. The evidence on the crime-reduction potential of the police is summarized in James Q. Wilson, *Thinking About Crime* (New York: Basic Books, 1975), chap. 5.

13. These studies are summarized in Wilson, chap. 8, and Gordon Tullock, "Does Punishment Deter Crime?", *The Public Interest* (Summer, 1974), pp. 103-111. Methodological criticisms are forthcoming from Daniel Nagin of Carnegie-Mellon, David Greenberg of New York University, and Brian Fiorst. The entire issue is being reviewed by a special panel of the National Research Council.

14. Estimates of the incapacitative effects of imprisonment can be found in David F. Greenberg, "The Incapacitative Effect of Imprisonment: Some Estimates," *Law and Society Review*, vol. 9, pp. 4 (Summer, 1975), pp. 541-580, and Reuel and Shlome Shinnar, "The Effects of the Criminal Justice System on the Control of Crime: A Quantitative Approach," *op. cit.*, pp. 581-612.

15. Frankel, pp. 118-124.

16. Hirsch, pp. 104, 136-139.

17. In Hirsch, p. 177.

18. Reviews of labeling theory are numerous. See, for example, Nanette J. Davis, "Labeling Theory in Deviance Research," *Sociological Quarterly*, vol. 13 (Fall, 1972), pp. 447-474; Clarence Schrag, "Theoretical Foundations for a Social Science of Corrections," in Daniel Glaser, ed., *Handbook of Criminology* (Chicago: Rand McNally, 1974); pp. 707-711; W.R. Gove, *The Labeling of Deviance* (New York, Halsted/Sage, 1975).

19. Marvin F. Wolfgang, Robert M. Figlio, and Thorsten Sellin, *Delinquency in a Birth Cohort* (Chicago: University of Chicago Press, 1972), p. 254.

20. See the studies summarized in Greenberg at p. 558.

Chapter Seven

Pursuing Justice in Corrections

David Fogel

As a result of aimlessness and public neglect the system of corrections in America has come to a standstill. The continuing problems of corrections still receive one or another of the old answers. In order to break the log-jam of correctional theory we need a new approach. One such approach might be the "justice model" of corrections which I wish to propose in this study. The "justice model" focuses upon the consumers of the criminal justice system—the offender, the guard, the victim, the witness, and the taxpayer—rather than upon the processors of criminal justice.

The following suggestions are based upon a two-pronged strategy: (1) the immediate and short range, and (2) the middle range. No long range is offered because of the critical urgency to move rapidly; since "progress" in corrections is usually counted in decades. The distinguishing characteristics between the two strategies is that the short range requires no legislation or new appropriations while the middle range requires both.

Immediate and Short Range

We need to conceptualize imprisonment differently and narrow our rhetorical claims. A penal sanction should *only* mean a temporary deprivation of liberty. It is the legal cost for the violation of some laws. The prison is responsible for executing the sentence not

Adapted from Chapter IV of "*. . . we are the living proof. . . " (The Justice Model for Corrections)*, by David Fogel, copyright 1975, Anderson Publishing Co., Cincinnati, Ohio. Reprinted with permission of the publisher.

rehabilitating the convict. The sentence must be seen as a part of the continuum of justice—it must be experienced justly, reasonably and constitutionally. It is in the context of justice that a mission arises for the prison and its staff. The mission is *fairness*. Until sentencing and parole problems can be resolved discretion must be harnessed by as much voluntary administrative explication of norms as is necessary to produce a sense of fairness for both the keeper and the kept.

Since the prison sentence is to be seen as only a deprivation of liberty, all the rights accorded free citizens but consistent with mass living and the execution of a sentence restricting the freedom of movement should follow a prisoner into prison. The prisoner is volitional and may therefore choose programs for his own benefit. The state cannot with any degree of confidence hire one person to rehabilitate another unless the latter senses an inadequacy in himself that he wishes to modify through services he himself seeks. This should be evident from historical experience. We will shortly elaborate a prison mission of justice for our current fortress prison environment—but the fortress prison system must be ended if we are to expect further rationality in correctional development.

Middle Range

There are three elements which should govern the middle range strategy which will be elaborated later: (1) a return to flat time sentences with procedural rules in law governing sentence selection; (2) the elimination of both parole boards and parole agencies as we have known them; and (3) the transformation of the fortress prison into institutions for no more than 300 persons, further divisible into subunits of 30. The institutions will contain people sentenced to similar terms. Release will be determined by a narrow and reviewable system of vested good-time rules. We turn first to those elements of a short range which can be immediately implemented by administrators.

A Justice Model for the Fortress Prison

The period of incarceration can be conceptualized as a time in which we try to reorient a prisoner to the lawful use of power. One of the more fruitful ways the prison can teach nonlaw-abiders to be law-abiding is to treat them in a lawful manner. The entire effort of the prison should be seen as an influence attempt based upon operationalizing justice. This is called the "justice model."

It begins by recognizing, not by moralizing, what the prison stay is about. Simply stated, it is an enforced deprivation of liberty, the taking of some or all of the days of a person's life and his confinement within an area. When men are confined against their will in this country, the bottom line of the arrangement of life for both the keeper and kept should be *justice-as-fairness*. Opportunities for self-improvement should be offered but not made a condition of freedom.

Confinement and compression of large numbers of men, in a human zoo, who in the past have frequently resorted to the use of force, fraud and violence is at best a precarious venture. Prison administrators should not further confuse their staff with a mission either claiming moral or psychological redemption or with one that leans on brutality to create a Lyndsian type of orderliness. Life in prison can be made saner and safer for the keeper and kept by reconceiving its meaning. The justice model calls for all the ingenuity an administrator can muster to place the inmate population and staff within a lawful and rational arena. It appeals to both (resident or worker) to rationalize their stay in prison in a context of fairness.

Justice-as-fairness provides the keeper and the kept with a rationale and morality for their shared fates in a correctional agency. Considering the failure of most treatment methods within our current operating structure—the fortress prison—the justice model holds some promise, if not to cut recidivism, then to more decisively preclude Atticas. This model purports to turn a prison experience into one which provides opportunities for men to learn to be agents in their own lives, to use legal processes to change their condition, and to wield lawful power. Men who can negotiate their fates do not have to turn to violence as a method of achieving change.

It is a sad irony in our system of criminal justice that we insist on the full majesty of due process for the accused until he is sentenced to a prison, then justice is said to have been served. The entire case for a justice model rests upon the need to continue to engage the person in the quest for justice as he moves on the continuum from defendant-to-convict-to-free citizen. Our traditions and statutes support dysfunctionality. They first insist, in effect, that only volitional actors be sent to prison. Then corrections support treatment regimens which assume nonvolitional behavior on the part of prisoners.

The proponents of the psychiatric or medical model visualized themselves as reformers. They grasped the prisoner from the onerous custody staff which meted out punishment for prison rule infractions. The clinicians viewed the prisoner as sick while custody staff saw them as bad. Both operated, until most recently, in an environment of low visibility and wide discretion. But the convict, it appears, would rather be bad than sick. He can hang onto a soft determinism and still be volitional. The clinicians didn't permit him much room for responsible behavior. One needs only to look at the extremes of either style to see their similarities and illogical conclusions from Arkansas to Patuxent.

The justice model seeks to engage both the keeper and the kept in a joint venture which insists that the agencies of justice shall operate in a lawful and just manner. It simply means that we believe that the prisoners did not use lawful means to guide themselves outside the prison and should therefore be provided greater (not lesser) opportunities to learn lawful behavior while in the institution. The staff effort should be turned to teaching a prisoner how to use lawful processes to achieve his ends. This also implies that the convict accepts the legal responsibility for the consequences of his behavior. In the absence of a continuum of justice in the prison, most ends are reached unlawfully. When unlawful behavior is detected, it is frequently dealt with in absence of the very standards of due process we insist upon outside the prison. The result is a further indication to the convict that lawful behavior has little pay-off. He can be dealt with arbitrarily and usually responds by treating others in the same manner.

OPERATIONALIZING JUSTICE IN THE PRISON

The model of justice we propose affects several aspects of prison life. It attempts to create a lawful and rational arena for dealing with problems arising from an artificial environment which charges one group of men to restrain the mobility of another against their wills. While this can probably never be voluntarily achieved there are some immediate short range goals which we believe are realizeable: (1) a mitigation of harshness, (2) peaceful conflict resolution, and (3) a safer staff work environment, that will emerge from the operationalization of fairness in prison life. What follows are some crucial aspects of the organization of prison life which if reconceived and transformed could be put in the service of reaching the previously cited short range goals. We will be concerned with the micro-world and macro-world concerns of prison administration. There is nothing contained in the programs offered with which the author has not already had an administrative experience.

JUSTICE IN THE MICRO-WORLD

Citizens in a free society understand that the problems of everyday living in the home, marketplace, work, school, and church produce different perceptions of turf, claims, prerogatives and rights. Accordingly, society attempts to organize orderly processes for conflict resolution. Conflict neglected may explode into violence. Conflict, to be resolved, must be transformed into negotiation, a form of diplomacy. However, the same problems that present themselves in free society are grossly magnified in a prison. Here the least significant micro-world event can, in the absence of conflict resolution mechanisms, escalate aimlessly into major disturbances, violence and death. Memoranda and directives clarifying expectations are helpful but do not settle hotly disputed claims. We offer a few alternatives.

One of the most strongly debated aspects of prison life is inmate self-governance. Experiments have been carried out sporadically over the entire history of corrections. They can be fairly categorized as having been both poorly executed and poorly documented. The arguments arising over forms of inmate self-governance represent historical reflections of the differing views of the purpose of prison.

Self-governance is not to be conceived in the historical sense of the "inmate council" or the "gimme group." Rather we suggest the joint venture model. Both inmates and staff should be heard, should be involved and thereby form a constituency inside the walls with the purpose of improving the quality of life and work in prison. The formats can vary but the linkage of the inmates and staff is crucial to the sense of fairness herein proposed. The warden, with staff on the council, can feel easier about the "gimme" quality previous inmate council formats exhibited. Requests for programs and changes, he will realize, have been filtered through a staff prism. Inmates' perspectives will have been moderated by guards. Guards may finally become involved in program innovation, but more significantly a forum for communication with the central actors present is created. The seats on the council may be filled in several different elective and elective-appointive formats. Several prisons might experiment with different formats.[a] The inmate-staff council serves as a program planning and grievance mechanism. It is not, as were some earlier models, an internal court. The administration retains its veto power over proposals brought to it from the council.

A reasonable expectation for this type of council, with its thrust toward making behavior public on the part of both groups involved, is that it might serve as an early warning mechanism for future problems. If such proves to be the case then timely defusing (perhaps using other conflict resolution processes soon to be discussed) may help the administration avoid escalations leading to massive problems.

---

[a]Stillwater Prison, Minnesota, is the only one, to the author's knowledge, with an inmate-staff council currently in existence with a three year history.

A program of self-governance does not mean that the council will be involved at the level of choosing the school colors. Its vitality and credibility will be established by the range of tasks with which it is permitted to deal. Because of the *inmate* council's weak historical past the *inmate-staff* council may have difficulty in finding sympathetic adherents. However, the changed format of the inmate-staff council, placing both groups in the same boat, now permits it to undertake new tasks not previously available to the inmate councils of the past. The new format should not be brushed off with tired arguments about the older inmate council's shortcomings.[b] Unlike other attempts we do not visualize the council as a group of the "warden's boys" or an internal court for trying rule infraction cases.

Conflict Resolution

One of the new tasks is that of conflict resolution through a formal procedure by a representative body. As long as we are in the fortress prison we will have to assume that it will continue to be hazardous to the physical and emotional health of inmates and staff, that conflict is a normal ingredient of such compressed and pressured life and that the participants in this abnormal prison society will need a machinery for peacefully settling such predictable and inevitable conflicts. Again, formats may differ but the central point to be considered is that the new council should be entrusted with the prison's formal grievance procedure thereby becoming a vital agency in conflict resolution.

There is mounting evidence that now links weak inmate organization with rioting. Not permitting a formal public arena for negotiation (a sharing of power) forces inmates to withdraw to their own initiatives to ward off perceived assaults on their status. In general, Wilsnack and Ohlin[c] argue that institutions permitting negotiation will experience disturbances (if at all) of a nonriotous character. Those prisons not permitting inmates the opportunity to make life more tolerable, force prisoners to go beyond the prison walls to reach the public with a political message—the riot. Where prisoners learn that negotiation can make life tolerable they tend to use it as a vehicle and have no need to resort to violence. An inmate-staff council increases communication, provides a negotiative model and serves as an early warning system to guide preventive action. Convicts

[b]In 1960 the Wardens' Association by resolution, opposed inmate self-government. (J.E. Baker, *Inmate Self-Government*, p. 47.)

[c]Richard Wilsnack and Lloyd E. Ohlin in current research on *Prison Disturbances* (Winter 1973-74), pp. 1-41, unpublished manuscript (1974), p. 28. (Harvard Law School, Center for Criminal Justice.)

fully understand their less-than-equal power status when negotiating across the table from the administration, but even elsewhere negotiation partners are rarely truly equal. It is the negotiation model, however, that does offer the prisoner status enhancement. In the absence of official (lawful) validation of such status the prisoner seeks it unofficially (and frequently unlawfully). In the latter sense inmate organization is said to be weak, fragmented, and in the hands of charismatic leaders who crystallize predictable discontent—all are the preconditions associated in current research with rioting. Other findings concerned with attempts at violence reduction point out that honest communication with prisoner groups in efforts to quell violence *already underway* are doomed if they *did not previously exist.*

Empirical evidence also points in other directions: (1) liberalization of prison visiting reduces reported violence; (2) blacks and whites transgress violently at equal rates; (3) more severe punishment serves to increase the overall levels of prison violence; and (4) high aggression levels are most frequently related to high percentages of convicts with one year or more extensions of parole board dates and no visits.[1]

The inmate-staff council and other open communication vehicles suggested form one strata of a multitiered strategy for reducing tension, redressing grievances and using lawful means for change which modern correctional administrators need to consider, others follow.

Since the start of the *Commission on Correctional Facilities and Services* there has been extensive work done to involve the law profession in the operation and day to day functioning of the prisons. Much of the work has been to clarify administrative procedures and to set model correctional legislation and standards. Some of the more important work concerning the legal aspect of prisons is being carried out in the Resource Center on Correctional Law and Legal Services. They have produced a training handbook on prison law to be used by correctional workers. Monographs outlining rights to medical care, censorship, disciplinary due process and prison law libraries have been published as well as materials on the use of ombudsmen and grievance mechanisms for dealing with inmate complaints and problems.

Though prisoners clearly need legal advice in seeking post-conviction remedies or to deal with the conditions of confinement, many of their legal problems are civil. Divorce, child custody, the protection of property—all these are matters of deep concern to the prisoner. It seems clear that the civil legal assistance currently available to inmates is inadequate. A study done by Marvin Finkelstein of the Boston University Center for Criminal Justice (1972) indicated that 76 percent of the corrections personnel and eighty-seven of the eighty-eight law schools surveyed thought that prison legal services are not sufficient at present.[2] Existing programs tend to focus their energy on criminal law; of the law schools with prisoner legal assistance programs surveyed, 83.3 percent directed more than half their activities toward criminal law.[3]

Nevertheless, requests for civil legal assistance form a significant portion of the caseloads of legal aid programs. In a six-month period, 19.7 percent of the requests for assistance received by the Boston University program were for civil legal aid.[4] A similar program at the University of Minnesota reported 23 percent of its caseload as dealing with divorce and annulment (the second largest category of requests in the entire program, the first being appeals from conviction) and the third largest category being other domestic relations problems.[5] The University of Wisconsin Law School student interns found that the most common civil legal problems were domestic relations, financial matters such as insurance and the repossession of property, dealings with government agencies and complaints against the institution.[6]

Lawyers can also play an important role in helping to create structures for the orderly handling of grievances. A Minnesota report on model grievance procedures points to the importance of such a program.

> It seems essential, too, that the corrections field move toward organizing procedures and channels of communications which will give more tangible form to the due process principles which are relied upon to assure fair treatment in our society. Such development would seem not only to fit into sound criminal justice practice but might forestall need for the courts to prescribe such measures and procedures from outside the correctional system.[7]

In the long run, the changes in prison will come from properly functioning administrative procedures, not court ordered reversals of administrative decisions or individual cases. Legal aid for prisoners is becoming not a privilege but a right that society has an obligation to provide if it expects the prisoner to improve his circumstances legally. "Now there is a growing conviction that not only are people entitled to equal protection under law but that society must insure that they have equal opportunity to invoke its protection."[8]

Failure to meet the legal needs of inmates simply adds problems to the already burdened existence of the prisoner. "Inability to do anything effective about their legal problems results in added frustrations for the inmates and reinforces resentment towards the institution and the law in general."[9] Events outside the walls often have considerable impact on the inmate or his family, but he usually has no way to influence them. With legal advice, he can bring some leverage to bear on these events, lessening his sense of impotence. Furthermore, resolution of potentially troublesome legal problems before release can make the ex-inmate's reentry into society smoother.[10]

The role of the lawyer in a prison also extends to service for the guard. Usually the warden can call upon the state's attorney to represent the institution or himself against a legal attack but the guard is not, as we have seen, completely absolved of legal responsibility. He may have questions about the extent of his liability when he is called upon to dispense medicines, break up fights, pursue an escapee, deny a privilege, or when he fails to warn a prisoner of an impending action.[d]

Finally, legal aid programs can assist in ways other than either reviewing practices in the prison or assisting inmates with legal problems. The President's Crime Commission (1967) pointed out that: "They can provide increased visibility for a system that has generally been too isolated, helping to mobilize public opinion and bring political pressure to bear where needed for reform. The mere presence of outsiders would serve to discourage illegal, unfair or inhumane practices."[11]

The Justice of Administration

Corrections, as a public agency, represents an official governmental service of considerable power. It cannot escape its responsibility to provide administrative due process. One repeatedly hears the argument that correctional administrators are professional, that the broad discretion they exercise is necessary and that review of, or a narrowing of such discretion would place undue restraint upon them. In response we point out that the administrators come from many different professions; that we are not interested in eliminating discretion; simply having it under a public spotlight and that in a democracy no public agency can enjoy unbridled discretion.[12]

Discretion is a central problem in corrections; affecting its entire structure from the administrators to the convict. Its successful

---

[d]The National Association of Attorneys General published a *Special Report on Corrections*, January 18, 1974, which lists some 75 different kinds of prisoners suits calling prison officials' attention to the burgeoning of correctional case law and the variety of potential liability.

harnassing could go a long way toward instilling a sense of fairness to all concerned. More significantly, perhaps it would free the administrator from bondage in the rhetoric of the imperial perspective and permit him to take a position more suitably appropriate for an agent of justice. In this sense, freedom for the correctional administrator lies in the direction of voluntarily adopting a model based on justice for administering his official affairs. How may this be done? Professor Kenneth Culp Davis suggests several ways of structuring discretion.

> The seven instruments that are most useful in the structuring of discretionary power are open plans, open policy statements, open rules, open findings, open reasons, open precedents, and fair informal procedure. The reason for repeating the word 'open' is a powerful one: Openness is the natural enemy of arbitrariness and a natural ally in the fight against injustice.[13]

Properly understood this discussion is limited to the elimination of unnecessary discretion and the structuring of arbitrary discretion. It does not imply the total elimination of discretion, rather a lifting of the veil so that fairness can creep in to protect those affected. We all respond more positively to fair treatment and even to a punitive action when it is accompanied by a precise explanation of a violated norm.

In the context of prison, justice-as-fairness means having clear rules, insuring their promulgation and a procedure for determining and punishing rule infractions rooted in due process safeguards (for example: statement of the allegation, notice, counsel substitute, a hearing, the chance to cross-examine, written findings, appeal). Further, it means giving up the foot dragging which the litigation so vividly bares. Correctional administrators should not have to be brought to court to provide adequate law libraries and access to them, to provide more than ten sheets of paper or for punishing by segregation those who exercise their right to access to the court, the press or the public. A justice perspective assures that expressions of racism will be fought. We should be in the forefront of exposing the indignities of poor medical care, inadequate diets, servile labor, absence of recreational programs and inhumane segregative facilities. The record shows that in court we appear to be alibiing for the existence of such conditions instead of agreeing to seek remediation. The public and court will permit us reasonable precautions about what may freely enter prisons, but they look askance at the broad prison regulations surrounding mail, publication and visitors. Administrators need to make a dramatic break with the vestiges of the nineteenth century "buried-from-the-world" philosophy. Courts should not have to *force* modern administrators to adopt any of the above procedures. Quite aside from the embarrassment it brings to us as agents of justice, it embarrasses our claims to professionalism.

In our justice perspective, the guard must be treated fairly as well. Our study of guard turnover rate at Stateville prison (102 percent) also revealed some unexpected outcomes, which have fairness implications. A substantial percentage of a sample of dropouts reported taking new jobs at the same or *lower* wages elsewhere. One might assume that fear, abuse from convicts and other hazard attendant to being a guard would drive many from the work. The research shows, however, that a prime reason for leaving was instead *abuse from superiors*—sergeants, lieutenants and captains. There were other reasons as well but *working with criminals* did not surface high as a negative factor.[e] Fairness recognizes the quality of the work environment and takes steps to improve it. An agenda for fairness should include: clearly drawn work assignments, employment standards and salary on par with the state police, hazardous duty and malpractice liability insurance, a dignified but mandatory earlier (age 55) retirement, special benefits from duty-related death, the right to organize and bargain collectively, involvement in program planning, a grievance procedure, freedom from partisan political pressures,[f] merit procedures for promotion and mandatory training that is unambiguous about the guards' work role and that focuses on procedures of justice-as-fairness in addition to traditional custodial concerns.

In the micro-world of the prison the justice perspective calls upon the maker of rules to share legitimate power with the enforcers and consumers of the rules. It also urges that all rules and rulings be required to stand the test of being the least onerous way of reaching a lawful end.

The days of hiding behind the wall are effectively over. Correctional administrators can undergo the turmoil of being forced to go public or can take the initiative and voluntarily begin playing a more open hand. By this we mean a checks and balances system of scrutiny not another torrent of slick publications.

Overseeing Fairness—The Ombudsman

In response to public pressure for civilian review boards in the last decade, police uniformly asked "why us?" A fair question. We agree

[e]Derived from an attitude survey of guard employment attrition rates by "Why They Quit: A Survey of Prison Guard Drop-Outs," James B. Jacobs and Mary P. Grear, University of Chicago Center for Studies in Criminal Justice (Mimeo, p. 26), 1974. Some 26 percent of the sample of dropouts took higher paying jobs, 57 percent at lower salaries.

[f]At Menard prison in 1973, guards talked freely about purchasing and retaining their jobs, and being promoted as a function of routine payments to county party chairmen, ranging from $50.00 to $300.

with the police, even though we are sympathetic to the argument that all low-visibility public agencies need public oversight. The police should not be singled out. Correctional practice needs to be brought under the umbrella of public scrutiny as well.

The ombudsman has been an accepted institution in Sweden's civil administration since 1809. The concept has only recently been recognized in the United States and even more recently put into practice. The prison is an eminently well-suited setting for the Ombudsman. His clientele, by definition, is frequently cut off from opportunities to carry their complaints beyond their keepers.

Administrators' most frequent objections to the use of an Ombudsman are: (1) existing methods of complaint hearing are adequate; or (2) if inadequate, the agency should be able to modify its practices without outside oversight which leads to dichotomized authority. In corrections, both have proven wrong. Complaints continue to pile up at an increasing rate, and, because of non resolution, pour over by way of litigation into already overloaded courts.[g] The American experience with the Ombudsman, as meager as it is, shows no cause for alarm with the dichotomization-of-authority argument. The earliest Ombudsman type program dates from 1777 when the Continental Congress established the Inspector General of the Army.[h] The well-known General Accounting Office and auditors perform similar services in other settings. Bureaucrats used to these oversight agencies accept them without arguing the erosion of their authority. Corrections, for the most part, has not had an experience with oversight and like the police wants to know "why us!" A continuous history of conflict, brutality, rioting and killings simply requires a mechanism of public oversight. Several states have already adopted some form of the office of Ombudsman for all its citizens. Minnesota is the first to have an independent Ombudsman for its prisoners, parolees and correctional staff.[i]

At the request of the Department of Corrections (1971) The University of Minnesota Law School drew up an initial proposal which was first funded as an L.E.A.A. project and ultimately found

---

[g]Tibble states, "It seems obvious that if legal recognition of prisoner complaints will result in judicial pandemonium other avenues must be found." (*Ombudsmen for American Prisons*, p. 390.)

[h]The Inspector General of the U.S. Army testified in favor of an Ombudsman for the Department of Corrections in Sacramento in December 1970.

[i]"In the last session of Congress, the late Congressman William F. Ryan unsuccessfully introduced a bill that would have withheld L.E.A.A. funds from any state that failed to establish an ombudsman for prison." (Linda Singer and J. Michael Keating, "Prisoner Grievance Mechanisms," *Crime and Delinquency*, July 1973, p. 375.)

statutory authority in 1973. The basic purpose for the office of Ombudsman was to permit ". . . the release of inmate frustration by opening communication . . . (and) to ensure procedural safeguards which are so fundamental to our system of justice, (that is) . . . due process.[14]

More specifically the Ombudsman would seek to fulfill the following ends:

(1) The improvement and clarification of administrative procedures and regulations.
(2) Reorganization and revitalization of internal prison review procedures.
(3) Increased access to judicial review by cooperation and coordination with the various legal aid services.
(4) Encouragement of more active involvement of private and governmental agencies and interest groups in alleviating the grievances.
(5) Coordination of overlapping governmental agencies by means of increased flow of information from the agencies to inmate and staff regarding functions, programs, and procedures.
(6) (Seek) strengthening and corrective legislation by providing the Legislature with information and recommendations regarding the correctional institutions.
(7) Improving the relationship between staff and inmate by providing the inmates with information on the actions, motives, and design of administration actions.
(8) Alleviation of tension within the prison by means of more open communication, i.e., a 'release valve'.[15]

Initial anxiety melted when each of the state's institutional administrators and their executive staff met, analyzed and modified the proposal. They in turn trained their staffs and by written notice informed all inmates, parolees (and their families), guards and the department's field services of the new program.

Perhaps the key to successful initiation and operation of an Ombudsman program is the credibility the office attracts. Given centuries of mistrust it is of crucial importance that the Ombudsman be independent of the department of corrections. If it is this political distance which initially produces confidence in the Ombudsman, then it is his ability to meet the needs of his constituency which assures continuing success.

What should be obvious to the correctional administrator is that an Ombudsman can help bring change which they find difficult to manage themselves because, "An administrative agency head has difficulty investigating and criticizing his officers and employees while continuing to keep their loyalty and confidence."[16]

An Ombudsman is still another strata of the multitier conflict resolution system we are constructing in this chapter. Staff-inmate governance operates at the level of program innovation, grievance and dispute settlement, and concern about overall conditions of confinement. It brings the two major groups into a public arena for communication and problem solving purposes. The introduction of legal services assists both groups in seeking redress but also distinguishes and seeks local remedies before involving the courts. Through assisting the individual prisoner with civil legal aid the prison itself is removed as an obstacle for the convict to continue to be an agent in his own life. Lawyers also assist in establishing due process mechanisms for the internal court and other procedures. Finally, their presence has a salutory effect in a largely invisible agency. The introduction of an Ombudsman assures that the entire process operates fairly.

THE MACRO-WORLD CONCERNS

The prison's macro-world is comprised of confusing forces and attitudes which act as constraints on modernization. We cite some and offer some tentative answers which might rationalize and bring justice-as-fairness into operation: (1) we will first move outside the prison to discuss some other neglected areas of justice—the victim, witness, and taxpayer—as they affect prison life, and (2) sentencing practices and parole granting. In discussing these factors which heavily impinge upon prison life we will keep an eye on how the convict is viewed by the major actors in criminal justice.

The Victim—The Witness—The Juror
Historically the criminal law replaced earlier known kinship group settlement of wrongs. The consolidation of political power in a jurisdiction changed private vengeance seeking (vendetta) of a variety of forms into collective order. When one party's wrong against another was transformed from a personal injury to a disturbance of the "King's peace," distance was created between the victim and the offender, (and insulated the administration of justice from the people). Crime came to be seen as a harm to the state (society). Today, private vengeance may itself be a crime. If A harms B it is transformed into the "People v. A" and B is mainly a harmed spectator to the trial. The state retains a monopoly of power to exact a *public* restoration of the disturbed balance although it is B's life which was upset. But it does so unsatisfactorily:

The State cannot prevent crime, cannot repress it, except in a small number of cases, and consequently fails in its duty for the accomplishment of which it receives taxes from its citizens, and then, after all that, it accepts a reward; and over and above this, it condemns every ten years some 3,230,000 individuals, the greater part of whom it imprisons, putting the expense of their maintenance on the back of the honest citizen whom it has neither protected from nor indemnified for the harm alone by the crime; and all this in the name of the eternal principles of absolute and retributive justice. It is evident that this manner of administering justice must undergo a radical change. (Enrico Ferri, 1917)

Currently there is a major revival of interest in offender restitution and victim compensation occasioned largely by Margery Fry's essay "Justice for Victims" in the *London Observer* in July 1957.ʲ However, our immediate interest in the subject is in how the isolation of the victim creates a sense of injustice resulting in resentment and further cries for vengeance.

When a crime is committed the *state* (having assumed the burden) has failed to keep the peace. If we expect the private citizen to assist the state in prevention, detection and suppression of crime, a certain amount of jeopardy attends such a commitment. Assuming the citizen's readiness to accept it; should he not be insured against duty-related injuries? Remembering that the state prohibits private vengeance, the responsible citizen must seek to "right wrong" through the criminal justice system. But this is not a satisfactory outcome since it effectively cuts off a civil remedy. A prison sentence simply represents the state's intervention not the victim's. The victim now, in his role as taxpayer, will become a double victim and in consequence of an ineffective prison experience may yet again be victimized either generally or specifically.

A reading of Galoway and Hudson is convincing proof that victim compensation holds much promise as possible rehabilitative and reconciliation tools but our interest is limited to fairness. If we expect an involved public (with a sense of justice) then we need to offer civil remedies when in chance involvement some become

---

ʲA forthcoming anthology by Burt Galoway and Joseph Hudson *Considering the Victim: Readings in Restitution and Victim Compensation* (1974) is the most comprehensive multidiscipline perspective available on the subject. For their thoughts on operationalizing a restitution program, in which they have had experience, see Fogel, Galoway and Hudson, "Restitution in Criminal Justice: A Minnesota Experiment," *Criminal Law Bulletin*, Vol. 8 (1972), and Galoway and Hudson, "Issues in the Correctional Implementation of Restitution to Victims of Crime," *American Society of Criminology*, New York (November 1973).

innocent victims. This notion extends to the witness who is treated in a largely shabby manner and the jury member who gives much in return for a pittance. Our proposal would lead to reimbursement for the latter two at least on the level of the minimum wage law.

In a concern for a rational prison and fairness to the major private actors in criminal justice we can perceive of a strategy linking both. It is our belief that adequate compensation to the victim of crime, the witness and the jury panelist *is right in itself*, and as a matter of fairness, requires little justification. If victim compensation and offender restitution beyond this were widely implemented, it might lead to an atmosphere in which rational prison planning could progress or to at least mute the cry for further escalations of harshness. In a "pocket-book culture" where money is so important one might reasonably assume that reimbursement for injury may quell the urge to retributively punish. If a successful renaissance of restitution were to occur, more offenders would by definition have to be kept out of prisons, at work repaying their victim. If money is a plausible nexus between the exploitive offender and the isolated victim and if it can engage both in a vengeance-free relationship, then its expenditure may create a just and inexpensive path to restoring the balance without further deepening the sense of injustice for either.

Sentencing and Parole—Some Alternatives
In the area of sentencing we are a government of men not law. Prisoners entering our institutions burdened with a sense of injustice, living in its compressed tension, with ruleless procedures for parole, makes the entire prison venture unsafe for all. Yet we will need some form of separation of the dangerous for the foreseeable future. But sentencing which is the separation mechanism can be accomplished more sensibly and equitably.

1. Sentencing criteria should be statutorily required.
2. Sentencing should be based upon classification of offenders into risk categories.
3. Sentences should be more definite, (there are fairly broad variations but indeterminacy is substantially rejected) or fixed and graduated by seriousness of the offense.
4. Sentences should be reviewable.
5. Sentences of imprisonment should be substantially reduced.
6. Sentences of imprisonment should be justified by the state after an exhaustive review fails to yield a satisfactory community-based sanction.

Others have urged Commissions on Sentencing,[18] sentencing review councils,[19] separate sentencing hearings,[20] an end to plea bargaining (because it limits all other sentencing alternatives),[21] statutory authority for non incarcerative sentences,[22] an end to the capriciously excessive "emergency laws" which periodically panic legislatures[23] and for sentencing decisions to be weighted in favor of promoting a concept of individual liberty.[24] The current and persistent thrust may be fairly characterized as a *neoclassical con-solidation* of penal sanctions. We add the perspective of justice-as-fairness which insists upon tight procedural regularity, hence a narrowing of discretion, for the agencies of the criminal law.

A RETURN TO FLAT TIME

All this leaves the problem just where it was. The irresponsible humanitarian citizen may indulge his pity and sympathy to his heart's content, knowing that whenever a criminal passes to his doom there, but for the grace of God, goes he; but those who have to govern find that they must either abdicate, and that promptly, or else take on themselves as best they can many of the attributes of God. They must decide what is good and what evil; they must force men to do certain things and refrain from doing certain other things whether individual consciences approve or not; they must resist evil resolutely and continually, possibly and preferably without malice or revenge, but certainly with the effect of disarming it, preventing it, stamping it out and creating public opinion against it. In short, they must do all sorts of things which they are manifestly not ideally fit to do, and, let us hope, do with becoming misgiving, but which must be done, all the same, well or ill, somehow and by somebody.

If I were to ignore this, everyone who has had any experience of government would throw these pages aside as those of an inexperienced sentimentalist or an Impossibilist Anarchist. (George Bernard Shaw 1922)[25]

Richard A. McGee, President of the American Justice Institute, has proposed an alternative for California which returns to flat time sentences in a five degree felony plan ranging from a minimum of three months to three years in the 5th degree to seven years to life (and death, if lawful) for 1st degree felonies.[26] Considerable discretion is left to judges (with a built-in appellate review council) and state parole is collapsed into the existing probation system in the county that the released convict is expected to dwell. The prison therefore receives no discretion other than through the residual good time law which is not eliminated. Our suggestion, although closely paralleling McGee's, calls for a total flat sentence for different classes of felonies mitigated by substantial vested good time credit. Both plans return power to the judiciary, within statutory guidelines and eliminate parole boards.

We call for a system based upon a finding of *clear and present danger* to be necessary for the imposition of a term of imprisonment. Imprisonment should be the courts last available sanction following an affirmative action by authorities seeking other alternatives. When a finding of clear and present danger is made it should require incarceration. At this point we part with McGee, who, we believe, leaves too much discretion to the courts (even with the appellate review council, which we do support). If we can accomplish procedural regularity in sentencing we believe a system based upon categories of *demonstrated risk* will bring more certainty and fairness to the prisoner.

But the prison needs one other tool to make prison life more rational. We propose that the length on the flat time sentence be mitigated *only* by good time credit. This puts modest discretion closer to the source which can most usefully employ it. It simply says to the prisoner:

> Your stay has been determined to be four years, no more, you can get out in two years but that's up to you. We reduce your sentence one day for every day of lawful behavior. You can't get out any faster by making progress in any other aspect of prison life. Lawful behavior is the payoff. We trade you a day on the streets for every good one inside. For rule infractions, which may lead to a loss of good time, you will be able to defend yourself at a hearing, safeguarded by due process. We publish and issue a list of prison rules and the penalties for their violation. Our internal court does not deal with any actual crimes you may commit. If we have probable cause to suspect you committed a felony during your term with us it becomes a matter for the local district attorney. This may lead to another prison consecutive sentence. The good time you earn is vested. It's in the bank. Nobody can touch it. The internal court can only take up to 30 days time for an offense. You can appeal to the warden and the director of the department.

The basic idea behind each of the leading sentencing revision plans is a search for the classification of dangerous felons. They presuppose tight sentencing procedures and they propose a variety of ways of accounting for the more dangerous.

Proposed Flat Time System

Using the author's home state of Illinois as an example, it currently provides for four classes of felony sentencing and for

A. Model Penal Code*

Felonies	Ordinary Term		Extended Term	
	Minimum	Maximum	Minimum	Maximum
1st degree . . .	1-10 yrs.	life	5-10 yrs.	life
2nd degree . . .	1-3 yrs.	10 yrs.	1-5 yrs.	10-20 yrs.
3rd degree . . .	1-2 yrs.	5 yrs.	1-3 yrs.	5-10 yrs.

B. Model Sentencing Act[†]

	Ordinary Term		Dangerous Offender	
	Minimum	Maximum	Minimum	Maximum
First degree murder . . .	none	life	none	life
Atrocious crimes[1]	none	0-10 yrs.	none	0-30 yrs.
Ordinary felonies . . .	none	0-5 yrs.	none	0-30 yrs.

[1] optional

C. McGee's Plan

5th degree — 3 months to 3 years
These in most cases may be reduced to misdemeanors of the first degree in the discretion of the court.
4th degree — 6 months to 5 years
3rd degree — 12 months to 12 years
2nd degree — 18 months to 20 years
1st degree — 7 years up to life, or death, if the law permits[27]

*Model Penal Code 6.06-.09.
†Model Sentencing Act 5.7-9.

murder separately.[k] The law requires the court to impose an indeterminate sentence of imprisonment in most instances, by specifying both a minimum and a maximum term of imprisonment, each within certain specified statutory limits. The minimum term imposed also may not exceed one-third the maximum term imposed.

The present schedule of offenses is as follows:

Offense	Maximum Term Range	Minimum Term Range
Murder	Death, or any term in excess of 14 years, if compelling reasons for mercy are shown.	14 years, unless the court sets a higher term.
Class 1	Any term in excess of 4 years.	4 years, unless the court sets a higher term.
Class 2	Any term in excess of 1 year, not exceeding 20 years.	1 year or more, up to one-third of the maximum term set by the court.
Class 3	Any term in excess of 1 year, not exceeding 10 years.	1 year or more, up to one-third of the maximum term set by the court.
Class 4	Any term in excess of 1 year, not exceeding 3 years.	1 year in all cases.

[k]Illinois Code of Corrections, Article 8 1005, 8.1

Under this system, a convicted person gets a "bracketed" term of imprisonment—2 to 7 years, 1 to 10 years, 15 to 60 years, et cetera. His sentence is "indeterminate" in that he has no idea of how much of the range between his minimum and maximum sentences actually will have to be spent in custody.

Type A

Part or nonincarcerative felony sentences. It is first important to understand what is *not* recommended by our flat time proposal. We do *not* propose that all offenders committing felony offenses go to prison. Such a draconian measure would run afoul of the provision of Article I, Section 11 of the Illinois Constitution of 1970 which requires that "all penalties (must) be determined both according to the seriousness of the offense and with the objective of restoring the offender to useful citizenship," as it would in many other states with similar provisions.

Instead, our proposal broadens the flexibility available to the trial court in many respects. We anticipate a broadening of the court's power to employ mandatory supervision (probation), conditional discharge, periodic imprisonment, restitution and fines as sentencing alternatives—both alone and in combination. As part of a mandatory presentence investigation, we would require an affirmative showing by the state that the felon could not be safely supervised by a nonincarcerative program before permitting the imposition of a prison term.

FACTORS IN MITIGATION

The following grounds shall be accorded weight in favor of withholding a sentence of imprisonment:

(1) the defendant's criminal conduct neither caused nor threatened serious harm;

(2) the defendant did not contemplate that his criminal conduct would cause or threaten serious harm;

(3) the defendant acted under a strong provocation;

(4) there were substantial grounds tending to excuse or justify the defendant's criminal conduct, though failing to establish a defense;

(5) the victim of the defendant's criminal conduct induced or facilitated its commission;

(6) the defendant has compensated or will compensate the victim of his criminal conduct for the damage or injury that he sustained;

(7) the defendant has no history of prior delinquency or criminal activity or has led a law-abiding life for a substantial period of time before the commission of the present crime;

(8) the defendant's criminal conduct was the result of circumstances unlikely to recur;

(9) the character and attitudes of the defendant indicate that he is unlikely to commit another crime;

(10) the defendant is particularly likely to comply with the terms of a period of mandatory supervision;

(11) the imprisonment of the defendant would entail excessive hardship to him or his dependents.

If the court, having due regard for the character of the offender, the nature and circumstances of the offense and the public interest finds that a sentence of imprisonment is the most appropriate disposition of the offender, or where other provisions of this Code mandate the imprisonment of the offender, the grounds listed in paragraph (a) of this subsection shall be considered as factors in mitigation of the term imposed.

On the other hand, we do not believe that a comparably untrammeled degree of discretion in deciding on the range of time a person should serve *in prison* is desirable. To illustrate, if two judges were asked to impose sentence on a burglar under current law, one might decide on a sentence of 1 to 4 years while the other might elect 2 to 6 years. In so doing, each judge might have had the same degree of culpability in mind. Indeed, on any given day, each might have elected to use the other alternative. No standards can be devised to assess the correctness of such determinations, except within very broad limits. Yet that decision can cost a person two years of his life. Far more extreme examples easily come to mind.

Type B or C

A Sentence of Imprisonment. Type B and C are distinguished by length and the standard required for enhancement of the prison term. Type B is the ordinary term Type C is the enhanced term. The standard for the imposition of a prison sentence follows:

FACTORS IN AGGRAVATION

The following factors shall be accorded weight in favor of imposing a term of imprisonment, and in the instances specified shall mandate a term of imprisonment.

(1) that in the commission of a felony offense or in flight therefrom, the defendant inflicted or attempted to inflict serious bodily injury to another. Serious bodily injury as used in this Section means bodily injury which creates a substantial risk of death, or which causes death or serious disfigurement, serious impairment of health, or serious loss of impairment or the function of any bodily organ.

(2) that the defendant presents a continuing risk of physical harm to the public.

If the court so finds and in addition finds the factors specified in subsection (1) of this Section, and that an additional period of confinement is required for the protection of the public, the defendant may be sentenced as provided (see below for sentencing schedule) in this Code whether or not the defendant has a prior felony conviction. However, a sentence under this Section shall not be imposed unless the defendant was at least 17 years of age at the time he committed the offense for which sentence is to be imposed.

(3) that the defendant is a repeat offender whose commitment for an extended term is necessary for the protection of the public. A defendant of this type shall have sentence imposed pursuant to (the sentencing schedule of) this Code. Provided, however, a sentence shall not be imposed pursuant to this Section unless:

(a) the defendant was at least 17 years of age at the time he committed the offense for which sentence is to be imposed;

(b) the defendant has been convicted of at least one other Class 1 or Class 2 felony or two or more lesser felony offenses within the 5 years immediately preceding commission of the instant offense, excluding time spent in custody for violation of the laws of any state or of the United States.

(4) that the defendant committed a felony offense that occurred under one or more of the following circumstances:

(a) the defendant, by the duties of his office or by his position, was obliged to prevent the particular offense committed or to bring the offenders committing it to justice;

(b) the defendant held public office at the time of the offense, and the offense related to the conduct of that office;

(c) the defendant utilized his professional reputation or position in the community to commit the offense, or to afford him an easier means of committing it, in circumstances where his example probably would influence the conduct of others;

(d) if the court, having due regard for the character of the offender, the nature and circumstances of the offense, and the public interest finds that a sentence of imprisonment is not the most appropriate disposition under this Code, the grounds listed in paragraphs (a) (1) and (a) (4) of this subsection shall be considered as factors in aggravation of the sentence imposed (non imprisonment).

We do not propose mitigation reductions in the enhancement schedule because it appears to us to be contrary to the purpose of extending terms at all. We are mindful that good but not persuasive, in the author's mind, arguments can be made to adopt a mitigative schedule as well.

We propose to inform the convict at the outset of what the penalties for his crime will be. We would replace the present law with a series of determinate sentences, keyed to the present felony classification system. For each felony class, a fixed sentence is proposed, with a small range in mitigation or aggravation allowed around that definite figure to permit adjustments either for the facts of a particular case or for the seriousness of the offense as compared to others in the same class. In effect, then, a relatively small range of allowable prison terms would be associated with each offense. Whenever the court found imprisonment to be the appropriate disposition, it would select a fixed sentence from within that range and impose it. When a convicted person left the courtroom he would know his actual sentence to be served less good time. A schedule of sentences could be as follows:

Type B

Offense	Flat-Time Sentence	Range in Aggravation or Mitigation	Range of Allowable Sentences
Murder A	Death or Life	—	Death or Life
Murder	Life or 25 years	± up to 5 years	Life, or any fixed term from 20 to 30 years
Class 1	8 years	± up to 2 years	Any fixed term from 6 to 10 years
Class 2	5 years	± up to 2 years	Any fixed term from 3 to 7 years
Class 3	3 years	± up to 1 year	Any fixed term from 2 to 4 years
Class 4	2 years	± up to 1 year	Any fixed term from 1 to 3 years

In addition, enhanced sentences (extended terms of imprisonment) are available for especially dangerous or repeat offenders. A schedule of enhanced sentences appears below as an illustration:

Type C

Offense	Flat-Time Sentence	Range in Aggravation or Mitigation	Range of Allowable Sentences
Class 1	15 years	+ up to 3 years	Any fixed term from 15 to 18 years
Class 2	9 years	+ up to 2 years	Any fixed term from 9 to 11 years
Class 3	6 years	+ up to 2 years	Any fixed term from 6 to 8 years
Class 4	5 years	+ up to 2 years	Any fixed term from 5 to 7 years

A necessary corollary to this new sentencing structure is the vested good time credit provision. With the setting of a flat time sentence and the abolition of parole, the possibility of this day-for-a-day reduction in time served is essential to give prisoners a sufficient incentive to behave lawfully while in prison. Short of "maxing out" executive clemency is the only "escape hatch" for those serving life (or any other) sentences.

Even assuming the relevancy of our claim that the rationalization of parole along lines of a punishment-deterrence-justice model could bring more safety, sanity and fairness to prison life some have argued; "Why mess with the system?" Some critics reason that even if the present anomie in sentencing and parole *appears* to be unjust still most prisoners average a two year plus stay, the more the appearance of unfairness is exposed the more tightening up will be legislated. This might, in their view, bring more convicts into the system and keep them longer. Therefore modernization may contain the seed of an unintended consequence which could operate against the cause of lower numbers of prisoners with relatively shorter average stays as compared to actual sentences. Hence the rationale becomes: "leave it alone, you can't really affect the onerousness of prison life anyhow and you may open up a Pandora's Box for conservative legislators which will produce draconian prison stays rather than merely long sentences." This is not unattractive. It is even a bit seductive. But not convincing on several grounds.

We find it difficult to avoid dealing with injustice in practice by simply assuming that the period of unfairness is relatively (if haphazardly) short. With the continuing expansion of nonincarcerative sentencing alternatives we approach the irreducible minimum who will not be viewed as an attractive constituency for prison modernization by legislators. Legislatures are infrequently guided in their criminal justice decision-making by knowledge. Indeed the usual process of law making, except for revisions of penal and correctional codes which occur with the frequency of one a century, is fragmented. Different constituencies in the system of criminal justice advance collision course bills which are not usually in tandem with each other. This process produces overload on one or another part of the continuum with little or no reference to the other parts. A simple example was the burgeoning undercover narcotics enforcement establishment without the necessary accompanying resources in jails, courts, clinics and prison to absorb the street addicts who were crowded into the system as a result of employing so many more police charged with the responsibility of simply arresting them.

Some academicians have argued that flat time at the level we suggest (2, 3, 5, 8 years) will never survive in a state legislature. Legislators will increase the flat rates, at least doubling the order of magnitude (4, 5, 10, 16 years). Having done several computer simulations with the proposed (2, 3, 5, 8) scheme we believe that knowledge in this case *can* guide a legislature. As a matter of fact the legislature using a flat time, no parole model can now predict, with a higher degree of confidence: inmate populations, necessary bed space, staff coverage, etc. and as a consequence future costs and building needs.

We took the Illinois Department of Corrections population projections, without a change in the sentencing and parole laws, and found that in 48 months (using a straight line projection) the inmate population would rise from the current 7,000 (rounded) to 10,000. We then took the 1971 to 1974 intake population and had the computer "give" them 2, 3, 5, 8 year sentences, as appropriate. Further we added multipliers for a bad economy and heavier intake, varying but conservative rates for the accumulation of good time and a sped up process (another component of a broad legislative program calling for a 60 day fair trial law) of moving 7,000 jail prisoners (5,000 in Cook County alone) through the system.

The "2, 3, 5, 8" scheme produced an 11,500 population for the same period of time the "no action" indeterminate scheme projected a 10,000 population. But the flat time scheme was manipulable. If we reduced the five to four we "lost" eleven hundred prisoners from the population. When we dropped the eight to seven years we lost another thousand convicts. When we adopted the 4, 8, 10, 16 scheme we tripled the population. Several other simulations, using expanded probation, periodic imprisonment, decriminalization of certain crimes yielded different populations.

We found that we could project pessimistic and optimistic worldviews depending upon the sentencing scheme adopted. Perhaps most significantly we found that it was now possible to predict with a high degree of reliability at all.

We now have the knowledge to confront the *realpolitik* of the legislative process, namely *prediction reliability* and *cost tolerance*. The flat time plan permits those interested in modernizing the system to forcefully enter the fray instead of sitting on the sidelines hoping for a semblance of sanity in the unpredictable whirlpool of current practice. We can point out to the public the intolerable costs which must be undertaken when you trade in a 2, 3, 5, 8 plan in for a 4, 6, 10, 16 plan. Legislators may have to calculate the political cost of their politicized calls for longer and longer sentences. The flat time program while delivering a plausible sentencing format may also have the broader appeal of muting the cries for retribution and vengeance when associated costs are apparent. In the author's experience with the proposal he has found that police chiefs for example are more interested in certainty and swiftness of outcome than in severity, measured in length of years.

Consistent with the neoclassic approach taken throughout this work the organization of the justice-as-fairness prison is based upon the principle of maintaining that spark we all seek for validation of manhood (and womenhood)—responsibility. The prison sentence is punishment but it is not to be vengefully executed. The conviction was based upon his volition and now it forms the basis for his treatment as a prisoner. The new prison program can offer a reasonable array of services beyond the food-clothing-medical-shelter needs. We see the need for education, recreation, conjugal visitation, work and vocational programs.

We reject the idea of building a factory first (even one which pays prevailing rates) and then a prison around it. We are aware of its success in Sweden (and of other nonexportable programs). The historical lessons of prison labor should give us pause for the concern in trying to operate a "free enterprise" system in a state prison. A few assembly type, collapsible work enterprises at prevailing rates are attractive. With such a system, when the market for the product dries up we will not be left with an obsolete prison factory coupled with legislative demands requiring servile labor to produce revenue. Other collapsible or easy "turn around" formats may be conceived. All other prison support services requiring manpower should be paid for by convict or free labor at prevailing rates. When prevailing rates are obtained the prisoner should be charged a reasonable rate for his stay, pay taxes, pay victim restitution if appropriate, have allotments sent to his family (reducing perhaps some other public stipends they may be receiving), and have the remainder held until release. The prisoner is hereby offered the dignified status of remaining head of household while doing a prison term. The convict, as a resident should only be expected to take care of his immediate household chores without pay.

Education (academic and vocational) in our new prison program is akin to labor. There is no need for a full spectrum of remedial, elementary, high school and college programs. Prisons rarely have them anyhow. Education should be offered on a contractual basis after a prisoner (or group of prisoners) has selected a program he believes necessary for his own self-improvement. Counseling should be provided to assist in selection. New programs can be simply added and old ones discarded in response to need, not for the purpose of keeping dozens of civil service academicians busy without reference to user or market needs.

All clinical programs can be dismantled as well. The spectacle of organizing inmates into therapy groups or caseloads is embarrassingly tragic. It is best described as a psychic lock-step. When the indominatability of the human spirit could not be crushed by our "break the spirit" forefathers, we relinquished the task to the technology of psychiatry. It is our belief that a conception of the prisoner as volitional and his assumption of responsibility for his behavior provide the best chemistry for good mental health. "To punish a man is to treat him as an equal. To be punished *for an offense against rules* is a sane man's right," said W.F.R. Macartney, an English exprisoner.[28]

All of this means that the prisoner has to be given opportunities to call some of the tunes. If he feels he has an emotional problem requiring professional assistance the prison should make a timely response by providing a delivery system whereby private therapists are contracted for from the free world. J.D. Mabbott (1939) believed that:

> ... it would be best if all such (clinical) arrangements were made optional for the prisoner, so as to leave him in these cases a freedom of choice which would make it clear that they are not part of his punishment. If it is said that every such reform lessens a man's punishment, I think that is simply muddled thinking which, if it were clear, would be mere brutality.[29]

The central point to be made is that *the prisoner chooses*[1] and his release is not a function of clinical progress. We wonder, in an atmosphere of real choice (in the sense of "free enterprise") how many prison clinical programs would survive if survival turned on attendance and immunity for absence.

A diagrammatic outline of a new smaller facility is found on page 152. We recommend that such units be built in or close to urban centers because: (1) most prisoners come from urban areas and thus

---

[1]A voucher credit system might put on the "books" (a computerized account) $6.00 to $8.00 for each good day. A prison is free to use the credit (even borrow in advance) either inside for education and clinical services or upon release for "reintegrative" services. Reintegration is a term popping up more and more. It appears that rehabilitators, viewing the handwriting on the wall, are making still another rhetorical leap to save their empires. After decades of hiding the U.S. Parole Board is now promising to be the most visible. This welcome turnabout, however, comes at a time when the whole question of continuing parole boards at all is in question. Correctional agencies have, like many other governmental entities, once begun then threatened, learned extraordinary life sustaining adaptive behavior.

the maintenance of family ties is facilitated; (2) professionals we wish to attract (as well as industry) for the contracting of services are also urban-oriented; and (3) the new prison staff will have more in common with prisoners when both are selected from similar populations.

As the Twentieth Century comes to an end, the prison must act on the universally accepted axiom that the human animal is basically bisexual and that deprivation of opportunities for its expression, in the best of circumstances, leads to distorted behavior. Dignified, private and extended visitation is a minimal standard in our new scheme. It is not a reward. Like medical and food services it is minimally required for those from whom we expect responsible behavior.

Type B and C custodial facilities are distinguished by degrees of security. Secure custody architectural treatment can now be accomplished mainly by perimeter security. The internal arrangements can be of the Vienna character. The National Clearinghouse of Correctional Architecture at the University of Illinois, Urbana has developed several modern and more humane formats as alternatives to the fortress prison. When a 300 person facility is subdivisible into living

Type A or B Institution   Basic Layout—Type C has greater custody features

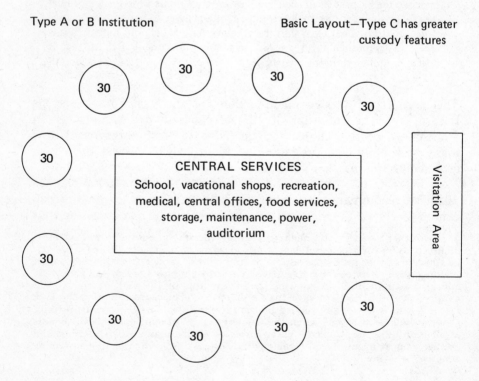

CENTRAL SERVICES
School, vacational shops, recreation, medical, central offices, food services, storage, maintenance, power, auditorium

Visitation Area

units of thirty, other advantages arise: (1) the oppressive features of large congregate living (counts, group movements, routinization, etc. . . .) are eliminated; (2) further refinements of classification (by work, education even treatment groups voluntarily devised) for residence selection are available; (3) staff can be assigned to manageable units and have their skills matched to the needs of the prisoners they supervise; and (4) finally, the guard as we have known him historically may find new roles for himself. In the last analysis it may provide a safer work environment.

We offer no single scheme for the course of transition from the fortress prison to a new environment. It will take a state-by-state struggle for each to find their particular way.[m] Some states, not yet committed to the rehabilitation approach, might leap over the next two decades by moving to a justice model now. Others, having already become disillusioned with treatment approaches but trapped into strict custody can begin a process of detente between the keeper and kept based on an agenda of fairness rather than one of increasing clinical services. And for the majority of states located somewhere in-between, it will take searing self-analysis and hard-nosed administrative decisions to redirect their efforts toward justice in prisons.

Transformation of the fortress prison will be expensive but not as expensive as building and operating new fortress prisons. There will be offsetting savings in locking fewer people up for less time (in our accompanying plan for rationalizing sentencing) and further savings are realizable by the dismantling of archaic clinical, industrial and educational programs. Our conception of the prison stay as reasonable and certain (if austere) is based upon the premise that the payoff will be an increase in the probability of safer streets.

Finally, we suggest a perspective that assumes crime and the criminal are not aberrations, that incarceration for some will be necessary, that in a democratic society the prison administrator's first priority is to accomplish it justly and that we stop seeking messianic "treatments" as a way of "changing" people. David Rothman has some timely advice along these lines:

> Such millenial goals and the true-believer syndrome they engender have helped generate and exacerbate our present plight. But pursuing a strategy of decarceration might introduce some reality and sanity in a field prone

---

[m]Richard McGee suggests a rational sentencing transition plan for California. With a history of strong commitments to county probation, California can reasonably collapse its state parole services into county operations. But there are too many variations in the U.S. to suggest (McGee does not) adoption of one transition plan for all or even many cases.

to illusion and hysteria. Americans will not escape the tradition of reform without change by continually striving to discover the perfect solution. Rather, we must learn to think in tough-minded ways about the costs, social and fiscal, of a system that has flourished for so very long on the basis of fanciful thinking. If we talk openly and honestly about what we can accomplish, if we demolish the myths of incarceration, regardless of how convenient to attractive they appear to be, if we put adequate funds and support behind the pilot programs that, when evaluated carefully, should lead us to fund large-scale measures, then we may begin to reverse a 150-year history of failure.[30]

NOTES TO CHAPTER SEVEN

1. Desmond Ellis, Harold Grasnick, and Bernard Gilman, "Violence in Prison: A Sociological Analysis," *American Journal of Sociology*, Vol. 80, No. 1, (pp. 16-43), July 1974.

2. Marvin Finkelstein, *Perspectives on Prison Legal Services: Needs, Impact and the Potential for Law School Involvement*, Summary Report (U.S. Dept. of Justice, February 1972), p. 2.

3. *Ibid.*, p. 4.

4. *Ibid.*, p. 1.

5. Jacob and Sharma, "Justice After Trial: Prisoners' Need for Legal Services in the Criminal-Correctional Process," *Kansas Law Review* 18: 493,501 (1970).

6. Comment, "Resolving Civil Problems of Correctional Inmates," 1969 *Wisconsin Law Review*, 574, 576 (1969).

7. *Legal Services and Development*, University of Minnesota (Mimeograph, 51 pages), p. 6.

8. *Op. cit.*, University of Minnesota, p. 1.

9. *Ibid.*, p. 4.

10. *Op. cit.*, "Resolving Civil Problems of Correctional Inmates," *Wisconsin Law Review*, p. 578.

11. *Op. cit.*, Dawson, 413.

12. *Ibid.*, p. 401.

13. *Op. cit.*, Davis, pp. 98-99.

14. *A Proposal to Establish an Experimental Ombudsman for the Minnesota Department of Corrections*, University of Minnesota, 1971, p. 1.

15. *Ibid.*, p. 2.

16. *Op. cit.*, Tribbles, p. 427.

17. Enrico Ferri, *Criminal Sociology*, Boston: Little, Brown, and Company, 1917, p. 514 as cited in Galaway, Burt and Hudson, Joseph, *Considering The Victim: Readings in Restitution and Victim Compensation* (forthcoming, 1974).

18. *Op. cit.*, Frankel, p. 118.

19. *Op. cit.*, Davis, p. 135.

20. *Op. cit.*, Dawson, pp. 383-84.

21. *Ibid.*, p. 398.

22. Larry I. Palmer, "A Model of Criminal Dispositions: An Alternative to Official Discretion in Sentencing," *The Georgetown Law Journal*, Vol. 62, No. 1, October 1973, p. 57.

23. *Op. cit.*, Rubin, p. 769.

24. *Op. cit.*, Palmer, p. 18.

25. *Op. cit.*, Shaw, pp. 61-62.

26. *Op. cit.*, McGee, p. 8.

27. *Ibid.*, p. 13.

28. J.D. Mabbott, "Punishment," in Olafson, Frederick A., *Justice and Social Policy*, New York: Prentice-Hall, 1961, p. 46.

29. *Ibid.*, pp. 52-53.

30. David Rothman, "Decarcerating Prisoners and Patients," (pp. 8-30) *The Civil Liberties Review*, Vol. 1, No. 1 (Fall 1973), p. 29.

Chapter Eight

Punishment and Prisons

Norval Morris

America, in its first two centuries, has done extremely well
in encouraging crime. The crime rate, particularly that for
violent crimes, stands grossly higher than in countries of
otherwise comparable culture. America *may* be the "land of the
free," but she *is* most certainly the "home of the brave." There is no
doubt about it. Our minority, ill-educated youths, lacking employment, have been gathered together in large pockets of desolation in
our inner city areas. Welfare programs have been created that
contribute powerfully to the breakdown of the families of the poor,
and which tend to criminalize their children. Government action has
fostered a drug culture that has increased crime in the city. A plague
of handguns, unchecked by governmental action, escalates the injury
flowing both from domestic conflict and from other pressures
toward crime.

A multiplicity of police forces comprised of more than 400,000
persons, have achieved low and declining rates of clearance of crime.
Prosecution and defense services, exiguous in relation to the incidence of crime, help to keep the jails and the courts of the cities
overcrowded. Continuances flourish, speedy trial is an idealistic
dream rather than a constitutional guarantee, and pressures of
expediency compel reliance on charge-and-plea bargaining. Finally,
prison, the residual punishment, the ultimate legal threat, is often
criminogenic rather than curative of crime, finding its typical
expression in cluttered fortresses of fear which impede rather than
facilitate the prisoner's self-direction away from crime.

America enters her third century with her criminal justice system

157

in considerable disarray. Her citizens have demonstrated their tolerance of high crime rates but their patience seems to be wearing thin,
and the danger in that has nothing to do with crime. The danger in
that has got to to with the delicate balance between political
authority and individual freedom which is at the pivot of the
criminal justice system. The present danger is that we will sacrifice
important freedoms in our efforts to control crime.

One of the most important elements in controlling crime, according to public opinion and that of many politicians, is a system of
imprisonment. The prison is, putting the rarity of capital punishment
aside, the ultimate legal threat to those who have committed crimes
or are considering committing crimes.[1] As such, it is viewed in the
public mind as the surest way to control crime, even though its
effectiveness has been widely challenged. In this study I wish to
make a prediction about the prison population of the future. On the
basis of that prediction I wish to offer several suggestions for devising
an effective but fair system of imprisonment and to provide a
justification for imprisonment as punishment.

It is my confident view that the prison population will continue
to increase steadily and it will increase into the mid-1980s and
nothing that we could do about it, even if we had political power,
would make much difference. Our present overcrowded, oversized,
ancient prisons will be almost certainly more crowded, more stuffed
for the next few years. Gang rape, riots, violence and terror will
increase. Attica will probably be reenacted. Drug habits continue to
be supported in virtually every big prison in this country. Big prisons
are run by the prisoners and (big secret) prisoners are not always
calm and peaceful types of people.

I have recently become a law dean and the similarity between law
schools and prisons interests me more each day. In law schools we
take an extraordinarily carefully selected lot of people of great
ability, who have demonstrated their capacity with astonishing skill
to pass examinations and scholastic aptitude tests, and we turn them
out as fine lawyers. They are so well selected that if we put them to
sea in a little boat in Lake Michigan with a library and told them to
row about and read for two and a half years, they would come back
and be fine lawyers. Prisoners are exactly the opposite of that, aren't
they? We select what turns out to be a worse and more violent
group—in behavioral terms, not moral terms—to go to prison. And we
are startled that it is hard to make much difference to them.

It is very hard to prove that the best law schools make much
difference to the average student who goes there. It is equally hard to
prove that prisons make much difference to the average prisoner who

goes there. But with increasing overcrowding, prison itself becomes more dangerous, more difficult to run.

Why are they going to be more crowded? Why more prisoners? Is it because the mood of the time changes, because people are getting more punitive? Perhaps they are, but that is not the reason. The basis is much less complicated. Males, aged 18 to 30, fill the world's prison cells except in political prisons where those who survive tend to be a little older. Women do not commit repeated crimes of violence, and men over 35 rarely commit crimes of violence unless their wives push them to it. Occasionally they get drunk in bars and use guns, but as a statistical matter, crime and prison is a young man's game. In this country the population curve for the 18 to 30 year olds is steadily rising and will peak about 1985. Put aphoristically, the baby-boom now hits the prison. As an absolute number and as a proportion of the total population, the larger wave of more prison prone males sweeps toward us. Do not think of population as a total number, the water in a tank. Think of it as waves in an ocean or in a lake. And the wave of the prison prone males swells to large degree. But that still is not the complete reason. There is an inner problem behind it. That wave of young males is particularly high among the poor, minority males who disproportionately fill our prison cells. Again, put aphoristically, the pill came late to the ghetto. I do not mean to be pejorative toward minorities here. I am simply trying to state what seems to be the reality—and not to make judgments about whether it is good or bad.

Is that all there is to it? No. I think that there are other reasons that one can predict an increase in the prison population, a substantial increase, independently of any change in punitive attitudes. If, as we should, we improve our police clearance rates, then the prison population will swell. If, as they should be, prosecution and public defense staffs are expanded, plea bargaining is made less unprincipled, continuance brought under better control, courts become more swift and even-handed in convicting and sentencing the guilty—then the growth in prison population will be even larger. Further, if mandatory minimum sentences are increasingly prescribed by federal and state legislatures, and if judges see the signals and respond, then the prison population will even further burgeon. Finally, all these predictions of an increased prison population are based on an assumption of stability of crime rates. And that is a tough assumption to make in America. If crime rates increase, then the prison increase will be even greater.

I am likely to be misread rather badly at this point. Predictions are often expressions of desires. When people say, "I think this will happen . . . " what they often mean is, "I hope it happens." I am not doing that. I think the prison population will increase, and I hate that fact. I have been visiting prisons and working in them and taking an interest in them for a long while in this country and in many countries. So I am serious in my efforts of scholarship here, in my efforts at understanding the prison. But I never get over my distaste of caging itself. If a necessity, it is a wholly undesirable necessity constantly to be justified by social need. Caging itself I find hateful. If caging is so disgusting then why can't we get rid of prisons? I can only sketch a brief reply to this rhetorical question. There are abolitionists of prisons and there are reductionists of prisons, and the three main mechanisms that both offer are the following: decriminalization, diversion, and locking up only the dangerous. I am in favor of decriminalization, of reducing the reach of the criminal law, but it does not much affect the prison. It affects the jail, not the prison. Reducing the prohibitory reach of the criminal law from what are inaccurately called "victimless crimes" does not much reduce the prison population. When you go to the typical prison, state and federal, and look at the crime records of the prisoners (even what is written down, which is less than they have done) you find few there for crimes which would be the subject of such decriminalization. The bulk of people now finding their way into the prisons of America have been convicted of serious predatory crime.

The mechanism of diversion is a plan to divert less serious offenders from the jails and the courts and the prisons, exercising less heroic powers over less serious offenders. A sound idea, but does it reduce the prison population? What happens is this: diversionary programs tend to take under control people who previously were not put under control and thus leave roughly the same number in prisons. I give you one example to suggest that somewhat unexpected result. Assume a hundred people are put in a familiar situation. Probably everyone has been stopped at some time by police for speeding or some other traffic offense. Now, assume that the policeman has a choice whether to arrest or to let you go and that he has not got power to issue a notice or summons to appear. Just an arrest power or a let-you-go power which is a not unusual situation. If we checked on a hundred such situations we would find that, in this typical flow, say 40 would be arrested and 60 would be let go. Now a law is passed saying that the police may issue a notice to appear or a summons. The idea is to divert offenders from being arrested when their crimes are not so serious or their residence is known and they are thought likely to appear. Instead of having a choice between arresting and letting go, the policeman may now arrest or issue a notice to appear or let you go. Previously it was 40-60. What will it be in the future? It will be something like 35-35-30. There will be a very slight reduction of arrests. There will be, of course, a great expansion of the middle position—the notice to appear—and there will be a reduction of the number let go. That happens with all diversion systems so far as I know. There are ways to prevent this result but they are rarely followed. So far, certainly, diversion has not reduced prison populations.

The third suggested technique of reducing the prison population is to imprison only the dangerous. The problem is that we are no good at prediction. It is not that the courts are no good at prediction, it is not that Morris is no good at prediction; nobody can do it. The only time we are even reasonably good at predicting violence is when the man has repeatedly done the same thing in the past and he is still young enough to do it tomorrow. Now those are rare situations in which, in any event, we are going to lock him up. The fact of the matter is that although it is a nice idea to lock up only the dangerous, it turns out to be beyond our capacity to achieve.

If we face the reality that crime will probably increase, and that the proposals for reducing prison populations would probably not work, then we are compelled to face the high likelihood of an increased prison population in this country. The question then becomes: What principles should guide the operation of the prisons?

The first insight, I suggest, is that we recognize that the important social values which must be maintained for the prison population of the future have little to do with the control of crime. The values involved are more important than crime control; they are values of minimum standards of freedom for every citizen, values of human rights, values of the balance between freedom and liberty. Within the ordinary sweep of prison policy, nothing that is done in prisons is going to make much difference to the crime rates of America. If every helpful program I wish to introduce were introduced, I think it would reduce crime in America somewhat. If the stupid, punitive processes, the bread and water and floggings that some people favor were introduced, I think they would increase crime in America somewhat. But both changes would be marginal. Neither humane nor brutal punishments would influence crime as much as do those serious questions of welfare, employment, race relations, housing, transportation, and education that beset this society. It is simply a vulgar error to think that prison policy and crime rates are closely interrelated. There is a long history of their independent movements. There is a long history of stability of prison populations over time in many different countries, staying constant, independent of a whole host of other social variables that move around.

The discussion of what should go on in prisons is usually cast in the form of a debate between treaters and punishers; between those who favor and those who oppose rehabilitation.

The extreme statement of the punishment position was made in 1822 by the Reverend Sidney Smith in his essay "On the Management of Prisons": "Prison should be a place of punishment from which men recoil with terror, a place of real suffering, painful to the memory, terrible to the imagination, that is, a place of sorrow and wailing which should be entered with horror, and quitted with earnest resolution never to return to such misery. With that deep impression, in short, of the evil which breaks out in perpetual warning and exhortation to others." Well, I think the Reverend Smith would be quite content with our larger prisons and jails; but I must say that those perpetual warnings and exhortations are rarely heard, or, at best, are thin on the ground. I don't think deterrence flows from the severity of conditions of imprisonment or even very much from the duration of imprisonment. I think it flows probably from the fact of imprisonment.

Now, as to rehabilitation, let me try to put my own position. The current cry is that "nothing works" and that, therefore, rehabilitation should be abandoned. This seems to be most superficial. What should be abandoned is the link between coercive efforts at rehabilitation and the duration of detention. The cage is not a sensible place in which to cure the criminal even when the medical analogy makes sense—which it rarely does. So, I want more rehabilitative programs in prison, even though rehabilitation is not a purpose of imprisonment. We need more voluntary programs. Prisoners must not be coerced into training programs by the hope that they can thus persuade a parole board of their dramatic conversions to virtue on the road to the main gate. But it is in the community's interest to provide an adequacy of relevant self-help programs.

Many of the principles which I believe should guide the operation of prisons have been incorporated into a new prison at Butner, North Carolina. Butner is intended to house 350 prisoners who have at least one to three years yet to serve. It is a voluntary prison in that prisoners can go to any other prison when they like and take their release dates with them. Butner is particularly important because 200 of its prisoners will be repetitively violent offenders, aged between 18 and 30. If Butner succeeds, its effectiveness will be much more convincingly demonstrated for having dealt with this kind of population than if it had chosen a less troublesome group. I will describe several features of Butner briefly.[2]

Intake and Release Procedures

The first four to six weeks will be a period of intense and concentrated work with the new prisoner. On arrival he will immediately be assigned to one of the small living groups of six to eight prisoners which make up an essential part of the pattern of life of the institution, and he will be integrated as fully as possible into the normal life of the institution. These early weeks are also the period when he will be most intensively interviewed by the staff of the institution. The purpose of these intensive weeks of intake procedure is to acquaint the prisoner as precisely as possible with the regimen of the institution, and in the light of all of the information about him and his crime, his psychological and sociological circumstances, and a lengthy and detailed anamnestic discussion with him, to settle with the prisoner the date of his first furlough from the institution, his first seventy-two-hour home leave, the date of his first work release from the institution (if a job can be found for him), the date of his first prerelease placement in a hostel or similar residential facility in the community (or in his own home, if he has one), and, most important, the precise date of his parole. All these tentative decisions will be recorded and the record made available to the prisoner. He must, if possible, be made to understand the basis for all these decisions.

What is in effect being developed in these early weeks is a graduated release plan. It is of fundamental importance that the prisoner's involvement in any treatment program in the institution must never be made part of the conditions of this graduated release plan. There is one exception to this. He must understand that if he stays in the institution he must remain part of the small living and discussion group to which he has been allocated. That fact will, of course, be an obvious and unavoidable issue for discussion with the prisoner by the small group in the early days of his intake procedure since on the day of his arrival he will become a part of such a group. It will be one task of the small group of prisoners and staff, as best they can, to give the new potential member of this prison community some understanding of the realities of life in that community.

The first four to six weeks should give the prisoner ample opportunity to test what resources of self-development are available to him. But the educational and vocational training, psychological self-understanding, and personality developing programs are all entirely facilitative and in no way coerced. He can be in the institution and can be guaranteed his graduated release opportunities entirely independently of participation in any program other than involvement in the small group discussions. This is the central feature of the proposed institution; it constitutes a liberation of the psychological and self-development educative and treatment opportunities from the crippling coercion that has characterized their functioning in other prison settings.

The environment within the new institution will be as free and permissive as possible; but it will in no wise be permissive of physical violence, or of other major disciplinary problems. It is an institution which aims to run overtly, as well as implicitly, by the consent of all who work in it, staff and prisoners alike.

The theme is to try to carry out the long-established belief that self-regeneration requires that the prisoner hold the key to his own prison. But that key is not his agreement to our view of a treatment program suitable to his self-development or better self-understanding. It is the simple proposition that we will gradually test his capacity to live without crime, particularly violent crime, first in the institutional setting and then more gradually by testing his fitness for a life in the community.

Staff Selection and Training

Inadequately trained and poorly motivated staff is a chronic prison problem. In maximum security prisons, staff turnover remains so high that continuities in programming become impossible. In addition, many so-called "rehabilitative" institutions evidence impregnable divisions between administrative, security, and treatment staffs that preclude creation of an environment facilitative of self-change.

It is clear that Butner will stand or fall on the quality of its staff. Does this mean that unusually highly trained and experienced staff must be selected to work in the institution? By no means. The whole institution must be seen as an innovative experiment in self-development and self-training efforts, and that means for prisoners and staff alike. A small clinical professionally trained staff of four or five will play their largest roles in the intake procedure, in negotiating the graduated release contract, in handling crises or assisting in handling crises in the institution, and in running a continuous staff training program which uses as its study material the day-to-day life of the institution. Other nonclinical professionals (lawyers and sociologists, for example) should be recruited to top administrative positions and be held responsible for coordinating a balanced treatment program. The linchpin of that program is the front-of-the-line staff member involved in the small group discussions, or working in the educational or vocational programs, or in the workshops or on the playing fields.

There is a need to redefine the role of line personnel in prison work if we are to upgrade their self-esteem and hence their morale. The Task Force on Corrections of the President's Commission spoke of a new kind of "collaborative" institution where all staff members are integrated into the primary rehabilitative tasks of the institution. Developing a truly collaborative institution will be a major challenge in the institution for the repetitively violent. The American Correctional Association's Joint Commission on Correctional Manpower and Training was wise in suggesting that determined efforts should be made to recruit members of minorities and women to this work. Ex-prisoners should also be employed.

Narrowing the racial and cultural chasm that today separates staff and prisoners would increase communication between these castes and might suggest role models for some prisoners.

Of the staff, 40 percent to 50 percent should be women and, further, minorities should be represented among the staff at all levels of seniority and training in roughly the same distribution as in the prisoner population. Given the realities of the American criminal justice system this would mean a disproportionate number of blacks and other minorities.

That the injection of women into the prison at all levels, including that of front-of-the-line-guard, will tend to reduce violence is offered as a confident proposition; it is certainly timely to test it. As a matter of observation, men behave better in the presence of women. The social skills of many male offenders in dealing with women are distorted and undeveloped. Frequent and constructive association with women as staff members of the prison will have a positive impact upon the prisoners' later social relationships. Of course, it need hardly be noted that front-line work in a maximum security prison is not the kind of work that will be attractive to a majority of women (or men, for that matter) or for which a majority will be suited. Women recruits will need to be made sensitive to the problems of sexual anxieties that are noticeable in many individuals who have been incarcerated for a long period of time. Fears of sexual inadequacy and hence of sexual readjustment upon release are substantial in prison. Not only younger women should be recruited; the work is suitable for more mature women also and mothers and other women coming back into the work force should be included. In view of the matriarchal nature of the black family and the generally idealized view of the mother in both black and Latino subcultures, minority women in the forty-plus age group should be particularly sought after.

Recent recruitment of ex-offenders and ex-prisoners into corrections in many states is a development to be emulated in the model prison. The creation of career opportunities in corrections for ex-prisoners not only affords an excellent rehabilitation technique for them but allows them to demonstrate that some prisoners do indeed "make it," in sharp contrast to the depressing presence of ex-prisoner recidivists who will be in abundant supply in this as in other prisons. The numbers of ex-prisoners on the staff need not be large; but applicants with criminal records certainly should not be rejected.

Institutional Program and Living Units

This is the heart of the matter, yet it can be treated relatively briefly. The operational structure so far suggested for this model prison for repetitively violent criminals has set it free to offer any and all treatment modalities, substantially unimpeded by the effects of coercion, hypocrisy, and condescension that have tended to corrupt other rehabilitative efforts in prisons.

The goal of Butner will be to help its inmates live without crime upon release, especially without violent crime, should they decide to try to do so. The overall program of the prison will be directed to developing a milieu conducive to that end. It will include treatment modalities—educative, vocational, clinical, and recreational—all on a voluntary basis. Only two aspects of the prison program will be obligatory. Every prisoner must participate in a small "living group" and he must fulfill his assigned stint in the daily work program.

All existing treatment programs within penal institutions that are thought worthy of emulation will be made available if funds and trained staff can be found. Some treatment modalities are suited to provision on a contract basis with those providing such treatments on the outside; to some, such as certain college courses, suitable prisoners will go out from the prison on a daily basis. Others will be intramural and provided by the prison staff. The range should be great, from literacy training to plastic surgery. And it merits repetition that this wide range of educational and treatment modalities should be introduced to the inmate as his awareness of his needs and wants increases and as he and the staff agree on the likelihood of any particular program being helpful to him. If he is illiterate, it must be entirely his decision whether he wishes to remain so or not. If he lacks a trade, he must be free to leave the prison with that lack. After all, the reason the institution is to be established is not for remedial education but because the community sees in it a means of banishing those who behave in an intolerable fashion and of fulfilling a faint hope that they might not, when they return, reengage in that behavior. That is the central reason for the assumption of power over the prisoner, and that fact must limit the coercive quality of any of our responses to him. The one exception to this principle of the substitution of the facilitation of change for an attempt to coerce cure is that certain rules which were negotiated at the time of intake remain part of the obligatory milieu of the institution, namely, his avoidance of any physical violence and his participation in a small group living experience.

If the prisoner is set free to develop his capacity to avoid violent crime in the future, this is likely to come less from the formal treatment programs than from the total milieu of the institution, and from the crucial small group discussions involving other prisoners and the staff. In these discussions, the prisoner with his fellow prisoners and staff will probe the lessons of the many ordinary human encounters which take place daily within the institution and on temporary absences from the institution.

The small living groups should consist of six to eight inmates and two to four staff members who share meals and discussions before and after the normal working day, every day, six days a week. The staff members will not be professional clinical staff but front-line staff, men or women working in the institution. The prisoner and staff group should also send representatives to a variety of committees whose work will be of importance to the life of the institution as a whole—a self-government committee, an institutional program committee, a discipline committee, committees on entertainment and recreation, and so on.

The organization of the small living groups should be directed toward an intense concern with their responsibilities to one another, with an examination of their crimes, the harm caused, and with the possibilities of a reconciliation with themselves and their victim or victim's family. Leadership of the group will be by the staff, but should be shared with the prisoners in terms of agenda and the intensity of examination of any particular prisoner's problems.

The small group experience should help the inmate establish new behavior patterns and new methods of adapting to life situations. The material for discussion at the small group meetings will encompass everything in the daily life of the institution and of the members of the group—prisoners and staff. Group work is immensely enriched by the fact that the members of each group are at different stages of their prison experience. At any one time in each such group there will be one or two recent arrivals, one or two approaching their first furlough or returning from furloughs, one or two "working out" or "studying out" from the institution, one or two beginning to face the promise and challenge of placement in a preparole hostel or of parole. The panorama of the life and progression of the institution and of each of its inmates should be captured in every small living group.

As well as academic, vocational, and recreational programs being available to the prisoner, there is need for some specialized medical, psychiatric, and psychological services. Such therapy opportunities may be individualized or offered in groups of various sizes. Larger groups for psychotherapy, say up to twenty-four participants, are more economical and there is evidence that they are as effective as smaller groups and one-to-one psychotherapy in treating many prisoners' violent behavior.

Educational, vocational training and treatment programs should normally take place after normal working hours. We are dealing with an adult group and only in special circumstances should arrangements be made for school or college work to be done as part of the ordinary work program. There are occasions when this is appropriate, calling for daily educational release to go to nearby schools or colleges, but the general pattern of life within the institution should be as similar as possible to the ordinary working life of a citizen in the community.

Whereas participation in the work program of the prison, its industries and its maintenance, is properly required of every inmate, there is a difficult problem of the quality and duration of work that should be provided. It is desirable to provide for the prisoner as near as ordinary vocational and industrial opportunities as exist outside; on the other hand, to do so will be to make this prison very different from most other prisons which face intractable problems in prison labor. Outmoded machinery, a lack of available industries, pervading idleness, make-work, maintenance in lieu of work, a pittance instead of a wage, all plague most American prisons.

A program of useful work should be established at the prison, not as a treatment program, but simply because this is regarded in our society as a substantial part of the life of the ordinary adult. There is no good reason that inmates should be exempted from this responsibility. By the same token, inmates in the work program should be compensated at a rate competitive with that paid for similar work on the outside and should return part of their salary for room and board. Those permitted educational leave in lieu of daytime work should be similarly compensated.

The general design, then, is that treatment of repetitively violent prisoners take place in a humane and secure setting, in which the prisoner has knowledge of his release date and of a graduated release program. Therapies are deployed as prisoner and staff work together to develop a voluntary treatment plan for each prisoner. The setting and participation in it offer the prisoner a relatively stable environment in which he is less fearful and therefore can use energies to examine his own fears, impulses, and crimes in a way which gives him a sense of control over himself and his behavior and in which he can develop confidence in his relationships within a small group, his social roles, and his work. He experiences increments of freedom and of responsibility which test his capacity to tolerate stress and help him to react without violence to troublesome environmental pressures and personal stimuli which previously precipitated his criminal violence.

Having described the kinds of practices which I think should be carried out in prisons, I will now state what I see to be the rationale for sending someone to prison, and, more broadly the principles governing punishment within which we would choose imprisonment as a form of punishment. We must avoid hypocrisy. We must recognize that the rationale for imprisonment is not rehabilitation.

We send men to prison for three reasons: first, as punishment for what they've done. Take the typical homicide, the typical spouse killer. He has solved his problem. He is cured. He will not kill again. But he will be imprisoned nevertheless to reinforce fundamental social values. In the view of all, a lesser punishment would grossly understate his punitive deserts.

The second reason we imprison is to deter others, and sometimes to deter the prisoner. The fact that punishment can be used as a deterrent is illustrated by the fact that we are led to pay our taxes partly due to the thought of punishment. We have a very effective, self-declared income tax system backed up by criminal sanctions, operating under deterrent processes, operating extraordinarily well compared with that of other countries, parsimonious in its use of imprisonment. Let me give you the figures: Over 80,000,000 tax returns were filed last year, but there were only a few over a thousand federal tax prosecutions, and less than 500 persons were sent to prison or jail on any sentence. That is an astonishingly cautious and discriminating use of the prison deterrent—and it is very effective. But there are many other areas where deterrent sanctions are used. Admittedly, the punishment of the prisoner is used to deter others.

But what he has done also falls within our collective view as deserving punishment. A just deterrence is thus the second reason we send people to prison.

And the third reason is very interesting: We imprison people because we don't know what else to do with them. We have tried other things and here the convicted criminal stands yet again before the bar of justice. Within the realities of the world and the political structure of our society, we don't know what to do other than to imprison him. And so we resort to the temporary banishment that is prison. At least he grows older, at least he is out of the way for a while. That is the third reason.

I submit that those three are the only three reasons why we ought to cage men. We should cage them only for what they have done. It is a cruel injustice to imprison men for what they are in order to attempt to change them or to cure them. There is a sharp difference between the purposes of imprisonment and opportunities for training and assistance and self-development that may probably be pursued within those purposes.

I want to make another point on the same theme of rehabilitation and punishment. Is the reason that I want to reject coercive rehabilitative purposes in prison because they don't work? Certainly not. People are not unchangeable. They can certainly be changed. I don't mean to be sacrilegious about the matter, but so far as I know, capital punishment is a complete cure of crime. Capital punishment cures criminals, of course it does. So if curing crime is your business, that would be one way. Let me offer another clear cure, this one actually suggested by some astonishing people who know how to cure violent recidivism. Lock up everyone convicted of a crime of violence to the person until he is over forty years old. I tell you as a matter of fact that you will have virtually no violent recidivism. The size of the reduction of violent crime generally by this means nobody knows, but I think James Q. Wilson and Marvin Wolfgang are probably right and that it would be quite a substantial reduction. But consider their age upon entry. Consider their color. Consider their number. And ask, "Do you want to build another Gulag Archipelago?" I hope we don't. But we could do it. We could have built concentration camps. But they would, I suggest, be punishment in excess of desert and a gross abuse of the power of the state. So what I am asserting is, I think, quite an important point. I think you should reject the model of coercive curing of criminals not on the ground that we lack power to change criminals, but on the more important ground that we lack power to change criminals within a proper regard for certain centrally important values of human rights, human dignity and human freedom. It is the relationship between individual freedom and state authority that should lead you to reject such concepts.

So I come to the conclusion that criminals should be locked up for only three reasons. Let me state my position with a little more formality. It consists of two principles governing *punishment*, and three conditions governing *imprisonment*.

First, there is a principle of parsimony in punishment which requires the application of the least restrictive or punitive sanctions necessary to achieve social purposes.

The second proposition is: no sanction should be imposed which is greater than that which was deserved by the last crime or series of crimes for which the offender is being sentenced.

Within these two principles, and recognizing our incapacity to predict dangerousness, only those who meet one or more of the following three conditions should go to prison: (1) that any lesser punishment would depreciate the seriousness of the crime committed; (2) that imprisonment of some who have done what this person did is necessary to achieve socially justified deterrent purposes; (3) or other less restrictive sanctions have been frequently applied and failed.

Given the increasing prison population that we face in the near future, we can only hope that prisons will be created that are not a disgrace to our minimum standards of decency. Furthermore, however paradoxical it might seem, criminals will be handled more decently and more effectively if officials recognize that the aim is to punish and not to help. Punishment, not rehabilitation, is the business of the sentencing judge. The purposes of the criminal law are really quite easy to state, though extraordinarily difficult to achieve. The criminal law should use justice and mercy to parsimoniously punish those whose punishment is both deserved by their conduct and necessary for the common good. When the functionaries of the criminal law seek to extend their reach beyond those purposes, they imperil fundamental values on which this country was built—not the exuberant language of the Declaration of Independence but the really great and lasting values of the Constitution and the Bill of Rights.

NOTES TO CHAPTER EIGHT

1. Prisons are to be distinguished from jails, half-way houses, detention farms and other units of incarceration.

2. The following description is excerpted, with modifications, from my book, *The Future of Imprisonment*. Chicago: The University of Chicago Press, 1974.

※   *Chapter Nine*

Some Problems with Theories of Punishment

Richard Wasserstrom

Punishment, whatever else may be said of it, involves the intentional infliction of unpleasantness or pain upon human beings by other human beings. For this reason most persons believe, and I think correctly, that punishment is a problem that must be confronted by all human beings concerned to be moral. It is a problem in the sense that the pain it intentionally imposes requires justification in order for us to regard punishment as morally acceptable.

In this study I consider what I take to be the three main philosophical approaches, or responses, to the problem of punishment. The first approach advocates the abolition of punishment as a distinctive mode of action and the replacement in its stead of something variously called a system of treatment, reform, or rehabilitation. According to this view, the problem of punishment is solved by seeing that something other than punishment is what is justifiable. The second approach thinks that a system of punishment is justifiable, and wholly so on utilitarian, or consequentialist grounds. The pain inflicted is justifiable because of the greater amount of pain that would be present in its absence. The third approach agrees with the second in its insistence that a system of punishment is justifiable, but it insists that backward-looking, or retributivist considerations constitute the essential justification of punishment. I see things that are attractive and convincing in each of these three approaches, but I also see objections to which I am unable to discover wholly satisfying responses.

Many recent philosophical discussions of punishment, especially those that are either utilitarian or retributive, in an attempt to bring order and understanding to these competing solutions to the problem of punishment, proceed in the following way. First, they see the need to distinguish punishment from treatment, as well as from other things with which punishment might be confused. To do this they often begin by offering a description, if not an analysis, of the features of the standard case of punishment. In this way they make it possible both to identify what punishment is and to distinguish cases of punishment from all of those other cases in which an unpleasantness is imposed by some person upon another person, and which are not cases of punishment. And second, many of those that are utilitarian, offer what they take to be a way out of the apparent conflict between retributive and utilitarian theories. The reconciliation, they claim, is attainable once it is realized that there are two different questions, or issues, that may be being addressed. One question is concerned with whether a particular case of punishment is justifiable. The other question is concerned with whether the practice or institution of punishment is itself justifiable. Retributivism, it is claimed, is most plausibly construed as dealing with the former question; utilitarian justifications of punishment, it is claimed, are most plausibly construed as dealing with the latter question. Neither of these philosophical moves seems to me to be unproblematic. I see problems internal to each of these proposals, and neither seems to me to solve the problem of finding a wholly satisfactory theory that adequately describes and justifies punishment.

I begin with the accounts of what punishment is. Then I consider the case for replacing punishment with rehabilitation. Next, I consider the utilitarian justifications for punishment. And, finally, I examine the retributivist position. In each case I try in particular to bring out what is troublesome about the theory under consideration.

I

In his "Prolegomenon to the Principles of Punishment,"[1] H.L.A. Hart provides a characterization of punishment in which he acknowledges the similarity of his account to those provided by philosophers such as Baier, Flew, and Benn.

> So with Mr. Benn and Professor Flew I shall define the standard or central case of 'punishment' in terms of five elements:

(i) It must involve pain or other consequences normally considered unpleasant.

(ii) It must be for an offence against legal rules.

(iii) It must be of an actual or supposed offender for his offence.

(iv) It must be intentionally administered by human beings other than the offender.

(v) It must be imposed and administered by an authority constituted by a legal system against which the offence is committed.[2]

Hart then relegates to the position of "substandard" or "secondary" cases those which involve:

(a) Punishments for breaches of legal rules imposed or administered otherwise than by officials (decentralized sanctions).

(b) Punishments for breaches of nonlegal rules or orders (punishments in a family or school).

(c) Vicarious or collective punishment of some members of a social group for actions done by others without the former's authorization, encouragement, control, or permission.

(d) Punishment of persons (otherwise than under (c)) who neither are in fact nor supposed to be offenders.[3]

It is, I think, useful, if not essential, to give a characterization of punishment, and to do so in terms of the standard case of punishment. However, there are several things that are either puzzling or inadequate about an account such as the above. And the first thing that is puzzling is the decision to mark off the standard case from the substandard case in this way. For I see no reason to believe that the case of legal punishment is any more the paradigm of punishment than is, for example, the case of parental punishment. There are, of course, nonstandard cases, and they are worth distinguishing. They are of at least two sorts. On the one hand, there are those which are only metaphorically describable as punishment—as, for instance, when we talk of one team punishing another. On the other hand, there are those which are less clear cases of punishment because they lack one or more of the features of the standard or typical case of punishment—as, for instance, when persons who know that another is innocent inflict an unpleasantness on the innocent person in order to get others to believe that the guilty person has been apprehended and is being punished.[4] But cases such as these to one side, I see no reason to focus upon the law rather than the school, the family, or a voluntary association as the standard or central setting for punishment. This suggests, perhaps, that the standard case does suppose the existence of a set or network of institutional arrangements (so that all cases of one friend punishing another friend are nonstandard cases), but that seems to me to be the right feature to focus upon; not the existence of a legal system. Throughout much of the discussion that follows, nothing of great importance will turn on this point. However, at times, the idea of punishment within the law seems to me to obscure rather than illuminate what is centrally at issue.

Part of what I mean by this can be seen from an examination of the second thing that troubles me about these typical definitions of the standard case of punishment. It is that they seem to be circular, and in a way that is serious because the circularity is so abrupt. The circularity occurs in part because the idea of legal punishment invites the use of the concept of an offense, which concept is utilized to some degree in (ii), (iii), (iv), and (v).

The problem of circularity can be presented in the following way. There are many things that a legal system does or authorizes that may be done to persons that involve pain or other consequences normally considered unpleasant. Among those that any characterization of punishment would want to be able to distinguish (as not cases of punishment at all) are: being drafted into the army, being quarantined if one has an infectious disease, being required to pay damages to the person injured by your negligence, being involuntarily committed to an institution because one is insane, being required to pay damages to the person injured by your breach of contract, and being deported as an alien present within the country without permission. Obviously, it is the notion of an offense in these characterizations of punishment which carries the primary burden of differentiating punishment from these other unpleasantnesses.

But what is an offense? Well, we might say, it is a crime. But what is a crime? The most ready and familiar response is that a crime is a legal violation that the law deals with via punishment rather than other possible modes of response. The circularity is so immediate that this way of proceeding is obviously unsatisfactory. We cannot give meaning to the standard case of punishment through introduction of the concept of an offense, and also have it be the case that an offense can be understood only through the concept of a crime, which concept itself can be understood only through the invocation of the concept of punishment.

There are two possible ways out. On the one hand, we can try to give a definition or a characterization of the idea of crime which does not involve the concept of punishment. And, on the other hand, we can try to give meaning to the concept of an offense in a way that does not involve the concept of crime.

Consider the latter possibility first. Suppose we were to characterize an offense not as a crime but rather as a violation of the law. Here we would have a noncircular account of punishment which depended only on understanding the idea of a violation of the law. But is that idea sufficiently clear, or sufficiently strong to do the job required of it? What constitutes a violation of the law? Is it a violation of the law to breach one's legal obligation, e.g., by intentionally breaching a contract? Is it a violation of the law to operate one's car negligently thereby injuring someone? Is it a violation of the law to be in the country without a permit? If the answer to any of these questions is yes, then "violation" cannot be substituted for "offense" because even though paying damages for breach of contract is an unpleasantness, it is not a punishment; nor is paying damages for negligence a punishment; nor is deportation (at least obviously). If the answer is that these things are not violations of the law, the question is why not. And the response will probably be that these things are not violations because they do not involve the punishment of persons for these kinds of behaviors. But this response is, of course, circular because it, too, uses the idea of punishment to explain the idea of a violation.

As I have indicated, the other approach is to treat "crime" and "offense" as roughly synonymous and to attempt to give a characterization of the idea of crime that does not so directly or exclusively depend on the idea of punishment. The most plausible candidate to me seems to be that of wrongdoing. But even here there will clearly be problems. What is to be said in favor of building the idea of wrongdoing directly into the account of punishment or indirectly into it through the concept of criminality is that it seems to belong there. That is to say, any cases that we would identify as the core cases of criminality do involve behavior that is seriously wrong. Typically, it is behavior that, viewed just as conduct, is seriously harmful or dangerous. Typically, too, it is behavior that, viewed in terms of the actor's culpability, was seriously culpable, i.e., it involved either the intentional or knowing infliction of injury on another. The core idea of criminality does, I think, necessarily involve this idea of moral wrongdoing—coupled, I believe, with the added idea that it is wrongdoing of the sort that is appropriately publicly condemned or denounced. And it seems to me to be both less circular and more illuminating to construct an account of punishment which utilizes this idea of criminality (or just serious, denounceable wrongdoing in the nonlegal context) instead of one which takes the undefined notion of an offense as central.[5]

But, as I have said, even this approach is not without its difficulties. And the most serious one, I think, is that many activities

can be and are crimes even though they do not involve wrongdoing—
or to put what I take to be a similar point somewhat differently—
even though they do not involve something that we can properly call
seriously blameworthy behavior on the part of the actor. Thus, in
our own society, it is a crime, for example, to possess various
weapons, to use drugs of various sorts, and to engage in various
consensual sexual behaviors. The point is not that there is disagreement over whether these things are morally wrong, over whether the
lawmakers all believe (although perhaps mistakenly) that they are
morally wrong and, hence, over whether they should be criminal.
Rather, the point is that it is both conceptually and empirically
possible to have behavior that is clearly and unmistakably understood and recognized as criminal, and that is thought by no one to be
"intrinsically" immoral. What is more, it seems plausible to assert
that even in an ideal society, some behavior would properly be
criminal, and hence punishable, although no one thought that it was
immoral.

Now, one way to deal with this problem is to keep this feature of
wrongness as a kind of necessary condition for crime, but to make
the wrongdoing, what might be termed, "second order" rather than
"primary" wrongdoing. On this view what would be a necessary
characteristic of any crime would be the fact either that the behavior
itself was wrong, or that the behavior was wrong in virtue of its being
an intentional (or otherwise culpable) violation of a law. While this
may help to account for how it is that some nonintrinsically
wrongful behavior is *properly* punished, the problem is, of course,
that it reintroduces the circularity, previously discussed, latent in the
idea of a violation of the law.[6]

I do not think that the definitional problems are wholly solvable.
The best that can be said, I believe, is that the core cases of
criminality do involve the idea of serious, culpable wrongdoing. But
there are things that are unmistakably illegal—that are clear and not
borderline cases of crime—and yet are not seriously, culpably wrong;
nor would they be even at most prima facie wrong or culpable were
it not for the contingent fact that they happened to be crimes in a
particular legal system. The characterization that I provide below is, I
believe, an improvement, but I do not take it to constitute a wholly
satisfactory, noncircular elucidation or definition of the standard
case of punishment by and in the law.

What I propose is that for the purpose of distinguishing between
some of the clearest cases of punishment and some of the clearest
cases of, what might be termed, unpleasant coerced treatments (and
one must do this if we are to assess the view that wrongdoers ought

always to be treated rather than punished), the following constitutes a relatively helpful elucidation of many of the key features.

I think that we would be punishing someone if:

1. We believed that he or she had done some action; and
2. We believed that he or she was responsible at the time he or she acted; and
3. We believed that his or her action was blameworthy; and
4. We publicly inflicted some unpleasantness upon him or her; and
5. We publicly inflicted that unpleasantness upon him or her in virtue of the fact that he or she did the action in question, that he or she was responsible when he or she acted, and that he or she was blameworthy for having so acted; and furthermore
6. We determined—within at least some limits—at the time of our decision to punish what the nature and magnitude of the unpleasantness would be; and, finally,
7. In making the determination we would regard any of the following factors as relevant—although none need be decisive:
   a. The immorality of the actor and his or her action,
   b. The way in which others similarly situated were dealt with,
   c. The probable effect of the punishment upon the actor's future conduct,
   d. The probable effect upon others of punishing the actor.

As for treatment, we would be treating someone if:

1. We believed that he or she was in a certain state or condition, and
2. We acted in a certain way toward or upon him or her, and
3. We acted in this way in virtue of the fact that acting in this way would alter his or her condition in a manner beneficial to him or her, and
4. The decision as to what constituted appropriate treatment was always subject to revision upon a showing either:
   a. That an alternative response would be more beneficial to him or her, or
   b. That his or her condition has altered so as no longer to require that, or any other, further response.

If I am right in thinking that these are among the significant and distinguishing characteristics of punishment and treatment as we know them, then several things become noteworthy. First, alleged assessments of responsibility and blameworthiness are simply irrelevant to what is involved in treating someone; whereas they are constitutive of an act of punishment. Secondly, punishment must have an aspect of publicity to it, whereas treatment need not. Thirdly, it would not make sense to treat someone for something which had happened to him or her but with which he or she was no longer afflicted or by which he or she was no longer affected. The question of the appropriateness of any particular treatment can be answered by referring to the state or condition of the person only at the time the question is asked. Such is not the case with punishment. And fourth, there are many things which we do to people, which may in addition involve unpleasantnesses wholly comparable to those of severe punishments or radical treatments, but which are, nevertheless, neither instances of punishment nor treatment. Confining someone who is a carrier, but not a sufferer, of an infectious disease is one example; drafting someone into the army is another.

II

There is a widespread view, held most prominently by persons in psychiatry and some of the other helping professions, as well as by some within the law, that we ought never punish persons who break the law and that we ought instead to do something much more like what we do when we treat someone who has a disease. According to this view, what we ought to do to all such persons is do our best to bring it about that they can and will function in a satisfactory way within society. The functional equivalent to the treatment of a disease is the rehabilitation of an offender, and it is a rehabilitative system, not a punishment system, that we ought to have in anything that might deserve to be called a decent society.

Karl Menninger has put the proposal this way:

> If we were to follow scientific methods, the convicted offender would be detained indefinitely pending a decision as to whether and how to reintroduce him successfully into society. All the skill and knowledge of modern behavior science would be used to examine his personality assets, his liabilities and potentialities, the environment from which he came, its effects upon him, and his effects upon it.
>
> Having arrived at some diagnostic grasp of the offender's personality, those in charge can decide whether there is a chance that he can be redirected into a mutually satisfactory adaptation to the world. If so, the most suitable techniques in education, industrial training, group administration, and psychotherapy should be selectively applied. All this may be

best done extramurally or intramurally. It may require maximum 'security' or only minimum 'security.' If, in due time, perceptible change occurs, the process should be expedited by finding a suitable spot in society and industry for him, and getting him out of prison control and into civil status (with parole control) as quickly as possible.[7]

It is important to see that there are two very different arguments which have been, or which might be made in support of the claim that the functional equivalent of a treatment system is desirable, and ought in fact always be preferred to a system of punishment.

The two different arguments are these:

1. Punishment is only justified if the offender was responsible. No offenders are responsible; therefore no offenders are ever justifiably punished.
2. Punishment is only justified if the offender was responsible. However, the consequences of punishing even the responsible are sufficiently undesirable so that better consequences would flow if we always treated and never punished offenders.

A good deal of the confusion present in discussions—particularly nonphilosophical discussion of the evils of punishment, and the virtues of treatment—results from a failure to get clear about these two arguments and to keep the two separate. The first is superficially the most attractive and ultimately the less plausible. The reason why it is implausible is simply this: The first premise makes good sense. It is wrong to punish a person if he or she was not responsible at the time he or she acted. This is so primarily because if an individual was not responsible then the individual is not blameworthy. And if an individual was not blameworthy, then it is wrong to punish the individual, i.e., thereby publicly accusing him or her of wrongdoing.

The problem is with the second premise. There is just no reason to suppose that none of the persons who commit crimes is responsible. Of course, some of those who commit crimes are insane, are subject to irresistible impulses, or can otherwise be shown to have been nonresponsible at the time they acted. But not all criminals fall into any of these classes. So, as to them, if there is an argument against their punishment, it must lie elsewhere.[8]

The second of the two arguments identified above is the most likely candidate. In general form the second argument is this: The legal system ought to abandon its attempts to assess responsibility and punish offenders and it ought instead to focus solely on the question of how most appropriately the legal system can deal with, i.e., rehabilitate if possible, the person presently before the court—not, however, because everyone is sick, but because no good comes from punishing even those who are responsible.

One such proponent of this view is Lady Barbara Wootton.[9] Her position is an ostensibly simple one. She has called for the "elimination" of responsibility. The state of mind, or *mens rea*, of the actor at the time he or she committed the act in question is no longer to be determinative—in the way it now is—of how he or she shall be dealt with by society. Rather, she asserts, when someone has been accused of violating the law we ought to have a social mechanism that will ask and answer two distinct questions: Did the accused in fact do the act in question? If he or she did, given all that we know about this person (including his or her mental state), what is the appropriate form of social response to him or her?

Lady Wootton wants a system of social control that is thoroughly forward-looking, or, we might say, rehabilitative in perspective. With the elimination of responsibility comes the elimination of the need by the legal system to distinguish any longer between wickedness and disease. And with the eradication of this distinction comes the substitution of a forward-looking, preventive system for a backward-looking, punitive system of criminal law.

The mental state or condition of the offender will continue to be important but in a different way. "Such conditions . . . become relevant, not to the question of determining the measure of culpability but to the choice of the treatment most likely to be effective in discouraging him from offending again. . . ."[10] What is at issue, though, is the fact that

> . . . one of the most important consequences must be to obscure the present rigid distinction between the penal and the medical institution. . . . For purposes of convenience offenders for whom medical treatment is indicated will doubtless tend to be allocated to one building, and those for whom medicine has nothing to offer to another; but *the formal distinction between prison and hospital will become blurred, and, one may reasonably expect, eventually obliterated altogether. Both will be simply 'places of safety' in which offenders receive the treatment which experience suggests is most likely to evoke the desired response.*[11]

Two quite different kinds of arguments can be offered in support of this general call for the elimination of responsibility and punishment. There are first a couple of practical arguments and second, there is a more fundamental, theoretical argument. I will discuss each in turn.[12]

To begin with, by making irrelevant the question of whether the actor was responsible when he acted, we can simplify greatly the operation of the criminal law. More specifically, by "eliminating" the issue of responsibility we thereby necessarily eliminate the requirement that the law continue to attempt to make those terribly difficult judgments of legal responsibility which any definite system of punishment requires to be made. And, as a practical matter, at least, this is no small consideration. For surely there is no area in which the techniques of legal adjudication have functioned less satisfactorily than in that of determining the actor's legal responsibility as of the time he violated the law. The attempts to formulate and articulate satisfactory and meaningful criteria of responsibility; the struggles to develop and then isolate specialists who can meaningfully and impartially relate these criteria to the relevant medical concepts and evidence; and the difficulties encountered in requiring the traditional legal fact finding mechanism—the jury—ultimately to resolve these issues—all of these bear impressive witness for the case for ceasing to make the effort.

In addition, I think it fair to say that most people do not like to punish others. They may, indeed, have no objection to the punishment of others; but the actual task of inflicting and overseeing the infliction of an organized set of punishments is, I am sure, distasteful to most. It is all too easy, therefore, and all too typical, for society to entrust the administration of punishments to those who, if they do not actually enjoy it, at least do not find it unpleasant. Just as there is no necessary reason for punishments ever to be needlessly severe, so there is no necessary reason for those who are charged with the duty of punishing to be brutal or unkind. Nonetheless, it is simply a fact that it is difficult, if not impossible, to attract sensitive, kindly or compassionate persons to assume this charge. No such analogous problem appears to attend the call for treatment.

These are both serious and real practical objections to punishment. There is, as I have said, also a more sweeping theoretical objection. It is this. Even if a person was responsible when he acted and blameworthy for having so acted, we still ought to behave toward him or her in roughly the same way that we behave toward someone who is sick—we ought, in other words, to do something very much like treating him or her. Surely this makes more sense than punishment. The fact that he or she was responsible is just not very relevant. It is wrong of course to punish people who are sick; but even with those who are well, the more humane and civilized approach is one that concerns itself solely with the question of how best to effect the most rapid and complete rehabilitation of the offender. Thus, as I have said, the argument is not that no one is responsible or blameworthy; instead, it is that these descriptions are simply irrelevant to what, on moral grounds, ought to be the only singificant considerations, namely, what mode of behavior toward the offender is most apt to maximize the likelihood that he or she will not in the future commit those obnoxious or dangerous acts that are proscribed by the law. The only goal ought to be rehabilitation (in this extended sense of "rehabilitation"), the only issue how to bring about the rehabilitation of the offender.

The moral good sense of this approach can be perceived, so the argument goes on, most clearly when we contrast this forward-looking, rehabilitative point of view, with any conception of punishment. For if there is one thing which serves to differentiate any form of punishment from that of treatment, it is that punishment necessarily permits the possibility and even the desirability that punishment will be imposed upon an offender even though he or she is fully "cured"—even though there is no significant likelihood that he or she will behave improperly in the future. And, in every such case in which a person is punished—in every case in which the infliction of the punishment will help the offender not at all (and may in fact harm him or her immeasurably)—the act of punishment is, on moral grounds, seriously offensive. Even if it were true that some of the people who commit crimes are responsible and blameworthy, and even if it were the case that we had meaningful techniques at our disposal for distinguishing those who are responsible from those who are not—still, every time we inflict a punishment on someone who will not be benefited by it, we commit a seriously immoral act. This claim, or something like it, lies, I think, at the base of the case which can be made against the punishment of the guilty. For it is true that any system of social punishment must permit, and probably must require, that some people be made to suffer even though the suffering will help the sufferer not at all. It is this which the analogue to a system of treatment, a rehabilitative system such as Lady Wootton's, expressly prevents, and it is in virtue of this that such a system is clearly preferable.

There are, I think, both practical and theoretical objections to a proposal such as this. The practical objections concern, first, the possibility that certain "effective" treatments may themselves be morally objectionable, and, second, the possibility that this way of viewing offenders may create a world in which we all become indifferent to the characteristics that distinguish those who are responsible from those who are not. The ease, for example, with which someone like Menninger tends to see the criminal not as an adult but as a "grown-up child"[13] says something about the ease with which a kind of paternalistic manipulativeness could readily pervade this system of "places of safety."

These are, though, contingent rather than necessary worries. A system organized in accordance with the rehabilitative ideal could have a view that certain therapies were impermissible on moral grounds, just as it could also treat all of the persons involved with all of the respect they deserved as persons. Indeed, it is important when comparing and contrasting rehabilitative systems with punishment systems to make certain that the comparisons are of comparables. There are abuses present in most if not all institutional therapy systems in existence today, but there are also abuses present in most if not all institutional penal systems in existence today. And the practical likelihood of the different abuses is certainly worth taking seriously in trying to evaluate the alternatives. What is not wholly appropriate, however, is to contrast either an ideal therapy system with an existing penal one, or an ideal (or just) penal system with an existing therapy one.[14]

III

One of the chief theoretical objections to a proposal such as Barbara Wootton's is that it ignores the whole question of general deterrence. Were we to have a system such as that envisioned by Lady Wootton or Menninger, we would ask one and only one question of each person who violated the law: What is the best, most efficacious thing to do to this individual to diminish substantially the likelihood that he or she will misbehave in this, or similar fashion, again? If there is nothing at all that need be done in order for us to be quite confident that he or she will not misbehave again (perhaps because the person is extremely contrite, or because we are convinced it was an impulsive, unlikely-to-be-repeated act), then the logic of this system requires that the individual be released back into society forthwith. For in this system it is the future conduct of the actor, and it alone, that is the only relevant consideration. There is simply no room within this way of thinking to take into account the goal of general deterrence. H.L.A. Hart has put the case this way in explaining why the *reform* (if any is called for) of the prisoner cannot be the general justifying aim of a system of punishment.

> The objection to assigning to Reform this place in punishment is not merely that punishment entails suffering and Reform does not; but that

> Reform is essentially a remedial step for which *ex hypothesi* there is an opportunity only at the point where the criminal law has failed in its primary task of securing society from the evil which breach of the law involves. Society is divisible at any moment into two classes, (i) those who have actually broken a given law and (ii) those who have not yet broken it but may. *To take Reform as the dominant objective would be to forego the hope of influencing the second—and in relation to the more serious offences—numerically much greater class. We should thus subordinate the prevention of first offenses to the prevention of recidivism.*[15]

A system of punishment is, in short, justified on this view just because the announcement of penalties and their infliction upon those who break the laws induces the rest of us to obey the laws. The question why punish anyone at all *is* answered by Hart. We punish because we thereby deter potential offenders from becoming actual offenders. For Hart, the case for punishment as a general social practice or institution, rests on the prevention of crime; it is not to be found either in the inherent appropriateness of punishing wrong-doing or in the contingently "corrective" or rehabilitative powers of fines or imprisonments on some criminals.

This approach to punishment has several implications, some of which are not always as thoroughly acknowledged as they ought to be. In the first place, a view such as Hart's is less a justification of punishment than a justification of a threat of punishment. For it is clear that if we could somehow convince the rest of society that we were in fact punishing offenders we would accomplish all that the deterrent theory would have us achieve through our somewhat more visible punishments. This is so because it is the belief that punishment will follow the commission of an offense that deters potential offenders. The actual punishment of persons is necessary only to keep the threat of punishment credible. Punishment is, therefore, to be conceived of as a necessary evil rather than a positive good, a means to an end, rather than an end in itself. It follows that punishment is something that society ought always seek to minimize if not eradicate. It follows, too, that our attitude toward punishment be one of reluctance, if not regret. It may be right to punish, but only on balance, and never for its own sake.

More significantly, moreover, despite appearances, the utilitarian appeal to general deterrence is more a supplement than an opponent to the rehabilitative ideal. For the case for punishment of the kind put forward by Hart is an essentially instrumental one. Deterrence just as much as rehabilitation views punishment as a system of *social control*. It is a way of inducing those who can control their behavior to regulate it in such a way that they conform to the dictates of the law. Its disagreement with rehabilitation is only over the question of whose behavioral modification justifies the imposition of unpleasantnesses upon the criminals. Deterrence says it is the modification of the behavior of the noncriminals that matters; rehabilitation says it is the modification of the behavior of the criminals that is decisive.

IV

One thing that seems to be wrong with both of these is that they are merely undifferentiated systems of social control. As such, some have argued, they fail to capture either the essence or the moral point of any system that is in fact a system of punishment. What is missing is the idea of retribution; the idea that punishment is in some fundamental sense backward-looking; that it is an unpleasantness that is only properly imposed in the way that it is because it is deserved; it is an unpleasantness that has been preceded by culpable wrongdoing and is publicly responsive to it.[16] Most philosophical discussions of punishment do take up the claim of retributivism, but with various degrees of seriousness. Many discussions take it up only summarily to dismiss it.[17] Others take it up in order to show that it is assimilable into a utilitarian account. The problem, as I see it, is to sort out the different claims and issues that are involved and to see what is to be said for and against each.

To begin with, let us acknowledge that much that passes in the name of retributive theory is unintelligible, and some of it may be vicious. So when I talk about retributivism I am not, therefore, talking about what may be a kind of unreflective call for revenge upon people who hurt other people. Nor am I talking about that manifestly utilitarian argument that justifies punishment as a means to keep the lid on—people, so this argument goes, demand that the guilty be punished, and unless we do it in an orderly way, it will simply get done anyway in a disorderly, socially disruptive manner.

The easiest way to defend retributivism, of course, is to construe it merely as a theory that is worth considering because of the importance that it places on the concept of a person. It can be understood in this light as a point of view which seeks to limit, for instance, things that can be done to human beings by other human beings—say, in the guise of treatment. In other words, it can in its most modest form be construed as establishing *necessary* conditions for the infliction of unpleasantnesses. As such, it is easily assimilated into the antitherapy critiques mentioned earlier, just as it is readily assimilable into rehabilitative and deterrent theories.[18]

Another way to defend retributivism is, as I have said, to adopt the position of Rawls, Hart, and Benn who argue that utilitarian and retributivist theories are not in conflict because they are asking two different questions. Thus Benn puts the case this way. Utilitarianism, he says, has

> ... the merit, as an approach to the justification of punishment, that it provides a clear procedure for determining whether the institution is acceptable in general terms. This the retributivist approach cannot do because it denies the relevance of weighing advantages and disadvantages, which is what we ultimately must do in moral criticism of rules and institutions. Consequently, a retributivist justification of punishment as an institution usually turns out to be denial of the necessity for justification, a veiled reference to the beneficial results of punishment (a utilitarianism in disguise), or an appeal to religious authority.
>
> When it is a question of justifying a particular case of punishment, however, the retributivist is in a far stronger position. There would be no point in having a general rule if on every occasion that it had to be applied one had to consider whether the advantages in this particular case warranted acting in accordance with it. Moreover, the point of punishment as deterrent would be quite lost were there no general expectation, based on the general operation of the rule, that guilty men would be punished. Assuming, then, that a penal system can be justified in utilitarian terms, any offense is at least prima facie an occasion for a penalty. Equally, without an offense there is no question of a penalty. The retributivist contention that punishment is justified if, and only if, it is deserved is really applicable, therefore, to the justification of particular instances of punishment, the institution as such being taken for granted.[19]

This surely will not, and ought not, satisfy the retributivist. On a view such as Benn's, all of the interesting questions concerning whether it is right to punish people, and if so why, are the utilitarian questions. Retributivism is reduced to a special instance of the general case for having a system follow and apply its own rules whatever they may happen to be. This is a general view of doubtful plausibility,[20] but even if it were plausible as a defense of rule— applying behavior, it would miss most, if not all, of the retributivist's point. And that point is, essentially, that there are some important facts that need explaining and that neither rehabilitative nor deterrent theories can explain; namely, that there are cases in which punishment seems appropriate and in which appeals either to the aim of deterrence or rehabilitation appear to be quite beside the point.

The retributivist might say something like this. Consider the following thought-experiment. Suppose that somehow Hitler had been found alive and well in Argentina, say, five years after the end of World War II. The Nazi apparatus had been fully dismantled, the East and West German governments were fully visible, and the Nazi ideology was now quite unpopular. Isn't it clear that if Hitler had been found it would have been right, perhaps even important, to punish him? Yet, surely the case for punishing him could not have rested very plausibly on the ground that punishment was needed to deter him from future acts of barbarism or in order to convince future Hitlers that they would be punished were they to do what he had done. More to the point, even if punishment in order to achieve deterrence or rehabilitation made some sense, would we not also want to say that these notions just do not get to the heart of what would be involved in punishing people such as Hitler?

Now, of course, the retributivist might add, if you regard these as marginal cases for punishment, then you can simply reject them as confusing borderline cases. But if you feel that these are central cases, then rejection of retributivism as a justification for punishment is less easy.

I think the retributivist is right in calling attention to the fact that there are these cases and that they are central rather than marginal cases just in the sense that they are clear cases of appropriate punishment. If anyone deserved to be punished for his or her wrongdoing—one might be tempted to say—it was persons such as the Nazi leaders. And if that is so, then any adequate theory of punishment must provide a convincing justification for punishment in instances like these. Since justifications focused upon deterrence or rehabilitation cannot do so, this at least counts as a mark against them both.

All of this is a special illustration of a more general point discussed earlier. The relationship between *blame* and *punishment* is both more important and more intimate than deterrent and rehabilitative theories allow.[21] While it would doubtless be too strong a view to propose that punishment *is* simply a harsher form of blame, it is not at all implausible to observe that *standard* case punishment is reserved to those cases in which at least blame is appropriate and in which mere blame is insufficient. Insufficient, however, not in the sense that blaming would not deter while punishment would, but rather insufficient in the sense that blaming would not do justice to the seriousness of the wrong. Thus, if punishment in the standard case is a more extreme version of blame, and if blame cannot be justified on deterrent or rehabilitative grounds, then this, too, casts doubt upon the justification of punishment by appeal to either of these ideals. They just do not neatly fit all the cases we would like them to fit.

In addition, there is a more affirmative case for retributivism that can be developed. There is, to begin with, one argument, typically thought of as retributivist, that is rather forward-looking in character, although it is certainly different from the typical utilitarian justification for punishing people. It is that punishment can be seen as a social mechanism by which an offender can best achieve expiation for his or her wrongdoing. As such, punishment may play an essential and humanizing role in the maintenance of any society. Submission to punishment may be the means by which an offender retains his or her membership in society despite the serious transgression. So we speak of punishment as involving the "paying" of one's "debt" to society, and, equally importantly, we speak of an offender's right to renewed acceptance in the society once his or her punishment has terminated and the "debt" to society has been paid by the offender. Perhaps, because this is a utilitarian argument of sorts, Benn and others would find it consistent with their general thesis, even though they seldom if ever mention it.

There are, then, these two "retributivist" arguments that can be fairly easily accepted and incorporated into nonretributivist theories: that retributivism can be construed either as a necessary condition for punishment or as a system of unpleasantnesses that ought to be made available to those who seek to deal with their wrongdoing in this expiative fashion. But retributivists do not wish to stop there. They see, they believe, still additional arguments for the punishment of the guilty, arguments that are not of the sort so far examined.

One argument goes something like this. As many of even the nonretributivist critics of utilitarianism acknowledge, it is unjust to punish those who are in fact innocent. Indeed, all of us would recognize the claim of any innocent person (no matter how fair the procedure by which he or she was found to be guilty and punished) that an injustice deserving correction had occurred. But if we can understand so readily and clearly that it is unjust to punish the innocent, that can only be because it is also the case that it is just to punish the guilty. To understand that the innocent do not deserve punishment is also necessarily to understand that the guilty do deserve it. That justice requires the punishment of the guilty is but a different aspect of the widely accepted idea that justice forbids the punishment of the innocent.

I find this a difficult claim to assess. I think there is something to it, but I am not certain how much. I do think that it is a fairly straightforward move from "It is unjust to punish the innocent," to

"It is not unjust to punish the guilty," although I am uncertain of the strictness of the logical connection between the two expressions. But even if it is one of entailment, there seems to me to be an important difference in meaning between "It is not unjust to punish the guilty" and "It is just to punish the guilty." And there seems to me to be an equally important difference in meaning between "It is just to punish the guilty" and "Justice requires the punishment of the guilty." I am clear that there is a special injustice in punishing the innocent such that *that* injustice is not present when the guilty are punished. In this sense, at least, it is true that it is not unjust to punish the guilty. Furthermore, I, for purposes of argument, am prepared to assume that, if anyone is to be punished, justice requires that it be the guilty, rather than the innocent. None of this, however, gets retributivism quite where it wants to go: to the claim that justice itself *requires* that there be the punishment of the guilty. If we are to be convinced of that truth about justice and punishment, then other arguments ought, I think, be forthcoming.

The two that are worth discussing the most are both advanced by Herbert Morris in "Persons and Punishment." The first argument involves the fairness of imposing those burdens that the criminal law imposes on us all. The second concerns the unfairness of letting the criminal keep the benefits he or she has unfairly appropriated through violating the law.

The first argument states:

> It is only reasonable that those who voluntarily comply with the rules be provided some assurance that they will not be assuming burdens which others are unprepared to assume. Their disposition to comply voluntarily will diminish as they learn that others are with impunity renouncing burdens they are assuming.[22]

There are two related points here. One is that the system will not work well, if at all, unless the guilty are punished. Not because the threat needs be made credible to those who have not yet broken the law, but who otherwise might.[23] But because those who have not broken the law will have no reason to continue to be law abiding (indeed, it will soon become extremely imprudent for them to continue to be law abiding) unless they can count on reasonably successful efforts being made to keep down the amount of dangerous crime.[24]

The other point perhaps to be extracted from the quotation above is more overtly retributivist. It is this. One way to understand the criminal law is to see it as a system of prohibitions which directs us all not to act in those various ways that it is wrong to act, although we are all inclined to do so. To act in accordance with the criminal law is, therefore, to take on a kind of burden—the burden that is connected with voluntarily restraining ourselves from doing many things that we would like to do. And this burden is only fairly assumed by anyone if it is equally assumed by everyone. Or, to put it another way, it is not fair that the criminal in committing the crime has thrown off the burden assumed by the rest. Punishment is fair—is required by justice—because it is the way to most nearly reinstate the missing burden where it properly belonged.

The other affirmative retributive argument is so closely related to this one that they can most profitably be discussed together.

> ... [I]t is just to punish those who have violated the rules and caused the unfair distribution of benefits and burdens. A person who violates the rules has something others have—the benefits of the system—but by renouncing what others have assumed, the burdens of self-restraint, he has acquired an unfair advantage. Matters are not even until this advantage is in some way erased. Another way of putting it is that he owes something to others, for he has something that does not rightfully belong to him. Justice—that is, punishing such individuals—restores the equilibrium of benefits and burdens by taking from the individual what he owes, that is, exacting the debt.[25]

Justice, in other words, requires that the guilty be punished because of two, interrelated facts: burdens have been unfairly assumed vis-à-vis the criminal by the law-abiding citizens and benefits have been unfairly appropriated by the criminal. The wrongdoer has obtained a benefit to which he or she is not entitled by not restraining himself or herself from acting on inclination and desire in the way in which the rest of us did. In punishing the offender we take away that benefit and thereby restore the social equilibrium which existed before the offense.

There are, I believe, at least two problems with this way of thinking about the justifiability of punishment. In the first place, it is not always plausible to think of criminal and law-abiding behavior in terms of benefits and burdens. Sometimes it is, but sometimes it is not. The basic scheme seems to fit best cases like that of tax evasion. Paying taxes is a burden. No one is naturally inclined or disposed to pay them. If everyone else does pay their taxes and I do not, I do benefit unfairly—and in two ways. I get to keep more of my income than the rest, and I also get the "public" benefits that are bought by the tax monies, e.g., the security provided by an army or a fire department. In addition, the taxpayers are unfairly burdened—also in two ways. They bear a burden that they ought reasonably be required to bear only if everyone bears it. And the burden is, perhaps, greater than it otherwise would have been, because of my evasion.

There are problems with this way of analyzing the injustice of tax evasion.[2][6] But even if there were none, the more central question is whether most cases of serious criminality are fundamentally analogous. I see some important respects in which they are not. Consider, for example, rape instead of tax evasion. If someone, who is inclined to rape a woman, fails to restrain that inclination and commits a rape, I do not see how he has unfairly benefited in respect to me. For I am not aware of any inclination on my part to rape another—irrespective of what the law does or does not prohibit. Because I do not see myself as having been burdened at all by the criminalization of rape, I do not see myself as having been unfairly burdened; nor, as I have said, do I see the rapist as having unfairly benefited himself, *as against those who abstain from rape.* Of course rape is wrong. Of course rape is a case of the rapist treating the victim very wrongly. But rape, torture, murder—many of the worst things one person can possibly do to another—do not neatly fit the model of the misallocation of benefits and burdens described by Morris and constituting the background justification for the punishment of the guilty.

In order for these cases to fit better there would have to be a retreat to a kind of second-order set of benefits and burdens. It is not, on this view, the inclination to do what a particular law prohibits that is involved. Instead, it is the inclination in each individual to do some of the things prohibited by the criminal law that underlies the analysis in terms of benefits and burdens. I restrain myself from doing those wrong things I am inclined to do and it is only fair that you restrain yourself from doing those wrong things you are inclined to do. You benefit from my law abidingness and I benefit from yours.

Maybe, but it does seem to me that much of the force of the original claim is dissipated once this retreat is made. What began as a powerful appeal to a direct and obvious sense in which committing a particular crime burdened unfairly those who did not commit that crime and benefited unfairly those who did, has been altered to become a far more abstract, less obviously correct appeal to the general benefits and burdens of law abidingness.

My second general objection—or reservation—concerns the relevance of an analysis such as Morris' (even if it were correct in terms of benefits and burdens) to punishment. For I do not understand precisely how it is that punishing the wrongdoer constitutes taking the wrongfully appropriated benefit away from him or her. Where the benefit is a tangible good still in existence, e.g., the payroll from the bank robbery, we do, of course, take it away from the bank robber and return it to the bank. But that is not even punishment; that is restitution. That seems to restore the social equilibrium in respect to the thing wrongfully appropriated.

Perhaps, though, the argument is that punishment can be seen as preventing the wrongdoer from enjoying the fruits of his or her wrongdoing. Perhaps in some straightforward sense, this is what is appropriately done to restore the equilibrium when, for example, we cannot find the stolen payroll and we know it has not yet been spent or enjoyed by the robber. But in many, if not most, cases the removal of the benefit and the resulting restoration of the social equilibrium will be at best metaphorical.

How, for instance, does punishment for rape take the unfairly appropriated benefit away from the rapist? How does it even keep him from enjoying the benefits of his wrongdoing? To speak of punishment for rape as restoring the social equilibrium does not seem thereby to explain why it is that the punishment of the rapist is justified. It seems no more or less illuminating than to speak of punishment for rape as deserved because of the seriousness of the wrong. It is to return, perhaps, to the very plausible intuition with which retributivism begins—that serious crime deserves to be punished—but it is not to give a wholly clear or distinct reason for moving beyond that intuition. We do not, I think, yet have in retributivism a set of moral arguments sufficiently sound, convincing, and worked out upon which to rest the justifiability of punishment.

This is why I have entitled by study, "Some Problems with Theories of Punishment." I start with the view that a theory, a justification for punishment is required. There are justifications, there are arguments, and they do work for some cases. But there is, when all is said and done, no one connected set of arguments, no one theory, that deals adequately with all of the cases that ought to be taken into account. There is more philosophical work yet to be done.

NOTES TO CHAPTER NINE

1. H.L.A. Hart, "Prolegomenon to the Principles of Punishment," 60 *Proceedings of the Aristotelian Society* 1 (new series, 1959), reprinted in Hart, *Punishment and Responsibility* (1968), p. 1.

2. *Ibid.*, pp. 4-5.

3. *Ibid.*, p. 5.

4. This example is, of course, typically offered as a part of the stock criticism—often taken to be decisive—of utilitarianism generally.

5. Hart's discussion of criminality does seem to me at times to come close to

this point. See, e.g., H.L.A. Hart, *The Morality of the Criminal Law* (1964), p. 28; and H.L.A. Hart, *The Concept of Law* (1961), p. 165. I have discussed this issue at greater length in my article, "H.L.A. Hart and the Doctrines of *Mens Rea* and Criminal Responsibility," 35 *The University of Chicago Law Review* 92 (1967).

Joel Feinberg also emphasizes the public, denunciatory aspect of punishment in "The Expressive Function of Punishment" in Feinberg, *Doing and Deserving* (1970), p. 95.

6. In addition, we would also need a theory that would explain why it is always immoral intentionally to disobey the law. I do not think such a defense is possible, and I have tried to show why in my article, "The Obligation to Obey the Law," 10 *U.C.L.A. Law Review* 780 (1963). See also, M.B.E. Smith, "Is There a *Prima Facie* Obligation to Obey the Law?," 82 *Yale Law Journal* 950 (1973).

7. Karl Menninger, "Therapy Not Punishment," reprinted in Jeffrie Murphy (Ed.) *Punishment and Rehabilitation* (1973), p. 136.

8. I have discussed at greater length what I take to be the difficulties with this first argument in "Punishing the Guilty," reprinted in Gertrude Ezorsky (Ed.), *Philosophical Perspectives on Punishment* (1972), pp. 330-333.

9. Barbara Wootton, *Crime and the Criminal Law* (1963).

10. *Ibid.*, p. 77.

11. *Ibid.*, pp. 79-80 (emphasis added).

12. The discussion that begins here and continues through page 184, *infra*, is taken from "Punishing the Guilty," *op. cit.*, pp. 334-335.

13. What Menninger says is this:

What might deter the reader from conduct which his neighbors would not like does not necessarily deter the grown-up child of vastly different background.

It is not the successful criminal upon whom we inflict our antiquated penal system. It is the unsuccessful criminal, the criminal who really doesn't know how to commit crimes and who gets caught. . . . The clumsy, the desperate, the obscure, the friendless, the defective, the diseased—these men who commit crimes that do not come off—are bad actors, indeed. But they are not the professional criminals, many of whom occupy high places.

Menninger, *op. cit.*, pp. 134-135.

For a more extended discussion of some of these objections see "Punishing the Guilty," *op. cit.*, pp. 335-337, and Herbert Morris, "Persons and Punishment," reprinted in Murphy (Ed.) *Punishment and Rehabilitation*, p. 40 at pp. 45-52.

14. Morris, I think, is to be criticized on this point. "Persons and Punishment" appears on the whole to contrast an Ideal, i.e., just, system of punishment with real, i.e., existing systems of treatment.

15. *The Concept of Law, op. cit.*, p. 181 (emphasis added).

16. Another objection is that there is a sense in which punishing the guilty person *in order to deter others* can be plausibly seen as a case of "using" that

individual merely as a means. I discuss this point, but not very fully, in "Punishing the Guilty," *op. cit.*, pp. 340-341.

17. I did, for example, in "Punishing the Guilty." I now think that was a serious mistake.

18. Some of Morris' argument in "Persons and Punishment" is of this form.

19. Stanley Benn, "Punishment" in Murphy (Ed.) *Punishment and Rehabilitation*, p. 25.

20. It is the central issue that divides act and rule utilitarians. For some discussions of why the rule utilitarian answer is at least not obviously correct, or even distinguishable from careful act utilitarianism see: David Lyons, *Forms and Limits of Utilitarianism* (1965); Rolf Sartorius, *Individual Conduct and Social Norms* (1975); and Wasserstrom, *The Judicial Decision* (1961).

21. It is much harder to develop a convincing consequentialist rationale for blaming than for punishment. We can and do blame others silently to ourselves. We can and do decide that those long since dead are properly to blame for things they did while alive; or that someone long considered blameworthy is, in fact, not blameworthy at all. These activities are clear cases of blaming. They play important roles in the lives of many persons. We can, of course, if pressed, construct a consequentialist account that takes these activities into account and justifies them on consequentialist grounds. But the arguments do not ring true. The theory can always be saved, but at a price. We do not always, or even typically, blame in order to deter or to reform—or even publicly to denounce.

Any adequate theory of blame would, I think, have to acknowledge this, and either account for all the important cases or urge that all of the nonconforming cases be extinguished from the repertoire of acceptable human behaviors.

22. "Persons and Punishment," *op. cit.*, p. 42.

23. This is what I take Hart's argument from general deterrence to be. See Part III, *supra*.

24. There is a sense in which this argument, too, is plausibly viewed as essentially utilitarian. Like the one concerning the redemptive benefits of a punishment system, it is an important one seldom discussed within the usual catalogue of utilitarian justifications.

25. "Persons and Punishment," *op. cit.*, p. 43.

26. If, for example, it is an empirical claim that everyone's taxes are made higher by my tax evasion, I see no reason to believe that such a claim is always true. The amount involved might just be too small to make a difference.

Bibliography

1. Acton, H.B. *The Philosophy of Punishment.* New York: St. Martin's Press, 1969.

2. Adkins, A.W.H. *Merit and Responsibility.* Oxford: Clarendon Press, 1960.

3. Alexander, J.P. "The Philosophy of Punishment." *Journal of the American Institute of Criminal Law and Criminology*, v. 13 (1922-1923), pp. 235-250.

4. Allen, Francis A. "The Rehabilitative Ideal." *Contemporary Punishment: Views, Explanations and Justifications.* Ed. by Rudolph J. Gerber and Patrick D. McAnany. Notre Dame: University of Notre Dame Press, 1972, pp. 209-218.

5. Ancel, Marc. "New Social Defense." *Contemporary Punishment: Views, Explanations and Justifications.* Ed. by Rudolph J. Gerber and Patrick D. McAnany. Notre Dame: University of Notre Dame Press, 1972, pp. 132-139.

6. Andenaes, J. "Choice of Punishment." *Scandinavian Studies in Law.* v. 2 (1958), pp. 55-74.

7. Andenaes, J. "Does Punishment Deter Crime?" *Philosophical Perspectives on Punishment.* Ed. by Gertrude Ezorsky. Albany: State University of New York Press, 1972, pp. 342-357.

8. Andenaes, J. "General Prevention: A Broader View of Deterrence." *Contemporary Punishment: Views, Explanations and Justifications.* Ed. by Rudolph J. Gerber and Patrick D. McAnany. Notre Dame: University of Notre Dame, 1972, pp. 108-119.

9. Andenaes, J. "General Prevention—Illusion or Reality?" *Journal of Criminal Law, Criminology and Police Science*, v. 43, n. 1 (May-June, 1952), pp. 176-198.

10. Annon. "Westermarck on the Origin of Punishment." *Annals of the*

American Academy of Political Sciences, v. 27 (January, 1901), pp. 151-153.

11. Aquinas, St. Thomas. "Of the Debt of Punishment." *Basic Writings of St. Thomas Aquinas.* Ed. by Anton C. Pegis. New York: Random House, 1945 (v. 2), pp. 708-720.

12. Aquinas, St. Thomas. "Those Who Have Sinned Involuntarily." *Philosophical Perspectives on Punishment.* Ed. by Gertrude Ezorsky. Albany: State University of New York Press, 1972, p. 185.

13. Aquinas, St. Thomas. "Whether Vengeance is Lawful." *Philosophical Perspectives on Punishment.* Ed. by Gertrude Ezorsky. Albany: State University of New York Press, 1972, p. 135.

14. Aristotle. "Nicomachean Ethics." *The Basic Works of Aristotle.* Ed. by Richard McKeon. New York: Random House, 1941, pp. 935-1112.

15. Armstrong, K.G. "The Retributivist Hits Back." *The Philosophy of Punishment.* Ed. by H.B. Acton. London: Macmillan, 1969, pp. 138-158.

16. Armstrong, K.G. "The Right to Punish." *Philosophical Perspectives on Punishment.* Ed. by Gertrude Ezorsky. Albany: State University of New York Press, 1972, p. 136.

17. Atkinson, Max. "Justified and Deserved Punishments." *Mind*, v. 78, n. 311 (July, 1969), pp. 354-374.

18. Babbage, S.B. "C.S. Lewis and the Humanitarian Theory of Punishment." *Interchange*, n. 12 (1972), pp. 192-200.

19. Baier, Kurt. "Is Punishment Retributive?" *The Philosophy of Punishment.* Ed. by H.B. Acton. London: Macmillan, 1969, pp. 130-137.

20. Balint, Michael. "On Punishing Offenders." *Psychoanalysis and Culture: Essays in Honor of Geza Róheim.* Ed. by G.B. Wilbur and W. Muensterberger. New York: International Universities Press, Inc., 1951, pp. 254-279.

21. Ball, John C. "The Deterrence Concept in Criminology and Law." *The Journal of Criminal Law, Criminology and Police Science*, v. 46, n. 3 (September-October, 1955), pp. 347-354.

22. Barnett, Anthony. "Reward and Punishment." *The Listener*, v. 66, no. 1695 (September 21, 1961), pp. 426-427.

23. Beardsley, Elizabeth Lane. "A Plea for Deserts." *American Philosophical Quarterly*, v. 6, n. 1 (January, 1969), pp. 33-42.

24. Beardsley, Elizabeth Lane. "Moral Worth and Moral Credit." *The Philosophical Review*, v. 66, n. 3 (July, 1957), pp. 304-328.

25. Bedau, Hugo Adam. "A Social Philosopher Looks at the Death Penalty." *The American Journal of Psychiatry*, v. 123, n. 11 (May, 1967), pp. 1361-1370.

26. Bedau, Hugo Adam. "Deterrence and the Death Penalty: A Reconsideration." *The Journal of Criminal Law, Criminology and Police Science*, v. 61, n. 4 (December, 1970), pp. 539-548.

27. Bedau, Hugo Adam. "Physical Intervention to Alter Behavior in a Punitive Environment." *American Behavioral Scientist*, v. 18, n. 5 (May-June, 1965), pp. 657-678.

28. Bedau, Hugo Adam, editor. *The Death Penalty in America.* Chicago: Aldine Publishing Co., 1964. Revised edition, 1967.

29. Bedau, Hugo Adam and Pierce, Chester M. (eds.) *Capital Punishment in the United States.* New York: AMS Press, Inc., 1976.

30. Bentham, Jeremy. *An Introduction to the Principles of Morals and Legislation.* Darien, Connecticut: Hafner Publishing Co., 1948.

31. Bentham, Jeremy. "Inefficacious Punishment." *Philosophical Perspectives on Punishment.* Ed. by Gertrude Ezorsky. Albany: State University of New York Press, 1972, pp. 186-188.

32. Bentham, Jeremy. "Utility and Punishment." *Philosophical Perspectives on Punishment.* Ed. by Gertrude Ezorsky. Albany: State University of New York Press, 1972, pp. 56-63.

33. Benn, S.I. "An Approach to the Problems of Punishment." *Social Principles and the Democratic State.* London: Allen and Unwin, 1959. Chapter 8.

34. Benn, Stanley I. "Punishment." *The Encyclopedia of Philosophy*, Ed. by Paul Edwards. New York: The Macmillan Co. and The Free Press, 1967 (v. 7), pp. 29-35.

35. Benn, Stanley I. and Peters, Richard, S. "The Utilitarian Case for Deterrence." *Contemporary Punishment: Views, Explanations and Justifications.* Ed. by Rudolph J. Gerber and Patrick D. McAnany. Notre Dame: University of Notre Dame, 1972, pp. 96-101.

36. Birks, W.R. and O'Flynn, F.D. "Some Problems in the Theory and Practice of Criminal Punishment." *New Zealand Law Journal*, v. 39 (1963), pp. 253-268.

37. Bittner, Egon and Platt, Anthony. "The Right of the State to Punish." *Contemporary Punishment: Views, Explanations and Justifications.* Ed. by Rudolph J. Gerber and Patrick D. McAnany. Notre Dame: University of Notre Dame, 1972, pp. 24-30.

38. Blanshard, Brand. "Retribution Revisited." in *Philosophical Perspectives on Punishment.* Ed. by E.H. Madden, Rollo Handy, and Marvin Farber. Springfield, Illinois: Thomas, 1968.

39. Blumenfeld, D. and Dworkin, G. "Necessity, Contingency and Punishment." *Philosophical Studies*, v. 16 (1965), pp. 91-94.

40. Bodenheimer, E. "Is Punishment Obsolete?" *Nomos III: Responsibility.* Ed. by C.J. Friedrich. New York: Liberal Arts Press, 1960, pp. 87-105.

41. Bradley, F.H. *Ethical Studies* (2d ed.). Oxford: Clarendon Press, 1927.

42. Bradley, F.H. "Some Remarks on Punishment." *International Journal of Ethics*, v. 4 (April, 1894), pp. 269-284.

43. Brandt, Richard B. "A Utilitarian Theory of Excuses." *Philosophical Review*, v. 78 (1969), pp. 337-361.

44. Brandt, Richard B. *Ethical Theory.* Englewood Cliffs: Prentice-Hall, Inc., 1959. Chapter 19.

45. Bridgman, Percy W. "Determinism and Punishment." *Determinism and Freedom in the Age of Modern Science.* Ed. by Sidney Hook. Washington Square: New York University Press, 1958, pp. 143-145.

46. Butler, Samuel, "Erewhorn and Erewhorn Revisited." *Philosophical Perspectives on Punishment.* Ed. by Gertrude Ezorsky. Albany: State University of New York Press, 1972, pp. 300-308.

47. Callard, P. "Punishment by the State: Its Motives and Form." *British Journal of Delinquency*, v. 9 (1959), pp. 36-45.

48. Cappon, Daniel. "Punishment and the Person." *Ethics*, v. 67, n. 3, (April, 1957), pp. 184-195.

49. Card, Claudia. "On Mercy." *The Philosophical Review*, v. 81, n. 2 (April, 1972), pp. 182-207.

50. Carmichael, E.K. "Crime and Punishment." *Howard Journal*, v. 3 (1930), pp. 74-79.

51. Carritt, Edgar Frederick. *Ethical and Political Thinking*. Oxford: Clarendon Press, 1947.

52. Charvet, John. "Criticism and Punishment." *Mind*, v. 75, n. 300 (October, 1966), pp. 573-379.

53. Clark, M. "The Moral Gradation of Punishment." *Philosophical Quarterly*, v. 21 (April, 1971), pp. 132-140.

54. Clemmer, Donald. *The Prison Community*. New York: Rinehart, 1958.

55. Cock, A.A. "Punishment: The Adjustment of a Disturbed Equilibrium." *Journal of Experimental Pedagogy*, (1915), pp. 198-201.

56. Cohen, Morris Raphael. *Reason and Law: Studies in Juristic Philosophy*. Glencoe, Illinois: The Free Press, 1950.

57. Committee for Revision of 1959 Manual. *Manual of Correctional Standards*. Washington, D.C.: The American Correctional Association, 1969.

58. Connolly, M. "Punishment of Crime." *Studies*, (1957), pp. 467-478.

59. Conrad, J.P. *Crime and Its Correction*. Berkeley and Los Angeles: University of California Press, 1965.

60. Cooper, David E. "Hegel's Theory of Punishment." *Hegel's Political Philosophy: Problems and Perspectives*. Ed. by Z.A. Pelczynski. Cambridge: Cambridge University Press, 1971, pp. 151-167.

61. Davis, Lawrence H. "They Deserve to Suffer." *Analysis*, v. 32, n. 4 (March, 1972), pp. 136-140.

62. Davitt, T.E., SJ. "Criminal Responsibility and Punishment." *Nomos III: Responsibility*. Ed. by C.J. Friedrich. New York: Liberal Arts Press, 1960, pp. 143-151.

63. Dawson, Robert O. *Sentencing*. Boston: Little, Brown, 1969.

64. del Vecchio, G. "Divine Justice and Human Justice." *Juridical Review*, v. 1 (1956), pp. 147-157.

65. Demos, Raphael. "Some Reflections on Threats and Punishments." *Review of Metaphysics*, v. 11, n. 2 (December, 1957), pp. 224-236.

66. Dershowitz, Alan M. "The Psychiatrist's Power in Civil Commitment: A Knife That Cuts Both Ways." *Psychology Today*, v. 2, n. 9 (February, 1969), pp. 42-47.

67. Devlin, P. "Criminal Responsibility and Punishment: Functions of Judge and Jury." *The Criminal Law Review*, (1954), pp. 661-686.

68. Dietl, Paul J. "On Punishing Attempts." *Mind*, v. 79, n. 313 (January, 1970), pp. 130-132.

69. Dietl, P.J. "Response to Charles E. Dwyer." *Philosophy of Education, Proceedings*, v. 25 (1969), pp. 58-63.

70. DiSalle, Michael V. and Blochman, Lawrence G. *The Power of Life or Death*. New York: Random House, 1965.

71. Dixon, K. "Discipline, Freedom and the Justification of Punishment." *Discipline in Schools: A Symposium*. Ed. by L. Stenhouse. Oxford: Pergamon Press, (1967), pp. 163-192.

72. Downie, R.S. "Forgiveness." *Philosophical Quarterly*, v. 15 (1965), pp. 128-134.

73. Doyle, James F. "Justice and Legal Punishment." *The Philosophy of Punishment*. Ed. by H.B. Acton. London: Macmillan, 1969, pp. 159-171.

74. Dworkin, Gerald and Blumenfeld, David. "Punishment for Intentions." *Mind*, v. 75, n. 299 (July, 1966), pp. 396-404.

75. Dwyer, C.E. "Punishment and Education." *Philosophy of Education, Proceedings*. Illinois: Southern Illinois University Press, v. 25 (1969), pp. 45-57.

76. Emmons, D.C. "The Retributive Criterion for Justice." *Mind*, v. 79, n. 313 (January, 1970), pp. 133-134.

77. Evans, I. "Is Punishment a Crime?" *Dublin Review*, v. 230 (1955-1956), pp. 4-11.

78. Evans, I. "Punishment." *New Catholic Encyclopedia*. New York: McGraw Hill, v. 11 (1967), pp. 1025-1028.

79. Ewing, A.C. "On 'Retributivism'." *Philosophical Perspectives on Punishment*. Ed. by Gertrude Ezorsky. Albany: State University of New York Press, 1972, pp. 137-141.

80. Ewing, A.C. "Punishment as a Moral Agency: An Attempt to Reconcile the Retributive and the Utilitarian View." *Mind*, v. 37, no. 143 (July, 1927), pp. 292-305.

81. Ewing, A.C. *The Morality of Punishment*. Montclair, New Jersey: Patterson Smith, 1970.

82. Eysenck, H.J. "Crime and Conditioning." *Contemporary Punishment: Views, Explanations and Justifications*. Ed. by Rudolph J. Gerber and Patrick D. McAnany. Notre Dame: University of Notre Dame, 1972, pp. 187-193.

83. Ezorsky, G. *Philosophical Perspectives on Punishment*. Albany, New York: State University of New York Press, 1972.

84. Ezorsky, G. "Retributive Justice." *Canadian Journal of Philosophy*, v. 1 (March, 1972), pp. 365-368.

85. Feinberg, Joel. *Doing and Deserving*. Princeton: Princeton University Press, 1970.

86. Feinberg, Joel. "Justice and Personal Desert." in *Nomos VI: Justice*. New York: Lieber-Atherton, Inc., 1974. Ed. by C.J. Friedrich and J.W. Chapman.

87. Feinberg, Joel. "On Justifying Legal Punishment." *Nomos III: Responsibility*. Ed. by C.J. Friedrich. New York: Liberal Arts Press, 1960, pp. 152-167.

88. Feinberg, Joel. "Problematic Responsibility in Law and Morals." *The Philosophical Review*, v. 71, n. 3 (July, 1962), pp. 340-351.

89. Feinberg, Joel. "The Expressive Function of Punishment." *The Monist*, v. 69 (July, 1965), pp. 397-423.

90. Feinberg, Joel, and Gross, Hyman (eds.) *Punishment*. Encino, California: Dickenson Publishing Co., 1975.

91. Findlay, R.C. "What Constitutes Punishment?" *Notre Dame Lawyer*, v. 39 (1964), pp. 594-606.

92. Finnis, John. "The Restoration of Retribution." *Analysis*, v. 32, n. 4 (March, 1972), pp. 131-135.

93. Fitzgerald, P.J. *Criminal Law and Punishment*. Oxford: Clarendon Press, 1962.

94. Flew, Anthony. "Crime or Disease?" *The British Journal of Sociology*, v. 5, n. 1 (March, 1954), pp. 49-62.

95. Flew, Anthony. "Definition of Punishment." *Contemporary Punishment: Views, Explanations and Justifications.* Ed. by Rudolph J. Gerber and Patrick D. McAnany. Notre Dame: University of Notre Dame, 1972, pp. 31-35.

96. Flew, Anthony. "The Justification of Punishment." *The Philosophy of Punishment.* Ed. by H.B. Acton. London: Macmillan, 1969, pp. 83-104.

97. Flew, Anthony. "The Justification of Punishment." *Philosophy*, v. 29, n. 3 (October, 1954), pp. 291-307.

98. Fogel, David. "Corrections in the Year 2000—Some Directions," in *Prisoners' Rights Sourcebook*, edited by Michele G. Hermann and Marilyn Haft. New York: Clark Boardman & Co., 1973, pp. 423-436.

99. Fogel, David. "Fate of the Rehabilitative Ideal in California Youth Authority Dispositions." *Journal of Crime and Delinquency*, v. 15, n. 4 (October, 1969), pp. 479-498.

100. Fogel, David. "The Politics of Corrections." *Federal Probation* (forthcoming).

101. Fogel, David. *We Are the Living Proof.* Cincinnati, Ohio: W.H. Anderson Publishing, 1975.

102. Fogel, David, Galaway, Burt, and Hudson, Joe. "Restitution in Criminal Justice: A Minnesota Experiment." *Criminal Law Bulletin*, v. 8, n. 8 (October, 1972), pp. 681-691.

103. Frankel, Marvin E. *Criminal Sentences.* New York: Hill and Wang, 1972.

104. Fuller, Lon L. "The Case of the Speluncean Explorers." *Harvard Law Review*, v. 62, n. 4 (1949), pp. 616-645.

105. Gahringer, Robert E. "Punishment as Language." *Ethics*, v. 71, n. 1 (October, 1960), pp. 46-48.

106. Gahringer, Robert E. "Punishment and Responsibility." *The Journal of Philosophy*, v. 66, n. 10 (May 22, 1969), pp. 291-306.

107. Gardiner, G. "The Purpose of Criminal Punishment." *Modern Law Review*, v. 21 (1958), pp. 117-129, 221-235.

108. Gendin, Sidney. "A Plausible Theory of Retribution." *The Journal of Value Inquiry.*, v. 5, n. 1 (Spring, 1971), pp. 1-16.

109. Gendin, Sidney. "The Meaning of Punishment." *Philosophy and Phenomenological Research*, v. 28, n. 2 (December, 1967), pp. 235-240.

110. Gerber, Rudolph J. and McAnany, Patrick D. *Contemporary Punishment: Views, Explanations and Justifications.* South Bend, Indiana: University of Notre Dame Press, 1972.

111. Glaser, Daniel. *Handbook of Criminology.* Chicago: Rand McNally College Publishing Co., 1974.

112. Glaser, Daniel. *The Effectiveness of a Prison and Parole System.* Indianapolis: The Bobbs-Merrill Co., Inc., 1964.

113. Golding, Martin P. *Philosophy of Law.* Englewood Cliffs, New Jersey: Prentice-Hall, 1974.

114. Goldinger, M. "Punishment, Justice and the Separation of Issues." *Monist*, v. 49 (July, 1965), pp. 458-474.

115. Goldinger, Milton. "Rule-utilitarianism and Criminal Reform." *Southern Journal of Philosophy*, v. 5, n. 2 (Summer, 1967), pp. 103-109.

116. Green, E. *Judicial Attitudes in Sentencing.* New York: St. Martin's Press, 1961.

117. Hadden, T.B. "A Plea for Punishment." *Cambridge Law Journal,* (1965), p. 117.

118. Hakeem, Michael. "A Critique of the Psychiatric Approach to Crime and Correction." *Law and Contemporary Problems,* v. 23, n. 4 (Autumn, 1958), pp. 650-682.

119. Haksar, V. "Aristotle and the Punishment of Psychopaths." *Philosophy,* v. 39 (1964), pp. 323-340.

120. Hall, Jerome. "Just v. Unjust Law." *Contemporary Punishment: Views, Explanations and Justifications.* Ed. by Rudolph J. Gerber and Patrick D. McAnany. Notre Dame: University of Notre Dame, 1972, pp. 49-58.

121. Hall, Jerome. "The Inclusive Theory of Punishment." *Contemporary Punishment: Views, Explanations and Justifications.* Ed. by Rudolph J. Gerber and Patrick D. McAnany. Notre Dame: University of Notre Dame, 1972, pp. 233-237.

122. Hargrove, B. "Some Recent Trends in Crime and Punishment." *Solicitor,* v. 26 (1959), p. 273.

123. Hart, Harold H. *Punishment: For and Against.* New York City: Hart Publishing Co., Inc., 1971.

124. Hart, H.L.A. "Prolegomenon to the Principles of Punishment." *Philosophy, Politics and Society.* Second Series. Ed. by P. Laslett and W.G. Runciman. Oxford: Blackwell, 1962, pp. 158-182.

125. Hart, H.L.A. "Legal Responsibility and Excuses." *Determinism and Freedom in the Age of Modern Science.* Ed. by Sidney Hook. Washington Square: New York University Press, 1958.

126. Hart, H.L.A. *Law, Liberty and Morality.* New York: Vintage Books, 1963.

127. Hart, H.L.A. "The General Aim and Limits for Punishment." *Contemporary Punishment: Views, Explanations and Justifications.* Ed. by Rudolph J. Gerber and Patrick D. McAnany. Notre Dame: University of Notre Dame, 1972, pp. 246-251.

128. Hart, H.L.A. "Principles of Punishment." *Philosophical Perspectives on Punishment.* Ed. by Gertrude Ezorsky. Albany: State University of New York, 1972, pp. 153-164.

129. Hart, H.L.A. *Punishment and Responsibility.* New York and Oxford: Oxford University Press, 1968.

130. Hart, Henry M., Jr. "The Aims of the Criminal Law." *Law and Contemporary Problems,* v. 23, n. 3 (Summer, 1958), pp. 401-441.

131. Hart, Henry M., Jr. "Criminal Punishment as Public Condemnation." *Contemporary Punishment: Views, Explanations and Justifications.* Ed. by Rudolph J. Gerber and Patrick D. McAnany. Notre Dame: University of Notre Dame, 1972, pp. 12-15.

132. Hawkins, Gordon. "Punishment as a Moral Educator." *Contemporary Punishment: Views, Explanations and Justifications.* Ed. by Rudolph J. Gerber and Patrick D. McAnany. Notre Dame: University of Notre Dame, 1972, pp. 120-128.

133. Hawkins, Gordon. "Punishment and Deterrence: The Educative, Moralizing and Habituative Effects." *Wisconsin Law Review* (1969).

134. Hazelrigg, L.E. *Prison within Society: A Reader in Penology.* Garden City, New York: Doubleday and Co., Inc., 1968.

135. Heath, James. *Eighteenth Century Penal Theory.* London: Oxford University Press, 1963.

136. Hegel, Georg Wilhelm Friedrich. *The Philosophy of Right.* trans. T.M. Knox. Chicago: Encyclopedia Britannica, Inc., 1952.

137. Hegel, Georg Wilhelm Friedrich. "Punishment as a Right." *Philosophical Perspectives on Punishment.* Ed. by Gertrude Ezorsky. Albany: State University of New York Press, 1972, pp. 107-108.

138. Hobbes, Thomas. "Of Punishments and Rewards." *Philosophical Perspectives on Punishment.* Ed. by Gertrude Ezorsky. Albany: State University of New York Press, 1972, pp. 3-5.

139. Hobbes, Thomas. *A Dialogue Between a Philosopher and a Student of the Common Laws of England.* Chicago: The University of Chicago Press, 1971.

140. Hodges, Donald Clark. "Punishment." *Philosophy and Phenomenological Research,* v. 18, n. 2 (December, 1957), pp. 209-218.

141. Hogarth, J. *Sentencing as a Human Process.* Toronto: University of Toronto Press, 1974.

142. Holborow, L.C. "Blame, Praise and Credit." *Proceedings of the Aristotelian Society,* New Series v. 72 (1971-1972), pp. 85-100.

143. Hospers, John. "Some Problems Concerning Punishment and the Retaliatory Use of Force." (Part I) *Reason,* v. 4, n. 7 (November, 1972), pp. 14-21.

144. Hospers, John. "Some Problems Concerning Punishment and the Retaliatory Use of Force." (Part II) *Reason,* v. 4, n. 9 (January, 1973), pp. 19-26.

145. Jensen, O.C. "Responsibility, Freedom and Punishment." *Mind,* v. 75, n. 298 (April, 1966), pp. 224-238.

146. Johnson, E.H. *Crime, Correction and Society.* Homewood, Illinois: The Dorsey Press, 1974.

147. Kant, Immanuel. *The Critique of Practical Reason.* Chicago: Encyclopedia Britannica, Inc., 1952.

148. Kant, Immanuel. "Justice and Punishment." *Philosophical Perspectives on Punishment.* Ed. by Gertrude Ezorsky. Albany: State University of New York Press, 1972, pp. 102-106.

149. Kasachkoff, T. "The Criteria of Punishment: Some Neglected Considerations." *Canadian Journal of Philosophy,* v. 2 (March, 1973), pp. 363-378.

150. Kaufman, A.S. "Anthony Quinton on Punishment." *Analysis,* v. 20 (1959-1960), pp. 10-13.

151. Kaufman, A.S. "The Reform Theory of Punishment." *Ethics,* v. 71, n. 1 (October, 1960), pp. 49-52.

152. Kelsen, H. "Causality and Retribution in the Evolution of Human Thought." *What Is Justice,* Berkeley: University of California Press, 1957.

153. Kenner, Lionel. "On Blaming." *Mind,* v. 76, no. 302 (April, 1967), pp. 238-249.

154. Klare, Hugh J. *Changing Concepts of Crime and Its Treatment.* London: Pergamon Press, 1966.

155. Kleinig, J.I. "Mercy and Justice." *Philosophy,* v. 44 (October, 1969), pp. 341-342.

156. Kleinig, J.I. "Punishment in Philosophical and Biblical Perspective." *Interchange*, v. 3 (June, 1971), pp. 29-45.

157. Kleinig, J.I. "R.S. Peters on Punishment." *British Journal of Educational Studies*, v. 20, n. 3 (October, 1972), pp. 259-269.

158. Kleinig, J.I. "The Concept of Desert." *American Philosophical Quarterly*, v. 8, n. 1 (January, 1971), pp. 71-78.

159. Kneale, William. "The Responsibility of Criminals." *The Philosophy of Punishment*. Ed. by H.B. Acton. London: Macmillan, 1969, pp. 172-196.

160. Lerman, Paul. *Community Treatment and Social Control*. Chicago: The University of Chicago Press, 1975.

161. Lerner, A. "Punishment as Justice and as Price." *Determinism and Freedom in the Age of Modern Science*. Ed. by S. Hook. New York University Press, 1958, pp. 180-182.

162. Lessnoff, Michael. "Two Justifications of Punishment." *The Philosophical Quarterly*, v. 21, n. 83 (April, 1971), pp. 141-148.

163. Lewis, C.S. "The Humanitarian Theory of Punishment." *Contemporary Punishment: Views, Explanations and Justifications*. Ed. by Rudolph J. Gerber and Patrick D. McAnany. Notre Dame: University of Notre Dame, 1972, pp. 194-199.

164. Lewis, C.S. "On Punishment: A Reply." *Res Judicatae*, v. 6 (1952-1954), pp. 519-523.

165. Lillie, W., Rev. "Towards a Biblical Doctrine of Punishment." *Scottish Journal of Theology*, v. 21, n. 4 (December, 1968), pp. 449-461.

166. Lindesmith, A.R. "Punishment." *International Encyclopedia of the Social Sciences*. v. 13 (1968), pp. 217-222.

167. Locke, Don. "The Many Faces of Punishment." *Mind*, v. 72, n. 288 (October, 1963), pp. 568-572.

168. Loftsgordon, Donald. "Present-day British Philosophers on Punishment." *The Journal of Philosophy*, v. 63, n. 12 (June 9, 1966), pp. 341-353.

169. Louch, A.R. "Sins and Crimes." *Philosophy*, v. 43 (January, 1968), pp. 38-50.

170. Lyons, David. "On Sanctioning Excuses." *The Journal of Philosophy*, v. 66, n. 19 (October 2, 1969), pp. 646-660.

171. Mabbott, J.D. "Punishment." *Philosophical Perspectives on Punishment*. Ed. by Gertrude Ezorsky. Albany: State University of New York Press, 1972, pp. 165-181.

172. Mabbott, J.D. "Punishment as a Corollary of Rule-Breaking." *Contemporary Punishment: Views, Explanations and Justifications*. Ed. by Rudolph J. Gerber and Patrick D. McAnany. Notre Dame: University of Notre Dame, 1972, pp. 41-48.

173. Mabbott, J.D. "Freewill and Punishment." *Contemporary British Philosophy*. Third Series. Ed. by H.D. Lewis. New York: The Macmillan Co., 1956, pp. 287-309.

174. Mabbott, J.D. "Professor Flew on Punishment." *The Philosophy of Punishment*. Ed. by H.B. Acton. London: Macmillan, 1969, pp. 115-129.

175. Madden, Edward H., Handy, Rollo., and Farber, Marvin. *Philosophical Perspectives of Punishment*. Springfield, Illinois: Charles C. Thomas, 1968.

176. Manser, A.R. "It Serves You Right." *Philosophy*, v. 37 (1962), pp. 293-306.

177. Marshall, John. "Punishment for Intentions." *Mind*, v. 80, n. 320 (October, 1971), pp. 597-598.

178. Martin, Rex. "On the Logic of Justifying Legal Punishment." *American Philosophical Quarterly*, v. 7, n. 3 (July, 1970), pp. 253-259.

179. Martinson, R. "The Paradox of Prison Reform." *Philosophical Perspectives on Punishment*. Ed. by Gertrude Ezorsky. Albany: State University of New York Press, 1972, pp. 309-327.

180. Martinson, Robert. "What Works?—Questions and Answers About Prison Reform." *The Public Interest*. nos. 34-37, (Spring, 1974), pp. 22-54.

181. Marx, Karl. "Punishment and Society." *Philosophical Perspectives on Punishment*. Ed. by Gertrude Ezorsky. Albany: State University of New York Press, 1972, pp. 358-359.

182. Marx, Karl. "Capital Punishment." *Marx and Engles: Basic Writings on Politics and Philosophy*. Ed. by Lewis S. Feuer. Garden City, New York: Doubleday and Co., Inc., 1959, pp. 485-488.

183. Marx, Karl. "Capital Punishment." *Punishment and Rehabilitation*. Ed. by Jeffrie G. Murphy. Belmont, California: Wadsworth Publishing Co., Inc., 1973, pp. 91-94.

184. Menninger, Karl. *The Crime of Punishment*. New York: Viking Press, 1968.

185. Middendorff, Wolf. *The Effectiveness of Punishment*. South Hackensack, New Jersey: Fred B. Rothman & Co., 1968.

186. Miller, W.A. "A Theory of Punishment." *Philosophy*, v. 45 (October, 1970), pp. 307-316.

187. Mitford, Jessica. *Kind and Usual Punishment*. New York: Random House, 1973.

188. Moberly, Walter, Sir. "Expiation." *Contemporary Punishment: Views, Explanations and Justifications*. Ed. by Rudolph J. Gerber and Patrick D. McAnany. Notre Dame: University of Notre Dame, 1972, pp. 73-82.

189. Moberly, Walter, Sir. *The Ethics of Punishment*. London: Faber and Faber, 1968.

190. Moore, T.W. "Punishment and Education." *Proceedings of the Philosophy of Education Society of Great Britain*, v. 1 (1966).

191. Morris, Herbert. "Persons and Punishment." *The Monist*, v. 52, n. 4 (October, 1968), pp. 475-501.

192. Morris, Herbert. *Guilt and Shame*. Belmont, California: Wadsworth Publishing Co., Inc., 1971.

193. Morris, Herbert. "Guilt and Punishment." *Personalist*, v. 52 (Spring, 1971), pp. 305-321.

194. Morris, Herbert. *Freedom and Responsibility*. Stanford, California: Stanford University Press, 1961.

195. Morris, Herbert. "Punishment for Thoughts." *The Monist*, v. 49, n. 3 (July, 1965), pp. 342-376.

196. Morris, Norval. "Prison in Evolution." *Federal Probation*, v. xxxiii, n. 4 (December, 1965), pp. 18-23.

197. Morris, Norval. *The Future of Imprisonment.* Chicago: University of Chicago Press, 1974.

198. Morris, Norval. *The Habitual Criminal.* Cambridge, Massachusetts: Harvard University Press, 1951.

199. Morris, Norval and Hawkins, Gordon. "Dangerousness and Prediction." *Contemporary Punishment: Views, Explanations and Justifications.* Ed. by Rudolph J. Gerber and Patrick D. McAnany. Notre Dame: University of Notre Dame, 1972, pp. 158-163.

200. Morris, Norval, and Hawkins, Gordon. "Rehabilitation: Rhetoric and Reality." *Federal Probation*, v. xxxiv, n. 4 (December, 1970), pp. 9-17.

201. Moser, S. "Utilitarian Theories of Punishment and Moral Judgements." *Philosophical Studies*, v. 7 (1957), pp. 15-19.

202. Motjabai, A.G. "Reflections on Punishment." *The Philosophical Journal*, (Glasgow), v. 5 (1967), pp. 1-17.

203. Mundle, C.W.K. "Punishment and Desert." *The Philosophy of Punishment.* Ed. by H.B. Acton. London: Macmillan, 1969, pp. 65-82.

204. Murphy, Jeffrie G. "Criminal Punishment and Psychiatric Fallacies." *Law and Society Review*, v. 3 (August, 1969).

205. Murphy, Jeffrie G. "Marxism and Retribution." *Philosophy and Public Affairs*, v. 2, n. 3 (Spring, 1973), pp. 217-243.

206. Murphy, Jeffrie G. *Punishment and Rehabilitation.* Belmont, California: Wadsworth Publishing Co., Inc., 1973.

207. Murphy, Jeffrie G. "Three Mistakes About Retributivism." *Analysis*, v. 31, n. 5 (April, 1971), pp. 166-169.

208. McCloskey, H.J. "A Non-Utilitarian Approach to Punishment." *Philosophical Perspectives on Punishment.* Ed. by Gertrude Ezorsky. Albany: State University of New York Press, 1972, pp. 119-134.

209. McCloskey, H.J. "A Note on Utilitarian Punishment." *Mind*, v. 72, n. 288 (October, 1963), p. 599.

210. McCloskey, H.J. "An Examination of Restricted Utilitarianism." *The Philosophical Review*, v. 66, n. 4 (October, 1957), pp. 466-485.

211. McCloskey, H.J. "The Complexity of the Concepts of Punishment." *Philosophy*, v. 37, n. 142 (October, 1962), pp. 307-325.

212. McCloskey, H.J. "Utilitarian and Retributive Punishment." *The Journal of Philosophy*, v. 64, n. 3 (February 16, 1967), pp. 91-110.

213. McPherson, Thomas. "Punishment: Definition and Justification." *Analysis*, v. 28, n. 1 (October, 1967), pp. 21-27.

214. McTaggart, J.E. "Hegel's Theory of Punishment." *Philosophical Perspectives on Punishment.* Ed. by Gertrude Ezorsky. Albany: State University of New York Press, 1972, pp. 40-55.

215. National Council on Crime and Delinquency. "Dangerousness and Sanction." *Contemporary Punishment: Views, Explanations and Justifications.* Ed. by Rudolph J. Gerber and Patrick D. McAnany. Notre Dame: University of Notre Dame, 1972, pp. 149-157.

216. New York Governor's Special Committee on Criminal Offenders. "The Penal System: Treatment as Prevention." *Contemporary Punishment: Views, Explanations and Justifications.* Ed. by Rudolph J. Gerber and Patrick D. McAnany. Notre Dame: University of Notre Dame, 1972, pp. 256-267.

217. Olafson, Frederick A. *Justice and Social Policy.* Englewood Cliffs, New Jersey: Prentice-Hall, 1961.

218. O'Shaughnessy, R.J. "Forgiveness." *Philosophy*, v. 42 (October, 1967), pp. 336-352.

219. Packer, Herbert L. "Conduct and Punishment." *Contemporary Punishment: Views, Explanations and Justifications.* Ed. by Rudolph J. Gerber and Patrick D. McAnany. Notre Dame: University of Notre Dame, 1972, pp. 16-18.

220. Packer, Herbert L. *The Limits of the Criminal Sanction.* Stanford, California: Stanford University Press, 1968.

221. Packer, Herbert L. "The Practical Limits of Deterrence." *Contemporary Punishment: Views, Explanations and Justifications.* Ed. by Rudolph J. Gerber and Patrick D. McAnany. Notre Dame: University of Notre Dame, 1972, pp. 102-107.

222. Palmer, H. "Principles of Punishment." *The Criminal Law Review*, (1957), pp. 155-159, 455-460, 536-539.

223. Perkins, Lisa H. "Suggestion for a Justification of Punishment." *Ethics*, v. 81, n. 1 (October, 1971), pp. 55-61.

224. Pincoffs, Edmund L. "Legal Responsibility and Moral Character." *Wayne Law Review*, (March, 1973), pp. 905-923.

225. Pincoffs, Edmund L. *The Rationale of Legal Punishment.* New York: Humanities Press, 1966.

226. Plamenatz, J. "Responsibility, Blame and Punishment." *Philosophy, Politics and Society*, Third Series. Ed. by P. Laslett and W.G. Runciman. Oxford: Blackwell, 1967, pp. 173-193.

227. Plato. "Punishment as Cure." *Philosophical Perspectives on Punishment.* Ed. by Gertrude Ezorsky. Albany: State University of New York Press, 1972, pp. 37-39.

228. Playfair, G. "Why Imprisonment Must Go." *Kentucky Law Journal*, v. 53 (1964-1965), pp. 415-431.

229. Playfair, Giles and Sington, Derrick. *Crime, Punishment and Cure.* London: Secker and Warburg, 1965.

230. Pope Pius XII. "Crime and Punishment." *Contemporary Punishment: Views, Explanations and Justifications.* Ed. by Rudolph J. Gerber and Patrick D. McAnany. Notre Dame: University of Notre Dame, 1972, pp. 59-72.

231. Powers, Edwin and Witmer, Helen. *An Experiment in the Prevention of Delinquency.* Montclair, New Jersey: Patterson Smith, 1972.

232. Privette, M. "Theories of Punishment." *University of Kansas City Law Review*, v. 29 (1962), pp. 46-90.

233. Quinton, A.M. "On Punishment." *Philosophical Perspectives on Punishment.* Ed. by Gertrude Ezorsky: Albany: State University of New York Press, 1972, pp. 6-15.

234. Radzinowicz, L. "Changing Attitudes Towards Crime and Punishment." *The Law Quarterly Review*, v. 75 (July, 1959), pp. 381-400.

235. Radzinowicz, L. "Toward a Pragmatic Position." *Contemporary Punishment: Views, Explanations and Justifications.* Ed. by Rudolph J. Gerber and Patrick D. McAnany. Notre Dame: University of Notre Dame, 1972, pp. 238-245.

236. Raphael, Daiches D. "Justice." *Philosophical Perspectives on Punishment.* Ed. by Gertrude Ezorsky. Albany: State University of New York Press, 1972, pp. 142-144.

237. Rashdall, H. "Punishment and the Individual." *Philosophical Perspectives on Punishment.* Ed. by Gertrude Ezorsky. Albany: State University of New York Press, 1972, pp. 64-65.

238. Rawls, John. *A Theory of Justice.* Cambridge, Massachusetts: The Belknap Press of Harvard University Press, 1971.

239. Rawls, John. "Two Concepts of Rules." *The Philosophical Review*, v. 64, n. 1 (January, 1955), pp. 3-32.

240. Robinsin, Louis N. "Contradictory Purposes in Prisons." *The Journal of Criminal Law and Criminology*, v. 37, n. 6 (March-April, 1947), pp. 449-457.

241. Rose, Arnold M. and Prell, Arthur E. "Does the Punishment Fit the Crime? A Study in Social Valuation." *The American Journal of Sociology*, v. 61, n. 3 (November, 1955), pp. 247-259.

242. Rose, Dennis J. "Retribution and Impartiality." *The Philosophical Quarterly*, v. 18, n. 73 (October, 1968), pp. 356-358.

243. Ross, A. "The Campaign Against Punishment." *Scandinavian Studies in Law*, v. 14 (1970).

244. Ross, W.D. "Punishment." *Philosophical Perspectives on Punishment.* Ed. by Gertrude Ezorsky. Albany: State University of New York Press, 1972, pp. 145-152.

245. Royal Commission on Capital Punishment. "The Deterrent Value of Capital Punishment." *Philosophical Perspectives on Punishment.* Ed. by Gertrude Ezorsky. Albany: State University of New York Press, 1972, pp. 249-261.

246. Samek, R.A. "Punishment: A Postscript to Two Prolegomena." *Philosophy*, v. 41 (July, 1966), pp. 216-232.

247. Sellin, T. "Correction in Historical Perspective." *Law and Contemporary Problems*, v. 23 (1958), pp. 585-593.

248. Shoham, Shlomo. *Crime and Social Deviation.* Chicago: Henry Regnery Co., 1966.

249. Shoham, Shlomo. "Moral Dilemmas in Rehabilitation." *Contemporary Punishment: Views, Explanations and Justifications.* Ed. by Rudolph J. Gerber and Patrick D. McAnany. Notre Dame: University of Notre Dame, 1972, pp. 200-208.

250. Shoham, S. and Slonim, Z. "The Moral Dilemma of Penal Treatment." *Juridical Review*, v. 8 (1963), pp. 135-157.

251. Sidgwick, Henry. *The Methods of Ethics.* London: Macmillan and Co., Limited, 1922. Book III.

252. Siegler, Fredrick Adrian. "Lyons on Sanctioning Excuses." *The Journal of Philosophy*, v. 67, n. 18 (September 17, 1970), pp. 620-625.

253. Silving, Helen. "A New Philosophy of Criminal Justice." *Contemporary Punishment: Views, Explanations and Justifications.* Ed. by Rudolph J. Gerber and Patrick D. McAnany. Notre Dame: University of Notre Dame, 1972, pp. 252-255.

254. Silving, Helen. "The Dual-Track System: Punishment and Prevention." *Contemporary Punishment: Views, Explanations and Justifications.* Ed. by

Rudolph J. Gerber and Patrick D. McAnany. Notre Dame: University of Notre Dame, 1972, pp. 140-148.

255. Smart, Alwynne. "Mercy." *The Philosophy of Punishment.* Ed. by H.B. Acton. London: Macmillan, 1969, pp. 212-227.

256. Smart, J.J.C. "Free-Will, Praise and Blame." *Mind*, v. 70, n. 279 (July, 1961), pp. 291-306.

257. Smart, J.J.C. "The Humanitarian Theory of Punishment." *Readings in Ethical Theory.* Second Edition. Ed. by Wilfrid Sellars and John Hospers. New York: Meredith Corp., 1970, pp. 651-653.

258. Smith, Adam. *The Theory of Moral Sentiments.* New York: Augustus M. Kelley, 1966.

259. Smith, James M. "Punishment: A Conceptual Map and a Normative Claim." *Ethics*, v. 75, n. 4 (July, 1965), pp. 285-290.

260. Smith, L.M.G. "On Baroness Wootton's Larceny." *Social Theory and Practice*, v. 1 (1970), pp. 101-112.

261. Spitzer, P.S. "Punishment vs. Treatment." *Federal Probation*, v. 23 (1961), pp. 3ff.

262. Sprigge, T.L.S. "A Utilitarian Reply to Dr. McCloskey." *Inquiry*, v. 8, n.(s) 1-4 (1965), pp. 264-291.

263. Squires, J.E.R. "Blame." *The Philosophy of Punishment.* Ed. by H.B. Acton. London: Macmillan, 1969, pp. 204-211.

264. Stern, L. "Deserved Punishment, Deserved Harm, Deserved Blame." *Philosophy*, v. 45 (October, 1970), pp. 317-329.

265. Stone, Julius. *Human Law and Human Justice.* Stanford, California: Stanford University Press, 1965.

266. Street, David, Vinter, Robert D. and Perrow, Charles. *Organization for Treatment: A Comparative Study of Institutions for Delinquents.* New York: The Free Press, 1966.

267. Strömberg, T. "Some Reflections on the Concept of Punishment." *Theoria*, v. 23 (1957), pp. 71-83.

268. Strong, Edward W. "Justification of Juridical Punishment." *Ethics*, v. 79, n. 3 (April, 1969), pp. 187-198.

269. Studt, Elliot, Messinger, Sheldon L. and Wilson, Thomas P. *C-Unit: Search for Community in Prison.* New York: Russell Sage Foundation.

270. Stürup, George K. *Treating the "Untreatable."* Baltimore: The Johns Hopkins Press, 1968.

271. Sykes, G.M. *The Society of Captives: A Study of a Maximum Security Prison.* Princeton, New Jersey: Princeton University Press, 1958.

272. Tarde, Gabriel. *Penal Philosophy.* Boston: Little, Brown, and Co., 1912.

273. Tay, Alice Erh-Soon. "Moral Guilt and Legal Liability." *The Hibbert Journal*, v. 60, n. 1 (October, 1961), pp. 44-52.

274. Taylor, Gabriele and Wolfram, Sybil. "Mill, Punishment and the Self-Regarding Failings." *Analysis*, v. 28, n. 5 (April, 1968), pp. 168-172.

275. Ten, C.L. "Mr. Thompson on the Distribution of Punishment." *The Philosophical Quarterly*, v. 17, n. 68 (July, 1967), pp. 253-254.

276. Thalberg, I. "Remorse." *Mind*, v. 72, n. 288 (October, 1963), pp. 545-555.

277. Thayer, Ezra Ripley. "Liability Without Fault." *Harvard Law Review*, v. 29 (1915-1916), pp. 801-815.

278. Thomas, D.A. "Theories of Punishment in the Court of Criminal Appeal." *Modern Law Review*, v. 27 (1964), pp. 546-567.

279. Thompson, D.F. "Retribution and the Distribution of Punishment." *Philosophical Quarterly*, v. 16 (January, 1966), pp. 59-63.

280. Toby, Jackson. "Is Punishment Necessary?" *The Journal of Criminal Law, Criminology and Police Science*, v. 55, n. 3 (September, 1964), pp. 332-337.

281. Tullock, Gordon. "Does Punishment Deter Crime?" *The Public Interest*, nos. 34-37 (Summer, 1974), pp. 103-111.

282. Van Den Haag, Ernest. "On Deterrence and the Death Penalty." *Ethics*, v. 78, n. 4 (July, 1968), pp. 280-288.

283. Van Den Haag, Ernest. "On Deterrence and the Death Penalty." *The Journal of Criminal Law, Criminology and Police Science*, v. 60, n. 2 (June, 1969), pp. 141-147.

284. Van Den Haag, Ernest. *Punishing Criminals.* New York: Basic Books, Inc., 1975.

285. Von Hentig, Hans. *Punishment: Its Origin, Purpose and Psychology.* Montclair, New Jersey: Patterson Smith, 1973.

286. Von Hirsch, Andrew. *Doing Justice.* New York: Hill and Wang, 1976.

287. Walker, Nigel, *Sentencing in a Rational Society.* New York: Basic Books, 1971.

288. Walker, Nigel, "Varieties of Retributivism." *Contemporary Punishment: Views, Explanations and Justifications.* Ed. by Rudolph J. Gerber and Patrick D. McAnany. Notre Dame: University of Notre Dame, 1972, pp. 83-92.

289. Wall, G.B. "Cultural Perspectives on the Punishment of the Innocent." *Philosophical Forum*, v. 2 (Summer, 1971).

290. Wasserstrom, Richard. "H.L.A. Hart and the Doctrine of Mens Rea and Criminal Responsibility." *University of Chicago Law Review*, v. 35 (Autumn, 1967), pp. 92ff.

291. Wasserstrom, Richard. "Punishment and Responsibility." *Contemporary Punishment: Views, Explanations and Justifications.* Ed. by Rudolph J. Gerber and Patrick D. McAnany. Notre Dame: University of Notre Dame, 1972, pp. 19-23.

292. Wasserstrom, Richard. "Strict Liability and the Criminal Law." *Stanford Law Review*, v. xii (1960), pp. 730-745.

293. Wasserstrom, Richard. "Why Punish the Guilty?" *Philosophical Perspectives on Punishment.* Ed. by Gertrude Ezorsky. Albany: State University of New York Press, 1972, pp. 328-341.

294. Weihofen, H. "Retribution is Obsolete." *Nomos III: Responsibility.* Ed. by C.J. Friedrich. New York: Liberal Arts Press, 1960, pp. 116-127.

295. Weiss, Jonathan A. "The Justification of Punishment." *The Review of Metaphysics*, v. 25, n. 99 (March, 1972), pp. 527-546.

296. Wheatley, J. "Comments on Professor Morris' Address." *Personalist*, v. 52 (Spring, 1971), pp. 374-378.

297. Whiteley, C.H. "On Retribution." *Philosophy*, v. 31 (April, 1956), pp. 154-157.

298. Wilkins, Leslie T. *Evaluation of Penal Measures.* New York: Random House, Inc., 1969.

299. Wilson, James Q. "Crime." *The Urban Predicament.* Ed. by William Gorham and Nathan Glazer. Washington, D.C.: Urban Institute, 1976.

300. Wilson, James Q. *Thinking About Crime.* New York: Basic Books, 1975.

301. Winch, P. "Ethical Reward and Punishment." *The Human World,* v. 1 (1970).

302. Woods, M. "Punishment Under Law." *Criminal Law Quarterly,* v. 1 (1958-1959), pp. 423-440.

303. Wootton, Barbara. "Crime, Responsibility and Prevention." *Contemporary Punishment: Views, Explanations and Justifications.* Ed. by Rudolph J. Gerber and Patrick D. McAnany. Notre Dame: University of Notre Dame, 1972, pp. 164-174.

304. Wootton, Barbara. *Social Science and Social Pathology.* New York: The Macmillan Co., 1959.

305. Zilboorg, Gregory. *The Psychology of the Criminal Act and Punishment.* New York: Greenwood Press, 1968.

Index

About the Editors

J.B. Cederblom is Assistant Professor of Philosophy and Coordinator of Humanities for the Goodrich Scholarship Program at the University of Nebraska at Omaha. He received a B.A. from Whitman College and a Ph.D. from the Claremont Graduate School, both in philosophy. He regularly teaches a course in the justification of punishment, and he developed a humanities course for criminal justice majors through the support of National Endowment for the Humanities Grant. Other areas in which he has lectured or written are aesthetics, moral and political philosophy, and epistemology. His publications include articles on the philosophy of community development, written with William Blizek.

William L. Blizek is Associate Professor of Philosophy at the University of Nebraska at Omaha. He received B.A. and M.A. degrees in philosophy from Southern Illinois University and the Ph.D. from the University of Missouri, also in philosophy. He has published articles on social philosophy, ethics, aesthetics, education, and community development in *The British Journal of Aesthetics*, *The Southern Journal of Philosophy*, *Metaphilosophy*, *The Journal of Experimental Education*, *Equality and Freedom: International and Comparative Jurisprudence*, and *The Journal of the Community Development Society*. He serves as a Senior Research Associate for The Institute for the Study of Contemporary Social Problems; Seattle, Washington.

About the Contributors

Hugo A. Bedau is Professor of Philosophy at Tufts University. He is the editor of *The Death Penalty in America* and *Justice and Equality*, and a member of the American Society for Political and Legal Philosophy.

David Fogel is presently Executive Director of the Illinois Law Enforcement Commission. He has been an innovative practitioner of criminal justice and he is author of "...*We Are the Living Proof*..."; *The Justice Model of Corrections*.

Martin Golding is presently Professor of Philosophy and Chairman of the Department at Duke University. He is secretary for the American Society for Political and Legal Philosophy. He is author of *Philosophy of Law* and editor of *The Nature of Law*.

John Hospers is Professor of Philosophy at the University of Southern California. He is editor of *The Personalist* and author of *Libertarianism* and *Human Conduct*, among other books and articles.

Norval Morris is presently serving as Dean of the University of Chicago Law School. He is author of *The Habitual Criminal, The Honest Politician's Guide to Crime Control*, and *The Future of Imprisonment*.

Edmund L. Pincoffs is Professor of Philosophy and Chairman of the Department at the University of Texas at Austin. He is the author of *The Rationale of Legal Punishment*.

Richard Wasserstrom is Professor of Philosophy and Law at the University of California at Los Angeles. He is the author of *Morality and the Law and The Judicial Decision: Toward a Theory of Legal Justification.*

James Q. Wilson is presently Henry Lee Shattuck Professor of Government at Harvard University. He has served as Vice-Chairman of The Police Foundation and a member of The Board of Directors of the Joint Center for Urban Studies (Harvard/M.I.T.). He is the author of *Thinking About Crime* and *Varieties of Police Behavior.*